SKETCHBOOK, 1966–1971

THE SWISS LIST

WORKS BY MAX FRISCH AVAILABLE FROM SEAGULL BOOKS

Sketchbook, 1946–1949
Translated by Simon Pare

Drafts for a Third Sketchbook
Translated by Mike Mitchell

An Answer from the Silence
Translated by Mike Mitchell

Biography: A Game
Translated by Birgit Schreyer Duarte

Correspondence: Max Frisch and Friedrich Dürrenmatt
Translated by Birgit Schreyer Duarte

From the Berlin Journal
Translated by Wieland Hoban

Gantenbein
Translated by Michael Bullock
Also available as an audiobook, narrated by Jonathan Davis

Homo Faber
Translated by Michael Bullock
Only available as an audiobook, narrated by Jonathan Davis

I'm Not Stiller
Translated by Michael Bullock
Also available as an audiobook, narrated by Jonathan Davis

Zurich Transit
Translated by Birgit Schreyer Duarte

Max Frisch

SKETCHBOOK, 1966–1971

A NEW TRANSLATION BY

Simon Pare

LONDON CALCUTTA NEW YORK

This publication has been supported by a grant from the Goethe-Institut Munich

Seagull Books, 2023

First published in German as *Tagebuch, 1966–1971* by Max Frisch

ISBN 978 1 80309 140 2

British Library Cataloguing-in-Publication Data
A catalogue record for this book is available from the British Library

Typeset by Seagull Books, Calcutta, India
Printed and bound by WordsWorth India, New Delhi, India

Contents

1967

1968

1969

1970

1971

Translator's Note

Max Frisch's second *Sketchbook* covers the period of his life when he was at the height of his international fame and a frequent visitor to the United States. There, he was confronted with race relations to an extent that was unfamiliar to him in Europe. He considers this issue in some detail, especially in the passages 'Murder as a Political Weapon', the later New York entries and 'School of the Arts'.

While conscious of the uneasy nature of this choice, we have chosen to translate the various occurrences of the German N-word—now universally considered to be derogatory and discriminatory—with 'Negro' in the text so as not to distort and sanitize the attitudes of the time. Although 'Negro' did not convey the same racist *mens rea* as it would now, it is representative of the latent racism and general lack of sensitivity to rhetoric concerning minorities pervasive even amongst progressive circles of this period. Otherwise, we have adopted the now-standard capitalization of 'Black' and 'White'. Frisch uses variants of 'Black'— 'schwarz', 'ein Schwarzer', the plural 'Schwarze'—although current usage would prefer 'Schwarze Menschen', the borrowed English term 'People of Colour' or words such as 'Afroamerikaner', 'Afrodeutsche/r', etc.

TRANSLATOR'S NOTE

This translation is based on the 1976 edition of Frisch's complete works published by Suhrkamp Verlag. Geoffrey Skelton's 1974 English translation of the second *Sketchbook* was based on the 1972 edition of the *Tagebuch 1966–1971*. This earlier edition, and thus Skelton's translation, did not contain, for example, the sections on Kabusch, Max Frisch's 1969 trip to Japan, the questionnaire about a sense of humour, and some of passages relating to the 'Vereinigung Freitod'—Frisch's witty and poignant spoof of an association that promotes voluntary suicide among ageing Swiss men. Some of these sections had been omitted on the advice of the second *Sketchbook*'s editor, the author Uwe Johnson, a long-standing friend of Frisch's, and were reinstated for the version in the complete works.

The translator would like to thank the Goethe-Institut in Munich and the Dietrich-Schindler-Stiftung in Glarus, Switzerland, for their generous support.

For Marianne

1966

Questionnaire

1.
Are you really sure that you're interested in the survival of the human race once you and everyone you know are no longer around?

2.
Why? Briefly list a few reasons.

3.
How many children did you choose *not* to have?

4.
Is there anyone you would rather never have met?

5.
Do you feel guilty towards someone who doesn't necessarily know how you feel, and do you hate yourself or the other person for it?

6.
Would you like to have total recall?

7.
Is there any politician whose death from disease or in a car accident would fill you with hope? Or do you believe that none of them is irreplaceable?

8.
Which dead person would you most like to see again?

9.
And whom would you rather not?

10.
Would you have preferred to be born in a different country (culture) and, if so, which one?

11.
To what age would you like to live?

12.
If you had the power to implement what you feel to be right, would you implement it against the will of the majority? Yes or no.

13.
Why not, if you feel it is right?

14.
Do you more easily hate a group or a specific individual, and do you prefer to hate alone or as part of a group?

15.
When did you stop believing you were getting more intelligent, or do you still believe you are? Give your age.

16.
Are you convinced by your own self-criticism?

17.
What do you think other people resent in you, and what do you resent in yourself? If they are not the same, for which do you tend to ask forgiveness?

18.
If you happen to imagine that you had never been born, do you find the idea unsettling?

19.
When you think of someone who is dead, would you like the deceased to speak to you, or would you rather say something to him or her?

20.
Do you love anyone?

21.
How can you tell?

22.
Assuming you have never killed anyone, how do you explain this?

23.
What would it take for you to be happy?

24.
What are you grateful for?

25.
Would you prefer to be dead or to live on for a while as a healthy animal? Which animal?

Statistic

The average human lifespan was 22 around the time of Christ's birth; by Martin Luther's day it had risen to 35.5; in 1900 it was still 49.2; and now it's 68.7 years. Longer life expectancy has brought about a shift in the age groups. In 1900 young people (under 20) made up 46% of the population; by 1925 it was only 36%; in 1950 it was still 31%; and the projection for 1975 is 28% young people. The proportion of elderly people (over 60) is growing accordingly: in 1900 they made up only 7% of the population, but by 1975 it will be 20%.

Bodega Gorgot

When his wife isn't interrupting him, everyone can see that she's no longer listening to him; that she finds it a drag when he speaks. He's a goldsmith. His work is prized. He takes an award (1939 National Exposition) down from the wall. An apprentice and two employees have noticed—what? They don't know, but they are aware that the old man thinks he needs to prove he's better than them and, even if he does manage to prove it, they're getting to him. He now spends almost every evening at the Bodega. He doesn't mind that the young beards and their loose-haired chicks in trousers, etc. aren't working at five in the afternoon. The Bodega is gloomy, even in daytime. He worked when he was younger, and it became second nature to him. Later, he goes to his workshop again. She comes to the Bodega once; he has been drinking and cuts a sad figure. She expected no less, and he knows that. She lays her hand on his and leads the goldsmith home. His father was a primary school teacher. There are many subjects, politics for example, he simply knows more about than his wife; others, less; the latter is enough to make him uncertain when she shows no interest in his political knowledge or opinions. He contradicts her when she claims that Trotsky was shot, but she isn't convinced; looking it up later, it enrages him that she caused him to doubt himself. He doesn't go to the Bodega for weeks. Maybe he's found another place she knows nothing about. She is a trained nursery teacher and had to stop working to bring up her own children; she keeps the goldsmith's book, which doesn't take much time; she is irreplaceable. Later, he is back at the round table in the Bodega; he watches the young beards, drinks and speaks to no one. When he picks up a newspaper, he feels as if he's read it all before. Maybe she has left him. What he is doing, as he sits there in silence, is defending himself. After all, he did set up his own firm; after all, his work is respected by other specialists, etc. His two children, now grown up and standing on their own two feet, realize that he needs their admiration; his bragging doesn't make this easy for them. She hasn't left him; she knows the goldsmith needs her and she bears her cross with good grace. She is in her mid-forties. Nothing will change now. He cannot really imagine what her life is like. She comes to the Bodega with her shopping bag and drinks rosé, like him. It might have been very early on, maybe on the first evening, that she noticed he can be made to feel insecure. He had a reputation as a go-getter; a lady's man, etc. He persuaded her to go for a boat trip so he could show off his ability as a rower, then considered it a failure on his part when it began to rain. His present failure doesn't alter her relationship with him; on the contrary, it reinforces it. The way he pays for the wine they've shared in the Bodega, picks up her shopping and holds out her coat for her and waits, not daring to say, 'Oh hurry up!' and the way he blames himself when she nearly forgets her gloves—

BERZONA

The village is a few miles from the border and has 82 inhabitants, who speak Italian; no   , not even a bar because it is slightly off the valley road. Every visitor from the city immediately says, 'Oh, the air here!' then somewhat anxiously, 'And the silence!' The terrain is steep: terraces with the customary dry-stone walls, a tangle of brambles, two large walnut trees, thistles, etc. You have to watch out for snakes. When Alfred Andersch, who had lived here for years, alerted us to the small property, the building was rundown—an old farmhouse with thick walls and a tower-shaped stable, now called the studio, all roofed with granite. The valley (Val Onsernone) is not flat bottomed; it has a deep, wild gorge in the middle, but we haven't climbed down there yet; its slopes are forested, rocky too, and probably boring over time. I prefer it in winter. The locals used to make their living from plaiting straw until Japanese baskets and hats and bags suddenly started appearing on the market in Milan; since then, the valley has grown poor.

RESOLUTION

After five years abroad (in Rome), I see many things more starkly, although such things are only noteworthy if they lead to new insights, and so far that hasn't been the case. This explains my resolution to make no more pronouncements about Switzerland—not publicly at least.

. . .

Foreigners living in Switzerland often seem to enjoy a happier relationship with this country than we do ourselves. They refrain from radical criticism; they find our own criticism a little embarrassing, and they would prefer to be spared it. What, other than Swiss banking secrecy, draws them here? All sorts of things, apparently: the scenery, the central location in Europe, the cleanliness, a stable currency, the people less so (the occasional disparaging cliche gives them away), but above all a kind of dispensation: here all you need is for your finances and papers to be in good order and to have no desire for change. Unless the immigration authorities come calling, Switzerland does not impinge on foreigners in Switzerland. What they enjoy is a comforting lack of history.

. . .

Unfortunately, I have already broken my promise not to make any pronouncements about Switzerland. ('A proud little master race feels under threat: they appealed for workers, but people came.') Maybe I came home too soon.

CASA DA VENDERE

Things that can happen: a villa has been standing empty for some time and its occupants have vanished without a trace. It looks as if the people just got up from the table without clearing anything away: a bowl of mouldy risotto, an open bottle of wine, the rock-hard remains of loaf. They didn't even take their clothes, their shoes, their personal belongings with them. It was weeks before the lights went off because no one had paid the bill, and someone noticed . . . Various things have been stolen in the meantime; the front door wasn't bolted; a porch with naive ________, above it a balcony with rusted railings; the green shutters are closed now, the plaster (the colour of raspberry yoghurt) has peeled off in slabs. There's a sign in the garden: CASA DA VENDERE. I hear it's been there for years.

The Goldsmith

He will come to a nasty end. He knows this as he sits in the Bodega. The Spanish waiter looks away as he places the small carafe of rosé on the table, already addressing the person at the next table. His father died of a simple heart attack; on the bus. Whenever someone who used to know the goldsmith enters the Bodega, the goldsmith doesn't stay long, paying as soon as his old acquaintance takes a seat. He cannot understand how an apprentice can get to him like this. As a young man, back after art college, he worked abroad (in Strasbourg), returning home in 1939. He sacked the apprentice and took on another: the new one leaves the tap dripping too. He's probably pedantic outside his workshop too (27 years working with a magnifying glass). He cannot stand a dirty kitchen when he gets home from work, for instance. Occasionally he is tempted to set fire to the building. She knows he can't stand a dirty kitchen and finds it absolutely absurd that this annoys him. The Spanish waiter at the Bodega treats him kindly but more sloppily than the other guests. He doesn't dare to insist she keep the kitchen tidy. She never has done, but he has clearly become touchier since failing as a man. Even his request that she not leave dirty dishes piled up for days because it disgusts him makes things tense. After all, she is a qualified nursery teacher and not his maid. The tensions over the kitchen always end with his realizing how ridiculous he is; then, and not before, she will wash up the dishes without a word. His shop and workshop are in a lane in the old part of town, where a blaze would cause a lot of damage, especially after midnight. If the goldsmith, with the flat to himself, washes the dishes and dries them and cleans the kitchen floor, he knows she'll have no cause to thank him; it's a blatant reproach. From time to time, he does it anyway because the unwashed dishes disgust him. Why doesn't she find herself another husband? If he doesn't wash up and waits for her to do it, he has to force himself not to apologize to her; she really isn't his maid. He feels pretty good after his first small carafe at the Bodega; he rarely drinks more. But the carafe doesn't last him long. Afterwards, he goes to the workshop again when the employees have left; he turns off the dripping tap. She once made a serious bookkeeping error, but he didn't mention it to her. He won't gain any respect by slighting her. When she spends a week at her parents', the dirty dishes in the kitchen don't bother him; he washes them up only on the eve of her return. He doesn't have much of an income, but it's enough. If it wasn't the dirty dishes in the kitchen, there would be some other sign that she doesn't feel the need to do what he wants. He knows this. It has nothing to do with the dishes of course. All this he knows. It's stupid. She pities him. She no longer comes to the Bodega to pick him up; he feels emasculated when she comes to get him. He's a difficult man. Every time he has ever fallen ill, she has been touching in her care. She still is. He used to have friends; he hardly ever calls them now, shunning them because his worries are so ridiculous. There is the odd incident known as a marital row, but he avoids such quarrels. Then he will say the precise thing he was determined not to say: the stuff about the dirty dishes, for instance. She makes an effort, sporadically. His interest in public affairs (the renovation of the old part of town) has faded, though he does read the *Tagesanzeiger* at the Bodega. Compared with the news in the paper, his worries are ridiculous. It is beneath him. If he does ever start a fire, this would be the cause.

He didn't use to have to put up with anything; a go-getter, a lady's man, etc. Even not so long ago, he didn't have to put up with very much because it never reached that point. For instance, she simply took the photo of Strasbourg off the wall and got rid of it. His wife is always worried he'll make a fool of himself now. He takes it personally if someone dials a wrong number and simply hangs up without saying sorry, repeating his name—'Huber!'—even after the other person has rung off. He sits at the back of his shop (mornings) under a neon light squinting through his loupe; his wife talks to the customers whereas he barely does now, or if a customer insists on speaking to the goldsmith himself, he hunches low over the table so the client cannot see his face. Some people still buy his brooches. He usually says nothing, nothing at all, and merely wonders what has gone so wrong that he puts up with all of this. Perhaps she thinks the goldsmith doesn't even notice. She asks every time, 'Did you really lock the front door?' Occasionally the goldsmith simply stares at her, as if he might hang himself. One of the waiters, the young Spaniard, has noticed too and become more friendly since the goldsmith has started keeping his coat on. He wears a beret. He unwraps some meatloaf from a rustling piece of paper; he obviously isn't going home for dinner. If the goldsmith is caught up in an argument, he knows in advance that she'll take the other person's side; there's no point in saying anything. She only ever wants him to be at his best and behaves as if he's constantly making mistakes. Sometimes he wants to end it. It doesn't bother him if the ashtrays in the Bodega are dirty. Once she has to tell him, 'You're to blame for all the dirt!' It can be proved. It's always preferable to say nothing. An hour after coming out of the toilets, the goldsmith notices that his flies aren't done up; this may have happened many times before without his realizing. He feels safer in his coat. In the Bodega he recalls a case he heard about while he was at school: a worker, a miner, with oesophageal cancer placed a detonator in his mouth; his brain was splattered all over the arcades on Hechtplatz. He was determined to go through with it, which the goldsmith isn't. The Bodega fills up around six and he vacates his seat; he's been sitting there in his coat anyway, so no one notices when he leaves. He puts the money down on the table first. Another case: when he was at art school and living with his mother in Wiedikon, he heard an unusual noise coming from the bathroom downstairs as he was brushing his teeth in their bathroom, not a very loud noise, a bit like someone shattering a mirror with a small hammer, but without the accompanying tinkle of glass. A gunshot; two hours later, they carried the coffin out of the block of flats. The older you get, the more straightforward you want it to be. He knows quite a few suitable spots in the Albis hills; it doesn't necessarily have to be on a Sunday when lots of people are out walking, families with kids. Sometimes he thinks: I'll hang myself! for example when she says, 'Don't talk—think!' He comes to the Bodega more and more regularly. When he has taken his seat, he looks at the other people first, then he thinks: What does he think? A young beard with long hair at the round table says: *Guten Appetit*. Later, from a neighbouring table, he hears the word 'prick'. The goldsmith mustn't fall into the trap of taking everything personally; he has to be very careful, all the time (not only coming out of the toilets). He has spent his whole life striving not to become disgusting, his whole life he has always opened the toilet window and pulled his coat over his face on the train when he felt like having a nap. The people in the Bodega only see the goldsmith in his coat now: an old man, content with meatloaf and rosé. Not the idiot she tells him he is at home, but he has to be careful. When he puts his money on the table in the Bodega, he counts it twice and, soon afterwards, a third time. Jumping off a viewing platform would make sure but, on further reflection, it would be disgusting for those left behind, and he has spent his whole life striving not to be disgusting. The goldsmith knows it has to be soon. Having been born near Zurich (in Adliswil) and grown up in the city, he is of course familiar with Mühlebachstrasse and Mühlegasse, and yet he still gives someone in the street the wrong directions. Luckily, she wasn't there. When they watch television, his opinions never impress her; he always supports people who don't impress his wife, for example Willy Brandt. One time, he thinks he could gas himself, but the flat isn't connected to the mains. She always wants him to be at his best: for example, to go out and socialize. His wife says afterwards that he monopolized the conversation again, didn't listen to anyone else, etc.; all the goldsmith knows is that no one is impressed if he does say something. The only method that would make sure and not be disgusting for those left behind is sleeping pills, but he thinks it unmanly; and yet in recent months he has started collecting sleeping pills and hiding them at the workshop. But even for this you have to be in the mood; it isn't sufficient not to be afraid. You don't take 30 sleeping pills just like that, tossing them from your palm into your mouth, 3 or 4 at a time, washing each lot down with water or Chianti. If, to get himself in the mood, the goldsmith starts a row over some trivial matter (she has thrown away that day's *Tagesanzeiger* again), she is reasonable, even motherly; she cooks him his favourite meal and lets him watch television. He later apologizes. She isn't to blame for the worsening situation. 'Childish!' is a common enough thing to say; she didn't mean it the way he takes it. She said many of these same things the same way 10 or 20 years ago, and it didn't bother the goldsmith when she called him an idiot. She doesn't mean it literally or else she wouldn't have spent her whole life with the goldsmith. Their beds are still side by side. It is not her fault that she has to tell him in front of people, 'It isn't "carfuncle"—you mean "carbuncle".' Completely neutrally, and she's already told him this at home. It's awful when you can no longer speak. One time she says, 'Now you're talking as if you're doolally,' but she doesn't apologize; she meant it—she has not said it again since.

It doesn't require a decision, in fact, as he is sitting on a bench in the woods; all he needs is the view of the city, the river Limmat, towers, the gasholder near Schlieren, lovers walking into the forest. The goldsmith has the sleeping pills with him in his bag. He will soon be 64. What's he waiting for? Since he has to go to the toilet in the night anyway: gulp down 10 lots of 3 tablets—it's doable. It just has to be sure. He no longer comes to the Bodega (no one misses the goldsmith, but he leaves a void: a couple of old people are as much part of the furniture as the old iron stove, the stovepipe running across the room, etc.,); suddenly he no longer knows why he would ever go in there. If he orders more headed letter paper or buys a new beret, this doesn't mean that the goldsmith is planning to wait until his first stroke. It would be too late then. His daughter-in-law in Sao Paolo writes to say that they'll be coming to Zurich in September; the goldsmith won't be bound by their timetable, however well meaning their suggestion of a family outing to Lake Lucerne to have some battered fish fillets. She thinks the goldsmith works too hard. If he goes to the toilet at night, it's four o'clock already, and if he doesn't appear for breakfast at nine, she'll call for help and he'll have his stomach pumped in an ambulance. It's only possible towards evening; not too late, so the ambulance doesn't come too soon; not too early so he doesn't fall asleep in front of the television. Snow flurries the next day, and to make sure she doesn't notice his resolution to take the sleeping pills around ten that evening, he spends the day in the usual manner: the morning at his workshop, the afternoon at the Bodega (his last), where he drinks no more than usual and reads the *Tagesanzeiger* to pass the time. All she notices is that he has been back to the Bodega: 'You'll go doolally at that Bodega.' When you're in control, there's no need to put up with anything; as the goldsmith doesn't look at her and flicks through the *Tagesanzeiger*, pretending he hasn't heard her, she repeats, 'You're going doolally.' This despite the fact that the goldsmith has a better grip of himself than he has had in a long time; for the goldsmith, the only pity is that she has said this today. It wouldn't be on for her to find the goldsmith dead the next morning; she would blame herself for saying those things. Their beds are still side by side. The goldsmith thinks about it almost every time the news comes on at 10 p.m. The goldsmith knows someone who has had a stroke. Apparently, only his eyelid is affected; he can hide it behind sunglasses; all of a sudden, everyone is very kind to him, uncertain whether he's still capable of thought. Does a man in that state know he babbles? He won't make a full recovery, but a second stroke is not a foregone conclusion. The goldsmith still has a grip on himself; he can still think. It is impossible a second time: his wife has to go to the doctor's, she says. They might have to operate, the doctor says, no reason to worry, a matter of eight to ten days . . . He has to put it off until afterwards.

The goldsmith is still alive. The meal of battered fish by Lake Lucerne in September with the grandchildren from Sao Paolo goes ahead. OK-OK! Only Grandma is not at her best; she tells the story of her operation in the spring, while the goldsmith is of the opinion that the battered fish isn't as tasty as it used to be. The son from Sao Paolo is principal agent for a Swiss-American company, and very American in the way he talks about Latin America while feeding the local swans. The goldsmith hears that money is no problem now, not even if he lives to 90, no problem at all. OK-OK, he doesn't say, but Grandma does; not to him, but to her little grandson.

Sitting there in the Bodega (the iron stove is still there, only the waiters have changed), unpacking the meatloaf from its crackling paper, then chewing it: his wife is dead, the shop has been sold, and he lives in a state-run old people's home.

BERLIN

We already know what there is to see. I've been to Berlin many times since and have decided not to visit the Wall. Uwe Johnson takes us around as an on-duty official would, without commenting. He is very tall, so he bends down politely when someone asks a factual question, removing his pipe from his mouth each time, dressed as always in a black leather jacket, his head clean shaven. He doesn't describe himself as a refugee, but he `can't go back to the other side. A sunny day with a cold wind, a big bright northern sky over barbed wire. When we see the Wall, there's nothing to say about it: and yet the sight prevents us from talking about anything else either. Only later in a pub (which is almost in no-man's land) do we talk about personal matters, although he doesn't take off his black leather jacket, for instance, the one he wore in Rome that summer. His uniform? The tobacco pouch I take out of my pocket is a gift from him because I apparently once said— not in Rome, no, in Spoleto, and not in that bar but at the kiosk . . . The man has a Homeric memory; Mecklenburg can count on it.`

Memories of Brecht

My first sight of Brecht: November 1947, a few days after he arrived in Europe: in the small, booklined flat belonging to Kurt Hirschfeld, dramaturge at the Zurich Schauspielhaus, which staged the first German-language performances of three of Brecht's plays. Brecht was sitting on the bench right in the corner, as we know him from the rare photos of him: grey, quiet, slim, hiding slightly, a man in a foreign country where they speak his language. He seemed glad to have walls by each shoulder. An account of the 'hearings' Brecht had just been through was interrupted when I joined them. I was 36 and an architect at the time. He didn't know Zurich, so I showed him the way down to Stadelhofen station. He didn't spare a glance at the city where he was intending to stay for an unspecified length of time. I told him as much as I knew about Germany from my travels, about Berlin in ruins. He said I should come to Herrliberg soon to tell him more. 'Maybe you too will one day find yourself in the interesting position,' Brecht said on the platform, 'of someone telling you about your homeland and listening as if they were telling you about some part of Africa.'

The flat had been put at his disposal, free of charge, by a young couple called Mertens. Brecht's financial position when he was living in Zurich was wretched: he had funded the journey to Europe by selling his house and furniture in America; his income at the time would barely have sufficed for a student. There were early negotiations with Peter Suhrkamp, but Suhrkamp had no capital either at the time. Maybe I was misled by his one and only luxury: good cigars. And by his hospitality. Brecht never mentioned his financial situation and seemed no harder up than later, and later he seemed no better off than then.

Did we see Brecht as a German? A Bavarian? A citizen of the world? As a Marxist, he wouldn't have stood for the latter. There was one respect in which, compared with other emigrants, he was very un-German: he never analysed things in national terms—not even the war Hitler had unleashed. (Once, later, in Weissensee, when asked for his thoughts about certain SED officials, he objected: 'Don't forget, Frisch, they are Germans!'—this tone was a rare exception, though.) Brecht had returned from emigration immune to 'foreignness': he was neither intimidated by the fact that other people had different customs, nor did he feel the need to assert that he was German. One social system inspired his rage, another his respect; he felt no call to act cosmopolitan, which almost always compensates for national inhibitions. He was a man from Augsburg who worked in Berlin, a man attached to his language, his origins not a badge of honour but an unchangeable condition. Accepting this fact, he could regard national flaws like self-hatred as relics of no concern.

23 August 1948: Bertolt Brecht's first public appearance in Zurich, and it was to be his last. In a small cellar, the antiquarian room of the Volkshaus bookshop, between 100 and 120 people are packed in between the bookshelves; the bookseller organizes this kind of reading from time to time. Brecht listens obediently to my short welcome speech, thanks me with a polite nod and sits down at the small table, needy rather than expansive, not looking at the audience; Brecht with his glasses on, a sheet of paper in his hand. It seems unlikely that those in the back rows heard the title, so quickly did he say it. Harassed by the audience's proximity—those at the front could rest their arms on the small table, though of course they don't; they sit with crossed arms—he reads the poem 'To Those Born Later', then jumps up, clutching his sheet of paper (no, three sheets) and steps aside into the darkness. He's finished. Those great artists Therese Giehse and Helene Weigel read, and everyone forgets Brecht is there. Afterwards, few of Brecht's writings are on sale up in the bookshop; many still haven't been published. Some audience members study the grey man from a distance as they take their coats; Brecht is not assailed. Later, the small group has a beer together: Brecht, Weigel, Giehse, the grateful bookseller, who can't pay very much for the reading—the usual 100 francs; Brecht seems quite content.

Once when I paid another visit to Herrliberg, two Brechts were sitting in the hallway, both with the same haircut and wearing the same grey linen jacket, one of them slightly thinner and gauche, friendly and embarrassed, the other Paul Dessau. Caspar Neher was often there. Brecht was laidback, almost jolly, different from usual; Brecht was happy.

When Brecht was in the company of people he didn't know very well—they were generally young people, and they would meet in a flat, rarely in a restaurant where unauthorized people could have listened in—he preferred to be one of the quieter participants, someone who asked questions: the centre of the small gathering but not its focal point, which was always a subject. I hardly recall Brecht telling any stories. He didn't like providing raw material. He didn't expound and if possible reduced things to anecdotes, which, even when told for the first time, sounded ready made. Only rarely did he feel the need to describe. I never knew Brecht to spin yarns, let his imagination run wild or spout random ideas for fun; but he could do what yarn spinners couldn't: listen with an encouraging, generous ear when someone was telling him something; he didn't need to say anything or virtually nothing—the speaker would automatically adopt his critical version of events. People tended to succumb to Brecht the listener more than to Brecht the debater.

Once, we visited estates for workers, hospitals, schools, etc. The man from the building department, an assistant from whom I had requested this official favour, drove us in his official car to all corners of the city but didn't understand our guest's questions, explaining the same things about one estate after another, while Brecht, who was initially taken aback by such comfort for workers, became increasingly irritated by this same comfort, which didn't seem to tackle the fundamental issues. Suddenly, in a nice new building, he found everything too small, much too small, inhumane, and in a fully equipped, sparkling kitchen, he tersely broke off the guided tour and said he was going to catch the next train back to his work, furious that working people should fall for such a trick;

he still had hope that Switzerland was the only country where it would be possible to stifle socialism by providing comfort for all.

Brecht must have been a manic note taker, but he never gave that impression. I never got the feeling that my visits were an interruption; he would clear a chair of papers or books, immediately switching from writer to listener, to questioner, and immediately shifting the focus of his interest as well. Not a word about his work; it had been turned off. When you left him after two or three hours, he seemed as alert as at the beginning; the evening never seemed to trail off. I have no idea if he worked afterwards, of course. I imagine him as being like Galileo: not industrious but always present, always open to discoveries. A standing desk would have been just the thing for him, in fact. I find it inconceivable that Brecht would sit over *A Little Organum for the Theatre* or the verses of his *Antigone* like a cat lurking outside a mousehole. Instead, I imagine him picking, finishing, noting, observing, trying something out, each movement extremely smooth. If not, the sheer abundance of his writings would be unfathomable, and it seems that even he was not completely aware of it. Peter Suhrkamp told me once that when they were discussing the proofs of the collected plays, Brecht pushed for larger type so his works would reach a certain scale—they should really encompass at least five volumes.

'Legend of the Origin of the Book Tao-Te-Ching During Lao-Tzu's Road into Exile'—I read this poem standing in the street during the war, the way you read the news; the carbon copy was virtually illegible. It came with a request to produce more copies and disseminate the poems; in my studio (I had two draughtsmen, no secretary) I typed out eight carbon copies:

We must seek to prise
Their wisdom from the wise,
So thank you to the customs man
For making this his first demand.

It is one of those memories you don't quite want to believe about yourself: I would sit in that flat in Herrliberg at least once a week, but it never occurred to me to ask Brecht for anything, even the time Helene Weigel gave away what was in the trunk in the corner. Brecht was 51 and, however friendly he was, still the master, and it didn't occur to the younger man that he might perhaps be pleased if I asked for something from that luggage, a classic edition of which now fills an entire bookshelf. He was working on *A Little Organum for the Theatre* among other things at the time. I, as the younger man, would not even have demanded this, had Brecht not offered it up of his own accord one day—as homework. He would like to know, he said, if it was comprehensible. I read it that same night, of course, but I didn't get in touch with him for several days. Returning the manuscript at the next opportunity, I still didn't genuinely think that Brecht was waiting for my opinion, so I laid the manuscript shamelessly enough on the table, thanking him and talking about something else: I left it to Brecht to broach the subject. This was outside on the tar-and-gravel roof; Weigel was cooking, and Brecht questioned me as we walked up and down on the roof; Brecht was extremely attentive, unstintingly attentive, interested even in my misunderstandings, eager to check whether they were attributable to the reader or to his text. That was the only time I read one of his manuscripts. But I, a novice, thought it normal that the master asked to read something I had written and normal too that he didn't wait until our next meeting but sat down at his typewriter to write an immediate answer.

For a while Brecht urged me, as a Swiss citizen, to write a play about William Tell. It should show that although the peasant uprising on Lake Lucerne had been a success, it was in reaction to the Habsburg utopia, a crazy plot. He thought it needed to be written by a Swiss person. His theory, which he made sound attractive in a dramatic sense, does at least come closer to the historical truth than Schiller's hymn for which we honoured him with the Rütli memorial, but it seemed all too easy to use as a justification for modern-day barons. Whenever Brecht got clever, I never knew whether he thought his cleverness was inscrutable or not. Another time he suggested Henry Dunant, the founder of the Red Cross, as good material for me, as his compatriot; a peerless loudmouth, a benefactor opposed by all, who triumphs only to see his work perverted. And one final suggestion: that I should arrange De Roja's *Celestina* for Therese Giehse, with Brecht offering to write the songs I would need here and there. I sat in a public park with the borrowed book, which he had already marked with notes and titles for the songs he meant to write. It was tempting. I started to get cold feet. Brecht remodelled anyone who got involved with him.

Something about Brecht's thinking, in conversation and in his theoretical writings, gave the feeling that it was not the man himself; it was his mode of treatment. This explains why Brechtians are endangered: they perfect a treatment against a genius they do not themselves possess.

Something he clearly couldn't stand was flattery. An actor who tried it at dinner once got no more answers or questions from him for the rest of the evening. Too stupid. Brecht never intended anyone to have to prove they were a connoisseur of his work; praise soured his mood; praise as a substitute for analysis.

Down by the lake once, as a thunderstorm was brewing, I noticed that he was very fearful; when I drew on my local-weather knowledge and reassured him that we would be able to take cover in good time, he shrugged and said, 'I don't want to be struck by lightning. I wouldn't want to give the pope the pleasure.' He was genuinely anxious.

The first production Brecht directed (with Caspar Neher) took place almost behind closed doors in Chur, in February 1948. All we got to see in Zurich was *Antigone*, played by Helene Weigel, in an extraordinary matinee performance that didn't sell out; the main thing for Brecht was to be able to rehearse. He was not in a rush to make a comeback. In both Chur and Zurich Brecht was rehearsing for Berlin. The play he allowed the Zurich Schauspielhaus to premiere was a comparatively harmless one called *Mr Puntila and His Man Matti*, written a long time ago in Finland, and he was not overly sad that his immigration status prevented him from directing it. It was all preparation, and the less attention it attracted, the better. He kept a low profile during rehearsals, just the odd tip here and there. A talented young actress from a good background was supposed to be playing a maid, with a washing tub. When Brecht sniggered, she had no idea what she'd done wrong. She was carrying a weightless prop. Politely, and not without praising the talented middle-class actress, he merely requested that a pile of wet washing be placed in the bottom of the tub for the rest of the rehearsals. Three weeks later, he said: See! Her hips have got it now . . . Brecht on stage: always a little embarrassed, as if he didn't belong there; and yet everyone could see which particular gesture he wanted but was unable to demonstrate, performing a parody of it instead. He sometimes wavered. If something doesn't work today, it might work tomorrow or the day after; if there's no solution today, as long as everyone can cope with the frustration and not pretend to know if and how it will ever come good. He didn't rely on theory but watched and reacted; the effect took precedence; naturally, Brecht knew what he wanted to depict and never succumbed to the arbitrary or the ostentatious. During rehearsals (especially in Zurich, where he was largely working with 'nonpolitical' actors) he never used political vocabulary to argue his case. When the servant Matti is required to examine the landscape while Puntila raves about it, the landowner's gestures and facial expressions of indifference to silence his man were simply to be 'better', 'funnier' and 'more natural', just as it was 'better' if the maid with the washing tub, despite her youthful bearing, didn't walk with too straight a back (like a tennis player, for example). Matters of taste. I found one scene a touch vulgar. Brecht: 'Oh really?' He waved aside my enthusiasm about others: 'What do you think is vulgar about it?' I couldn't actually say. 'We'll meet afterwards,' he said, 'so have a think about it!' When we did talk about it, my unconscious political bias came to light. Brecht laughed: 'You want Puntila to behave like a lord, and that's exactly what he does by becoming vulgar.' During the rehearsals, actors were often surprised by a sudden burst of laughter from the back of the stalls: it was Brecht.

All of a sudden, at our next meeting, his face was like a prisoner's again: small, round eyes swimming in the flat face on top of a scrawny neck like a bird. At the same time, he could be very cheerful. A scary face, repulsive too, if you'd never met him before. The cap, the jacket: as if he'd borrowed them from the plump Paul Dessau; only the cigar was in its proper place. A camp inmate with a cigar. I felt like giving him a warm scarf. His mouth almost lipless. He was clean, but unshaven. Not a tramp: not Villon. Merely grey. His haircut looked like a delousing measure or as if he'd been abused. His gait had no shoulders. His head seemed small. He didn't resemble a cardinal. Nor did he look like a worker. Brecht never looked like a worker; that would be to misinterpret his outfit; more like a craftsman as stylized by Caspar Neher, a carpenter for example, with a head that would have made a presentable cardinal for the Roman Catholic Church. Now, though, he didn't at all resemble a cardinal; I would walk alongside Brecht and feel embarrassed, like being with a cripple. He had no complaints; on the contrary, he was praising Giehse. We were sitting in Café Ost, which no longer exists, near a table reserved for a student fraternity and decorated with its paraphernalia. What makes an actor? We pondered the question, as if Brecht had never written a single line about it. He had time and was eager to speak, and during the discussion he was alert and vivacious, quick thinking—not at all like a cripple. It was only when we were out in the street again that he once more began to walk like someone we needed to pity, a vagrant, his grey cap pulled low over his eyes. It was mainly his neck: so naked. He walked swiftly, but his arms couldn't keep up. The grey farmer's jacket: as if an institution had clothed him from its stocks, and only the bundle of pencils he always carried in his top pocket were his own, along with the inevitable cigar. Otherwise, he didn't know what to do with his hands and shoved them flat, like an exposed part of himself, into his jacket pockets.

5 June 1948, the premiere of *Puntila* in Zurich: the audience wasn't ecstatic, but Brecht himself was satisfied. 'You have to perform this kind of play over and over again before they get used to it,' he said, 'as they got used to Schiller. It takes a few years.' After this, he spoke just as he would after a rehearsal.

I only saw Brecht with a member of the bourgeoisie once; the municipal architect insisted on inviting a group of us to a small lunch in a place with a view of Zurich—Brecht, instead of praising Zurich as expected, asked me if I'd been to New York. I should go, it was worth it, but I shouldn't wait too long, who knew how long New York would still be standing . . . The municipal architect stopped making conversation.

The once unavoidable ideological discussions gradually petered out—not because I contradicted him, but because I was too unschooled, and Brecht had better things to do than school me; he preferred me to lead him around my building site and explain structures, architectural problems and more simple matters such as how to organize a relatively large construction project. Technical expertise, especially when displayed in action, inspired his respect. Ruth Berlau was with us but, as women do, soon became bored, while Brecht dutifully if anxiously climbed the scaffolding and lastly even a ten-metre diving platform which offered the best view of the site. Up here, though, he had no time for explanations, only for respect: 'Impressive, Frisch. Very impressive!' and when Ruth Berlau, with her camera to her eye, invited Brecht to step farther out on the platform, he refused. Only after we were back on the ground was he receptive to a lesson in structural engineering calculations. 'Yours is an honest profession.' His goodbyes were sometimes perfunctory when we parted, never condescending but brief and simple. Now though, after visiting my building site, he was expressive—collegial even.

When we crossed the border between Kreuzlingen and Constance in August 1948, Brecht had not set foot on German soil for 15 years. It was only an evening outing. The explicit reason, which was a welcome pretext for Brecht, was a performance directed by Heinz Hilpert of the Deutsches Theater in Constance of my first play, which I would have preferred not to see again. (Later, in November of that year, Brecht travelled to Berlin via Prague and then returned to Zurich for a few more months before moving to East Berlin for good in 1949.) A stagehand from Zurich who owned an old Lancia drove us as far as the border barrier. Brecht said, 'Let's walk!' The passport checks, still a minor sensation at the time, went smoothly. Brecht was ostentatiously unbothered. So we walked into the small town, a conspicuously German town, unscathed, the restaurant signs in Gothic lettering. After 100 metres, in the middle of some conversation or other, Brecht stopped to relight his cigar, which had obviously gone out, glanced up at the sky and said, 'The sky's no different here!' with the same involuntary gesture he often made: he waggled his skinny neck around in his collar, and this tic relaxed him. Later, a welcome from Heinz Hilpert and his circle. Exuberance always made Brecht feel awkward, and he concentrated on his beer as a young actor (who had heard of *The Threepenny Opera*) wouldn't stop praising the undertaking in Constance; Brecht was stunned into silence by the vocabulary he used. After the performance Brecht expounded on German beer, which he maintained was still the best beer anywhere, and said shortly afterwards, 'Let's go!' He kept silent until we were back in Kreuzlingen, but then a comment from Wilfried Seifert, who was accompanying us, suddenly made him boil over. It began with an icy cackle and then he started shouting, white with rage; Seifert didn't know what was wrong. The vocabulary of these survivors, however innocent they were, and their attitude on stage, their light-hearted cluelessness, the intolerable fact that they simply carried on as if only their mere houses had been destroyed, their blissful belief in art, their overhasty peacemaking with their country—it was all worse than he had feared. Brecht was distraught, his speech one long imprecation. I had never heard him like this before, never as explicit as he was during this declaration of war in a sleepy pub at midnight after his first visit to Germany. He suddenly demanded that we drive home, as if he were in a hurry: 'We have to start again from scratch.'

'Take this photo with you to Poland,' he said. 'You'll probably meet some government people, so ask them if this is true.' He handed me a magazine containing no reports but some pictures suggesting ill-treatment in Silesia and concentration-camp-like conditions. 'Ask everyone you meet if it's true!' Brecht urged me, and I found it hard to imagine that government people, at a banquet for instance, would comment on the magazine's allegations; Brecht: 'No harm in asking.' He was serious. 'If such things exist in Poland,' Brecht said, 'then something must be done.' When I returned from Poland, he was eager to hear about it, calling as soon as he heard that I was back. So I cycled out to Herrliberg with an abundance of material: Breslau, now Wrocław; *Congrès International des Intellectuels pour la Paix*, Warsaw. I expected a difficult conversation. The news I had was ambiguous, Brecht expectant.

Greetings from Anna Seghers. Once alone with Brecht, who had not yet seen the Eastern Bloc with his own eyes, I started talking: dubious news, heartening news, upsetting news, cryptic news. I gave him details. Impressions of a journey through Silesia; a conversation with a Polish farmer who spoke flawless German—a peasant back in East Prussia, where he taught himself and saved up enough money to get his own farm in eastern Poland, then came the war; driven out of his home by the Russians, now settled in Silesia; the story of a life. Brecht was an open-minded listener, which made it easier for me to give my account; I saw his shock or joy respectively, but concern was his overwhelming response. He was irritated by Fadeyev's and the brilliant Ehrenburg's manoeuvres: 'If you insist on holding a conference, that shouldn't happen.' Now and then he would call to Weigel, but we sat there alone, Brecht in turmoil, often silent, openly upset, not inclined to dispute inconvenient facts. Once he upbraided me for not asking certain questions directly at a state reception where hundreds of intellectuals were gathered around a buffet. I gladly told him about what I had seen of the nascent reconstruction and planning in Warsaw (the project was cancelled after Gomulka's downfall) and the lively, frank, happy people I had met in basement bars under ruined buildings, away from the official optimism. Brecht saw this as proof that I wasn't being polemical, which only made him take my negative impressions, which he shared, all the more seriously. 'That's not right,' he said several times, 'that has to change.' Helene Weigel joined us later, and Brecht asked me to tell them more and occasionally to repeat things; but it was not the same. It wasn't just that Weigel had a ready-made interpretation, delivered in a hectoring tone, of all my eyewitness accounts;

Brecht also seemed a man transformed, suddenly indignant not with Fadeyev but with me. It was like an examination I couldn't help but fail. Having received my lecture on Polish affairs, I got on my bike.

Warmth was certainly not the first thing you noticed about this man who shied away from sharing raw material—and feelings are raw material. It wasn't even possible for the other person to express warmth in words; the fact that Brecht's vocabulary remained virtually unchanged in private, whether he was showing forbearance or respect or affection, made it initially seem as if he were sitting in judgement. His gestures (I keep mentioning his gestures, even though they were very limited and sometimes almost mechanical or stereotypical) tended to be parodic. Why this need for parody? Brecht must have been very conscious of sentimentality, and he outlawed anything that might have suggested the start of the slippery slope towards it. His politeness, which he did not express in commonplaces but in his attitude when greeting you or during a meal, this elegant courtesy was all he allowed himself by way of expressing his affection. He would immediately torpedo any hint of familiarity, fairly rudely if called for. He clearly didn't feel at ease. Only in poetry—under artistic control, therefore—did Brecht tolerate what he otherwise fended off with jokes and gestures: emotions. Brecht was prudish. Unlike most other men, Brecht wouldn't change his behaviour in the presence of women, and he made no gestures calculated to impress. In company, women were either comrades and thus neutered; or they were dumb and, once acknowledged and treated as such, did not disturb the conversation for long. On these occasions, more than at other times, Brecht showed more warmth towards men than usual.

Spring 1950, Berlin: the Berliner Ensemble's version of Jakob Lenz's *The Tutor*; for the first time the curtain with Picasso's white dove; and afterwards, Brecht on the square outside the Deutsches Theater, aura-free. He was obviously delighted that people were coming to Berlin to see the Ensemble's work. No famous actors, a few acquaintances from Zurich: Hans Gaugler, Regina Lutz, Benno Besson. It was quite a shock: my first encounter with real theatre. A vindication of his theory? You forgot the theory now that you could see its fruits—probably very imperfect in comparison with the Berliner Ensemble's later productions or the Piccolo Teatro's in Milan, which are now in danger of growing sterile . . . Brecht looked younger than usual. He suggested that I stay overnight in Weissensee as he wished to discuss things; the only problem was that there was a May Day party at the theatre, a duty. Not a rally; there had been one of those out in the streets during the day. Now there was dancing, a social occasion from which ties were pointedly absent; everyone wore determinedly cheerful expressions, the good mood fuelled by vouchers you could exchange at the buffet. The question—'So how do you like it here?'—embarrassed me somewhat. Wolfgang Langhoff, another old acquaintance from Zurich, greeted me warily. Whether I liked it or not, I saw myself assigned the role of a Westerner snooping around in East Germany and secretly out to observe a lack of freedom, and poverty and desolation. I felt uncomfortable. Brecht was there, fittingly, but largely inconspicuous. Though excited by the performance I had just seen, this party filled me with bleak unease; even the buffet (I was hungry) appeared designed to teach me what life was like here; and the way people greeted one another here: such camaraderie! There was a hint of duress about the whole thing, and if you tried to resist it, you immediately felt that your reaction had been misunderstood, which accentuated the compulsion to see everything in a positive light; even silence came across as hostile. Helene Weigel, festively exuberant, invited this outsider to dance, but I was beyond saving by now: everything struck me as demonstrative and therefore suspect. There was a firework display over black ruins outside; Brecht stood smoking with everyone else at a window, waiting for the noisy final flourish, and soon afterwards he came over to me and said, 'We can go now, Frisch, or would you rather stay a little longer?' Our leaving was discreet, and once we were outside in the dark street again, he talked about work. The ruins were not news; there was nothing less important than ruins. Brecht was on top form—supple, light hearted.

The rumour that Brecht had been housed in a palace by the Russians and lived like a prince amid the poverty of East Berlin, while Weigel bought up precious antiques from the impoverished East Zone, was, as expected, unfounded. Theirs was a villa like a thousand others in Berlin: unscathed but a little decrepit in an overgrown garden, spacious and, if I remember correctly, almost devoid of carpets. A nice old wardrobe, a few pieces of rustic furniture, all in all very little; temporary, as always with Brecht. I slept in an attic room, formerly the maid's quarters; walls lined with Marxist classics. The next morning: Brecht is already working, but he has time; for five minutes he stands with his guest, who has never seen the Weissensee, down by the lake, but then we sat in his study rather than under a willow in the first flush of spring. The tutor's self-castration as a staging problem. It would be hard to prove my suspicion that our conversation in Weissensee was different from the ones in Herrliberg, but that was my impression at the time. 'Now is the time for plays by people who know this country's concerns from experience,' Brecht said, 'and that can't be done from over there.' There was no Berlin Wall as yet, but there was already a 'here' and an 'over there'. He was very concerned that there shouldn't be a boycott, though; he asked me to speak to Barlog about an actor who was having problems over there because he had acted for Brecht. Otherwise, I don't recall our long conversation, but I do remember how easily Brecht rearranged the bourgeois villa for his purposes without converting it. He didn't need to resist the architecture; Brecht was stronger; and it didn't seem like a requisitioning or even a change of ownership; the question of who the villa belonged to didn't even arise. Brecht used it the same way the living always use the buildings of the dead—that's the rule of human history. Later we drove to the theatre: Brecht with cap and cigar at the wheel of an old open-topped car, the banners of yesterday's May Day celebrations in traffic-free streets, ruins all around under the thin Berlin sky, and Brecht said cheerfully, 'When are you going to move here?'

Another time in Weissensee: 'You've been accused of formalism. What do the people making these accusations mean by formalism?' Brecht tries to shrug it off: 'Nothing.' He is irritated when I follow up; he leans back in his work chair, smoking, and pretends to be unconcerned, amused: 'Formalism means that certain people don't like me.' The angry words that follow reveal his irritation: 'They would probably call it something different in the West.' We change the subject and only later, when I'm no longer expecting it, does he toss out the real answer: 'We learnt during our time in emigration that our work was destined to be shelved. Maybe a time will come when people will dig out our work and can use it.'

I have met very few people who are acknowledged as great individuals and if someone were to ask me how Brecht's greatness expressed itself, I would be lost for words. In fact, it was the same every time: only when you left Brecht did you feel the full force of his presence. The impact of his greatness was delayed, always a little belated, like an echo; and it was only by seeing him again that you could resist it, helped by his physical inconspicuousness.

I later asked two members of the Berliner Ensemble, Egon Monk and Benno Besson, about Brecht's behaviour during the workers' uprising on 17 June 1953. Did Brecht give a speech to his colleagues that morning as the first news came in from Stalin-Allee? What is known is that rehearsals (*The Broken Jug* and *Don Juan*) were cut short. Where did Brecht go during the day? What was his view of events, insofar as he was aware of them? Did he think it was a demonstration by rightfully unhappy workers, or a mutiny? What information did Brecht have? Did he suspect the West might take advantage of this leaderless popular uprising and war might break out? Did he have any chance to intervene? What was it? Was Brecht torn? Indifferent? Helpless? Passive? Did he tell his colleagues what to do? Was Brecht (as was whispered at the time) a coward, a traitor to the working class? Or did he despair that the workers' romantic illusions were luring them into danger? Was Brecht outraged by the intervention of the Soviet tanks, or did he think it inevitable to deter the West from attacking? Even the two Ensemble members I asked gave interpretations rather than evidence, and their interpretations were incompatible. Peter Suhrkamp sent copies of Brecht's letter to Ulbricht—the full-length version.

My last visit before his death was a short and slightly stiff one I paid to Chaussee-Strasse in September 1955. A flat looking out over a cemetery. I was self-conscious; Benno Besson happened to be there; I knew him better than the other people from the Ensemble, and there was a misunderstanding between us at the time that had blinkered us politically. Benno and I had argued a lot in recent times and not yet made up, and our greetings as I entered Brecht's flat were correspondingly cold; neither of us so much as looked at the other. Was Brecht aware of this? I'd walked in on a work conversation, and we stood there for a few minutes until courtesy required Brecht to dismiss Besson with a signal that cut their urgent discussions short. Now alone with Brecht, I found the atmosphere of our first reunion in a long time quite formal. Brecht: The Ensemble was now well established, and so he would be able to leave others to run it. It sounded as if he needed to write. He looked sickly and grey; his movements were economical. I had come from rehearsals in West Berlin; Hanne Hiob, his daughter, was playing a leading role, and Caspar Neher was the set designer. Over lunch: what do people in the West make of the threat of war? Now, if you came from the West, you were coming from far away. The usual question 'What are you working on?' was not forthcoming. Helene Weigel was with us; she asked me for my position on the persecution of Konrad Farner in Switzerland. There were spells of silence during our meal. No jokes. I felt ill at ease. The conversation wasn't open—in fact it wasn't a conversation; the feeling that I was to blame for this lack of openness distressed me and couldn't be redeemed by my report on how Suhrkamp was doing—badly. Reunification? Brecht on this subject: 'Reunification would mean emigrating again.'

It remains a mystery why Brecht requested a steel coffin. What was this steel coffin supposed to protect him from? Rulers? Resurrection? Becoming 'carrion with much carrion'?

There is a fitting sentence for Brecht, though it wasn't written about him: 'His doctrine may have been one-sided, but this magical man was infinitely multi-facetted' (Maxim Gorky about Leo Tolstoy).

ZURICH
Mother's dying. She sometimes thinks we're in Russia together. She's 90. She wonders if Odessa has changed much since 1901.

POSTSCRIPT TO MY JOURNEY

At night, in a room, someone shows a piece of paper, a form in Russian script, a worn-out, grey sheet of paper: on the back is a scrawl, from one side to the other, in tiny handwriting that can only be read with a magnifying glass. A comrade was deported, and she never found out why. After a year in a camp, she asked for a single cell, which was worse: rats. Her second request: paper. Eventually, both of her wishes were granted. She received forms like these from the camp administration and spent three years in solitary confinement. She translated Lord Byron's *Don Juan* from memory. When she had finished, she asked to be released from solitary. Back in the collection camp and during farm work, she carried the manuscript concealed on her person. After a total of eight years (if my account is accurate) she was declared innocent, and released. Her Byron translation is now being printed, in 1966, and a reading has been programmed by a major theatre.

. . . .

I have some roubles, my fee for the publication of a novel in the magazine *Inostranya Litteratura*. 900 roubles. As much as a worker earns in half a year. I can't do anything with it: hotels and flights can only be paid for in dollars. Nor can I take the roubles out of the country. So the only option is to drink champansky and eat caviar. Neither is available in Odessa. It isn't possible to fly to Crimea: firstly, I can't use my roubles; secondly, we don't have any dollars left; and thirdly, we would need another visa from Moscow. And so we while away the time (we have seen the Potemkin Steps by now; the Liebknecht kolkhoz, lauded as a model in a colourful brochure, can only be reached with a dollar taxi, and though our dollars will just about stretch that far, it is not open to visitors due to foot-and-mouth—'a disease that also exists in the West')—and so we pass the time at a football ground; the tickets we bought through INTOURIST are numbered. By chance, a young man sitting next to us speaks German and is a lover of literature; he's read Heinrich Böll, Erich Maria Remarque; and then he pulls out of his case the famous magazine featuring a German novel he is currently reading—how miraculous that I wrote it, yes, me. Our friend knows less about football. An evening with champansky. We talk about God and the astronauts. Boris is a lecturer and earns 80 roubles per month; he lives in one room with his wife who is currently writing her thesis or her dissertation, I'm not sure which: in any case, Boris is at our disposal if there's anything we'd like to know. Second evening with champansky, but I still have 630 roubles left on the eve of our departure. What should I do? The next morning, three hours before our flight, Boris gets in touch, his voice odd, saying he needs to speak to me. Right away. We can't meet in the hotel foyer (though I get the feeling the staff know him, but no one's supposed to notice). Out on the avenue above the harbour: he cannot accept the money I slipped inside his magazine. Impossible. I explain my situation. Should I leave my roubles on this wall here? No Soviet person would take them, he says. Money as wages for work, yes, but not like this. Am I supposed to get myself arrested at customs because of these roubles I earnt in Moscow? I say: Boris, listen! with one eye on the clock, the bundle of notes in the other hand. This was the most expensive journey I'd ever made. One rouble equals one dollar. If I don't want to go to the state bank (which disappoints Boris), then I could buy something. The two fur hats I bought in Moscow are enough; vinyl records are too cheap. Tell me, I ask, what costs 630 roubles? A motorbike. Or something easier to take with me, like a camera. But I don't take photographs, nor does my partner, and my children already have one. But this is the best camera in the whole Soviet Union. I must buy it. Boris leads me there. Did I really have to ask after Isaac Babel's house on our way there? Without Boris, I would have been lost in the department store he takes me to; he has an identity card that eventually compels the assistant to serve us, but she still looks sullen. Several people gather round to see what this Westerner is buying; I know nothing about cameras, the assistant even less, but Boris assures me that it works. I don't doubt this, but someone needs to explain the thing to me. Boris explains something else to me: she is very happy, you know, because now she's fulfilled her daily quota—surpassed it in fact. I believe him, even though the assistant doesn't say goodbye; Boris takes the roubles to the till. It's done. We manage to spend the last few roubles on drink at the airport . . . In Warsaw, I don't get far into my story about the meeting at the football ground in Odessa before they laugh: most of them are called Boris. Maybe so, but our Boris was nice.

Warsaw

Should you want something here, it would be hard to find, but all the same I have the impression that they live better than the Russians do. They are self-deprecating. The things they put on display are good taste without the goods, imagination and grace. It almost seems like overconfidence.

In 1948 this was nothing but ruins and rubble—I remember Wiska, our guide back then, and our argument over whether there was any point in restoring the historic facades. Now I can see that she was right: even the dummy house fronts are taking on a patina. I sit on the public square in a Biedermeier armchair because they're unloading furniture and the young female photographer asked me to sit in the chair. She's right: 20 years on from my last visit, I feel like a relic of history.

This heir to a royal title doesn't toe the Party line. Born a large landowner, he was denounced at the time as the Red Prince and spent years in a concentration camp under Hitler. Over lunch at the Polish Society of Authors (he translates from German—Musil at the moment) he tells me that he frequently visits the farmers on his former estate: they don't live well, no, but still better than ever before. He is a Catholic. Some people are doing less well than before, but he is in favour of 90 per cent doing better.

Chinese people at the airport—a delegation in Mao jackets. Are we as inscrutable to them as they are to us? A man I know from Switzerland, a professor, who has attended a scientific conference here, speaks to me and says he finds Warsaw poor, dirty, desolate, etc.

[1966]

ZURICH

In the small restaurant (Wolfbächli), I gradually engage the younger man eating fried eggs opposite me in conversation. A master painter-decorator with six employees, enough clients, working through the night today. Via all kinds of tangents (rates for night shifts, sport, arrogant architects, spraying methods, foreign workers, etc.) I finally come to my question: Which type of work do you enjoy most? I prefer painting a wall to a window frame, and colour to insipid tone on tone. What's it like? He doesn't understand the question. What does he prefer: renovations or new buildings? They do both, and tonight it happens to be a renovation. Does he dread the night shift? It needs doing, that's all. Since he's the boss and can choose what he does, I ask him: Which part of the job do you pick for yourself? I reckon that doing the undercoat must be boring, stripping off old paint even more tedious. What's more enjoyable, painting with a brush or spraying? His speciality, he says, is hard lacquer; that's worth his while. So, back to the going rates: I gradually learn about his annual turnover, even his own average income after swearing I'm not a tax informer. His income isn't high, but it's decent; he has regular clients; but it's hard nowadays to find workers who do a good job, and then one of them quits or bunks off work; none of it's easy: the appointments, the prices for materials, botched jobs, etc. Back to my question: Which part of your job do you sometimes enjoy? His answer: spraying is more lucrative, redecorating doesn't pay much, the rates for windows are too low, but it's worth his while, after all he has a wife and kids, and working nights is lucrative. My subsidiary question: Doesn't it annoy you to paint something that isn't to your taste? Of course he works to make a living, I get that, but still: Don't you sometimes feel like choosing a different colour? You hold a sample up against the wall, but it can sometimes come as a shock when the whole staircase is painted; I mean: Do you look forward to seeing what it's like when it's finished? He doesn't know what I'm getting at with all these questions; he's told me how much he earns. Do you sometimes feel like doing a different job? Of course he does: if a job doesn't pay because the rates are far too low, except for hard lacquer, his speciality, then he can earn less. So hard lacquer is fun? He wouldn't go that far; not everyone can do hard lacquer, which is why the rates are a bit higher . . . Finally (he should be going actually, so his workers don't laze around, but I've just ordered two more beers) I ask if he thinks the workers would laze around less if it was their own business, i.e. if they had a stake in the profits and his understandable worries, i.e. if he thinks that a business on socialist principles could work too, and if not, why not. What would that business look like? he asks. A brief explanation, which largely proves that I don't have a clue about decorating: someone has to get the orders, someone has to do the accounts, and the workers understand nothing about those things and don't care; someone has to keep the appointments so they don't lose customers and make sure they don't botch the job, because as soon as the boss takes his eye off the job, it gets botched. That's just how the way is. And that's why he has to go now, without shaking my hand, without enthusiasm—

SKETCH

There's nothing to say . . . But he doesn't even say that. His wife does everything in her power to get him to speak including picking fights recently—to the point of tears because he doesn't argue back. He stands at the window with his hands in his pockets as if trying to come up with an answer. Silently. When he eventually turns round, he asks if the dog has been fed.

. . .

It gets worse every year.

. . .

Guests, all talking and no one notices that he, ever busy as the host, doesn't speak. Most of the guests think it was a pleasant evening. Only his wife is put out, and afterwards she says, 'You used to have opinions.' He doesn't dispute this. 'Don't you have anything to say?' Of course he can say something if he forces himself to; it just seems as if he's said everything before; at best, his words might still interest other people.

. . .

He's in his mid-forties, so not old.

. . .

At first, his wife puts it down to their marriage. There are couples who have nothing left to say to each other. She goes away on trips, etc. to revive their marriage. When she comes back after three or four weeks, he stands at the station or the airport and waves, immediately takes her bags and gives her a kiss—but there's nothing to say.

. . .

Words he never utters—he knows what they mean when he hears other people say them, but when he utters them himself, the same words mean nothing.

. . .

And yet he's a lawyer, director of an accountancy and tax consultancy firm, chair of the homeowners' association. He has a lot to do, lots of boring tasks, but he doesn't even complain about that. He meets lots of people every day, experiences all sorts of things. 'Why don't you ever tell me anything?' He turns on the TV. 'You and your football!'

. . .

One time as a kid, at the zoo, he thought the fish couldn't speak because they were underwater; they would, otherwise—

. . .

People appreciate him. His quiet manner. There are enough people with things to say; it's usually fine merely to listen. He's the kind of guest who sits there, not noticing that it's time to leave, just sitting there quietly . . . Nothing comes to his mind, even when he's alone.

. . .

When she says, 'But there must be something going on inside your head!' he stands up as if the conversation were over, goes out and feeds the dog, which is content to wag its tail and eat, and is not intent on getting him to talk.

. . .

Clients value the fact that he doesn't say what he's thinking; it's sufficient that he's mindful of their interests.

. . .

His hobby is playing chess. None of his chess partners would ever think of asking: What are you thinking right now? It's sufficient that he makes his next move in his own time, as silent as the pieces themselves. His patience when the other player is thinking, his composure, etc. He feels no pressure when the other player suddenly says, 'Check!' There's nothing you can say to that. He's grateful for every game, even when he ends up losing after two hours—hours without any conversation.

. . .

He immediately turns on the car radio.

. . .

Opinions about Nasser and Israel, about heart transplants, about Ulbricht, about Franz Josef Strauss, about Saridon, about *Der Spiegel* magazine, about women's suffrage in Switzerland, about mutual acquaintances, about the statute of limitation for war crimes—everybody has an opinion, you can't not have one. Which is why his wife says, 'Heiner thinks so too!' as he uncorks a bottle.

. . .

The dog becomes increasingly important. He walks the dog for hours on end. His wife can't stand walking next to or in front of or behind a man who has to make an effort even to say, 'Look, a hare!' And when she talks, he listens until he has to reply, and then he suddenly stops: experiencing nature is an excuse for not talking . . . When he walks the dog on his own, he doesn't notice that for hours he doesn't say what he's thinking, and the dog doesn't notice if he doesn't have any thoughts.

. . .

What he does like are films. If opinions on a film diverge, however, he tends to avoid it. He prefers westerns.

. . .

Only people who don't know him ask the usual question: What do you think? So he says something, when he could just as well say the opposite, then he's confused—like in his school days when the teacher said, 'Absolutely right!'

. . .

When he has been drinking, yes—then he does talk, without wondering if he has anything to say. The next day he can't remember and it torments him; he can't figure out what he might have had to say from nine in the evening till four in the morning.

. . .

His daughter has now noticed that he has nothing to say. He is fatherly, nothing else. He knows quite a few things when she asks him, but he doesn't expand on them; he merely knows what 'idiosyncrasy' means (the dictionary definition) and then he pretends he's busy again. He pushes the lawnmower around. When their daughter gets bored at home, he wonders what might be upsetting her; he asks her. He lets her do almost anything she wants. He reads Mao to understand her—then they play table tennis.

. . .

The doctor has banned him from smoking. He can't stop, not with people waiting for him to say something.

. . .

Once he goes into hospital for an operation. He enjoys those three weeks; the only thing he needs to say is that he is almost pain-free now while the visitor tells him about the weather outside, how hot it is in the city, about friends getting divorced, etc.

. . .

One day, he and the dog cease to get on. The dog won't chase when he throws a pine cone. The dog doesn't come when he calls. The dog amuses itself.

. . .

One time, for a public inauguration, he has to make a speech on behalf of the board. He does a wonderful job, addressing two cameras with no little wit. When he sees himself on television, he too thinks he's done a wonderful job. That kind of thing isn't a problem—as long as he doesn't have to say what he thinks.

. . .

When alone at home, he will sometimes suddenly fry himself two eggs, even though he isn't hungry. Do nothing and at any moment you might think something.

. . .

It's true that he used to have opinions. He can remember. For instance, he (more than Doris) was of the opinion that they should get married. Even about that he has no opinion now.

. . .

Sometimes in his dreams he has something to say, but then the idea that he had wanted to say something wakes him up—

. . .

This has nothing to do with Doris.

. . .

How people can get together in a room and immediately know what they're going to say; or how no sooner have they said hello on the phone or out in the street, they immediately know what to say.

. . .

He now avoids any situation in which he can hear his own silence. He stops outside building sites: the noise of pneumatic drills, the noise of a digger, etc. but all noises cease at some point.

. . .

For a time, in the past, he might talk to himself when he was silent; now he still knows, word for word, what he isn't saying.

. . .

Nobody can tell.

. . .

A suicide plan that fails because he feels he owes his wife a letter but has nothing to say—

. . .

Funerals were never difficult for him, even when he liked the deceased person. Everyone in black, some grieving, everyone admitting they don't know what to say; a handshake: there really is nothing to say.

. . .

He does it later, minus the letter.

BERZONA, June

A phone call from Moscow:
appeals for a protest against the bombing in North Vietnam. Immediately. They're going to ring back tomorrow at the same time, 12:00.
'You ask what Western writers have to say about the American bombing of North Vietnam. You assume that we can speak our minds freely, which is indeed largely true. If you can promise Western writers that you will publish our protests, even if they are not aimed at the United States but for example at the

```
sentencing of Soviet writers, then I would be
grateful if you would publish the following
statement on the American bombing of North
Vietnam.' The agreed phone call at 12:10. The
person who takes down my dictated words speaks
effortless German, but turns sour at the
mention of Soviet writers. I demand a
commitment—the whole text or nothing. Ten
days later, a phone call from Moscow: they
didn't publish my contribution. A very
friendly voice. Their reason: I didn't stick
to the question.
```

Questionnaire

1.
Is marriage still problematic for you?

2.
When are you more confident about marriage as an institution: when you look at other people's or your own?

3.
What have you more often advised other people to do:

a. to separate?

b. not to separate?

4.
Do you know of any couples who have got back together without either or both sides being scarred?

5.
What problems does a good marriage solve?

6.
How long do you live with a partner on average before your candour with yourself starts to dwindle, i.e. you no longer even secretly dare to think things that might shock your partner?

7.
How do you explain to yourself your inclination to blame yourself or your partner when you think of separating?

8.
Would you have ever invented marriage?

9.
Do you feel attuned to your shared habits in your present marriage? And if not, do you think your spouse feels attuned to these habits, and what makes you believe that?

10.
When does marriage set you on edge:

a. in daily life?
b. when travelling?
c. when you're alone?
d. in large gatherings?
e. in private?
f. in the evenings?
g. in the mornings?

11.
Does a married couple develop shared tastes (as the furnishing of a marital home would suggest), or do you experience the purchase of a lamp, a carpet, a vase, etc. as a silent capitulation?

12.
If you have children: does separating make you feel guilty towards your children, i.e. do you think children have a right to unhappy parents? If yes, until the children are what age?

13.
What was your motivation for getting married:

a. a need for security?

b. a child?

c. the social disadvantages of not being married, e.g. awkward situations in hotels, bothersome gossip, tactlessness, problems with the authorities and the neighbours, etc.?

d. custom?

e. simpler household arrangements?

f. consideration for your families?

g. the experience that an unmarried relationship is just as likely to become a habit, a drag, a routine, etc.?

h. the prospect of an inheritance?

i. a belief in miracles?

k. the idea that it is just a formality?

14.
Would you like to add anything to the marriage vows used at the registry office or in church:

a. as a woman?

b. as a man?

(Please give the precise wording)

15.
If you have been married more than once, which parts of your marriages were more similar—the beginnings or the ends?

16.
If you hear that your partner continues to blame you after your separation, do you conclude that you were more loved than you thought at the time, or are you relieved?

17.
What do you usually say when there's another divorce in your circle of friends, and why did you not tell those involved before?

18.
Can you be equally candid towards both partners in a married couple if they are not candid with each other?

19.
If your current marriage can be considered happy, to what factors do you attribute this? (Give a short list)

20.
If you could choose between what is considered a happy marriage and inspiration, intelligence, a vocation, etc. that could potentially threaten this marital happiness, what would come first for you:

a. as a man?

b. as a woman?

21.
Why?

22.
Do you believe you can guess how your current partner would answer this questionnaire? If not:

23.
Would you like to find out his or her answers?

24.
Conversely, would you want your partner to know how you answered this questionnaire?

25.
Do you believe that having no secrets from each other is a necessity in marriage, or do you believe that it is in fact people's secrets from each other that bind them together?

ZURICH, December

A morning awards ceremony at the Schauspielhaus; the recipient gives a speech—people listen to his acknowledgement solemnly and confirm it with applause. At long last, it is once more possible to say that there is such a thing as degenerate literature. He doesn't say which authors he means: the German literature scholar from Zurich, dignified and conscious of his bravery, and solemn rather than impulsive in his determination to speak the simple truth, here and now, in the language of Eckermann, wonders: What circles do they move in? Authors, I mean . . . We have long been on friendly terms. I am indebted to him for his generous approval of my early work and we used to go mushroom hunting and smoke cigars together; he will have trouble understanding that I will from this day on be his open adversary.

'Look at the subjects of recent novels and plays. They are teeming with psychopaths, people who are a danger to the public, with outrageous atrocities and sophisticated perfidiousness. They are set in dimly lit rooms and display a rampant imagination for all forms of base behaviour. And yet if people try to convince us that these kinds of things attest to profound indignation, unease or an earnest concern for the common good, we signal—often, but not always—our well-founded doubts.

'And today? We encounter the slogan "littérature engagée". This will upset anyone who truly loves fiction as fiction. Literature is losing its freedom; it is losing the true and convincing language that ensures that it will outlive changing times when it is all too immediately and deliberately employed to advocate predefined humanitarian, social and political ideals. We see "littérature engagée" purely as a degeneration of the will that drove the authors of times past to forge a community.

'—this legion of authors across the whole Western world who spend their lives wallowing in all that is disgusting and base—

'When these authors claim that the sewer is the image of the real world, that pimps and whores and drunkards are representatives of the true, unvarnished world, then I ask: What circles do they move in?

'Let us relay the simple and dignified foundations on which the edifice of every great culture was built.

'Let us go back to Mozart!'

Emil Staiger at the awards ceremony
for the Zurich Literature Prize on 17 December 1966.

Marriage beyond the Grave

A relatively young widow is suddenly shaken three years after her husband's death: the character still held in great esteem by the public never existed. His professional achievements are known in the city and beyond; his public achievements were real, and virtually no one disputes this. The obituaries were over the top as usual; and despite her grief she recognized this; but they would have made him happy. The widow doesn't tell anyone this, incidentally. When someone mentions Marcel (although this happens less and less) she acts the model widow; it is possible to negotiate with her; she is understanding and does not pretend that the deceased is still superior to his successors, so to speak; all she requires is for her husband to enjoy the same respect as before his death. She has read his early letters; but they aren't the cause. They're nice letters; funny too. Nor has anything come to light since his death that might have distressed her—no facts that would have revealed him to be a different character. A brief affair, which she might not have been as indifferent to then as she is now, is in keeping with the lively character he presented. She still lives in the same flat; his collection of crystals, kept glittering with a feather duster, too many photos of regattas (he sailed in his free time) and Indian souvenirs of a journey they made together: they are all still there, as is the same maid, who still refers to the deceased as Herr Doktor. Now that she's thinking less about Marcel, much to her surprise one of his common expressions appears from thin air. In actual fact, he always deluded himself without realizing it, not strikingly so but always to a certain extent. It would seem that his friends still believe in him, and in that they are united with the widow, or so they think. Once or twice, when she bursts into tears, people comfort her with words that could be from Marcel. This shocks her. Eight years of marriage, a good marriage on the whole; he fell to his death in the mountains; the children are school age now. He would undoubtedly wish her to remarry; she can hear exactly what he would say. Yet the longer he's dead, the less she believes him. It is still a marriage. In fact, the only thing about him she believes in now is his death—

ZURICH LOCHERGUT

He stands outside the door (I let the doorbell ring, but it didn't stop) and would like to talk to me; a young Jew who bears a resemblance to early pictures of Kafka, hat in hand, dressed for the Sabbath. Couldn't he come back another time. In his eyes: this was the answer he'd feared. Fortunately, I alter my firm resolution: Do come in. What is it? He gives his first name, and since I ask for his surname, he says, Do you really need to know? Several times he has stood outside on the covered walkway, a 60-metre drop. He is extremely calm, but it is easy to believe. No personal details. He read my name in the newspaper, then saw it on the door of my flat which is why he rang the bell. He cannot sing with his people in the synagogue and he can't live among us—

PS

He has often phoned (only ever giving his first name) and often come round, even though I have never tried to offer him any advice, less and less as time goes by. Some details about him: he grew up in the fourth district of Zurich, a tailor's son, destined to learn the trade. I never found out any more. Literature? He knows nothing about it. He talks only about himself and reveals absolutely nothing about himself. What I say about Israel is of no interest to him. He keeps his visits to me a secret from a psychiatrist I suspect of trying to cure him of his metaphysical intelligence. He stays for an hour each time, asking at the end if he may come again. The latest news: he says he has now told the psychiatrist and no longer goes to see her. He's keeping a diary and attending school; he won't do it.

1967

Text for the Rosenhof fountain

HERE LIES	1967 NOBODY
no great	conTEMPORARY
ZURICH-BORN	patriot
thinker and	REFORMER
SWISS	STATESMAN
or REBEL	in the XXth century
farsighted	FOUNDER
PLANNER	of the FUTURE
of freedom	which will come whatever

etc. 1967

no famous exile lived here or died near- by for the glory of our hometown. no heretic was burnt here. this spot marks no victory. no glorious legend warrants a stone memorial. here, think here of our deeds today this monument is free

no cold warrior lies here
this stone is silent
and was erected during
the war in VIETNAM
1967

BERZONA

Elias Canetti, who was here on a two-day visit, is resolutely opposed to death, i.e. to any thinking that acknowledges death—

PRAGUE, February

Public ownership does not yet seem to act as an incentive to look after things. I enquire why, two years on, the access road to an estate containing approximately 500 flats still hasn't been surfaced. A few diggers are burrowing around on the site. When it rains, the residents have to trudge through a mire. Apparently, two departments cannot coordinate their work. Haven't the residents complained? They're going to keep their heads down—too many people are waiting for flats like these. There's a lot of keeping silent.

A visit to a large hospital: here too, the final approach road makes the ambulance jump and jolt. The medical staff have been complaining for years without success. Our guide is a friendly surgeon, reserved but willing to provide us with facts; a loyal civil servant. A major new hospital is under construction. The old one, built by the Germans, is reminiscent of a field hospital, a stopgap still in use 20 years after the war; much of it is out dated and inadequate. We have to help the sick, the surgeon says, with the means at our disposal. Medical drugs? They get everything there is from the West too. He would like to go to a professional conference in the West one day, but he can't get approval. Specialist journals? They have them—not at the hospital, but in the town library; the authorities are saving foreign currency and won't accept that it would be essential for doctors, who are already overworked, to be able to pick up a medical journal whenever they have a free moment. They have to go into town whenever they wish to update their scientific knowledge. Why don't the authorities understand despite years of petitioning by medical staff? They're officials, they serve the Party and they don't owe their jobs to suitability but purely to the Party. I guess that the room where the surgeon gets ready, and maybe also sleeps, is about 6 or 7 square metres. I visit some wards. It's sad . . . Yes, the surgeon says, we all hope it will improve some day!

My handler, ever solicitous only to give information that she judges will give a good impression and therefore anxious that we might run into the wrong people, is astonished that as a guest of the Czechoslovakian Society of Authors, I would like to see an ice-hockey match. Is this why they invited me to Prague? But, no problem—the guest should feel free, absolutely free. I haven't noticed any microphones in the hotel the hosts have booked for me; nor does it bother me; I don't think out loud. For two days the hotel tells a prestigious but unpleasant man whom my handler doesn't introduce that I have checked out. He argues with the concierge, assuring him that he has an appointment with me, but the concierge sticks to his guns: 'He's checked out!' even as I'm waiting upstairs. When we bump into each other in the lobby and rejoice at this coincidence, the concierge doesn't need to apologize; making mistakes is all part of his job. On a trip out into the countryside I meet a young writer, a rising star, and other artists. A sociable day. Among friends: no subversive comments, the state is completely absent, which makes the countryside, the people there and their work all the more present. We talk about poetry. Poetry as resistance? One evening, my visit to someone's flat goes on until late; people are happy to see foreigners. The man goes out on foot to hail me a taxi—midnight silence in a suburb deserted of people and traffic, but as my taxi pulls away I notice another car parked within sight which also turns on its lights and takes the same route as us into the city, at the same speed. It turns off only shortly before my hotel—it might have been a coincidence . . .

Ilya Ehrenburg is staying at the same hotel. After a week my handler is becoming pretty cheesed off by the fact that this guest meets so many people by himself or already knows people here, including some who wanted to pick me up at the airport and weren't allowed to; and Party comrades, who also keep their unavoidable encounters with her to a bare minimum—I feel sorry for her. My handler has been completely transformed since handing me a card from Ilya Ehrenburg, suddenly showing very little mistrust, her friendliness less diplomatic, more relaxed, as charming as if I'd been rehabilitated. I'm worried about this meeting with Ehrenburg. (An old acquaintance, a young follower of Gottwald at the time, gives a quick smile and say, 'Listen to him!' And: 'He's writing his memoirs, but other people have memories too.') I remember seeing Ehrenburg at a congress in Wrocław 20 years ago; I was angry with Ehrenburg and Fadeyev, a Stalinist who later committed suicide. Ehrenburg is ancient now. We sit in the hotel lobby, on display, and from time to time a flash goes off in Ehrenburg's direction. He knows one of my novels in Russian translation, a play that was performed; he knows Enzensberger and Böll. 'You were in Moscow a year ago?' I was. In Moscow I met theatre people, no well-known writers; they were by the Black Sea at the time. Ehrenburg: 'Who did you meet in Moscow?' There were three phases to our conversation (as I recall it), and it lasted two hours.

First phase: admiration for Isaac Babel. Ehrenburg tells me of his friendship with a contemporary whom he calls the greatest Soviet writer but is not recognized as such (according to Ehrenburg) because he was Jewish. Is that true? I ask. Ehrenburg talks, and Isaac Babel is more alive than anyone walking across the hotel lobby.

Second phase: after discussing Babel, it is logical that Ehrenburg should talk next about the victims of Stalin who survived and he describes the fate of one man of which I have already heard—from the man himself. I listen. Ehrenburg: 'Didn't you meet him in Moscow?' Moscow is a gigantic city and I was only there for a week, so I'm surprised that our conversation turns to this particular man. But Ehrenburg mentions a second man I met in Moscow, a man he describes as a good friend of his. What a small world! I know that this man spent ten years in a dungeon under Stalin and is now back in the Party, rehabilitated, yet once more in trouble for signing up to a protest (in the form of a petition). Ehrenburg is right: a *mensch*, a wonderful person. How do we come to be talking about him? Since Ehrenburg clearly knows that I met this man at meetings of the Union of Soviet Writers and the Gorky Institute, as well as alone, I send my greetings. (Three months later he thanks me in a letter for the greetings Ehrenburg passed on.) I ask Ehrenburg what is going to happen to Daniel and Sinyavsky. He is hoping for an amnesty to mark the anniversary of the Revolution. We agree: a *mensch*, a wonderful person, helpful and loyal, a brave person—

Third phase: in response to his question of how I'm finding life in Prague at the moment, I tell him about the theatre, the housing estate I visited, the hospital, the failures of official bureaucracy. Ehrenburg: You're telling me! A party that sees itself as governing in the name of the people should have a special interest in—, I say, but don't get to finish my sentence; Ehrenburg: 'You're telling me!' I assume that there are no microphones here; Ehrenburg is saying things no Czech could afford to say. What is my impression of the young people here? I can't properly judge after a week, but the patriarch wants to hear my impressions. One impression among many: politically apathetic. Ehrenburg: 'It's the same back home.' What is his explanation for a situation he deplores? Young people, Ehrenburg says, didn't experience either what it was like before the Revolution or the Revolution or the war. Soon, though, he accepts this is an insufficient explanation; it's more complicated than that, he says. And as Ehrenburg orders some tea (if I'm not mistaken, it was tea) and therefore obviously has time, I continue with my questions. Ehrenburg: 'That's how things are.' But why? Ehrenburg isn't criticizing young people; he doesn't think young people are to blame. I don't know quite how open this conversation is; there is, after all, a tactical pretend openness. Maybe I'm wrong, I don't know, which is what breeds a wariness which everyone here, as in Moscow, learns when they learn to write. Ehrenburg asks who I've met in Prague. I mention Professor Goldstücker, who successfully stood up to the ban on Kafka, and I steer our conversation to Kafka's grave, which I've visited that day. Someone calls out Ehrenburg's name again in the lobby. He doesn't get up. We have to understand young people, he says when the waiter has left; verbatim: 'Young people naturally ask us how the Stalin era could have happened and whether we were criminals or idiots. It's a difficult question to answer—'

DIAVOLEZZA

My companions are already at the top of the run as they want to enjoy the descent three times; we'll meet up later at the Bernina Pass. An odd feeling as I put on my skis; not anxiety, because the descent is easy and the snow perfect. I ski down without falling over too, but the odd feeling lingers. What is

```
different this time? Maybe it's the glasses,
so I stop halfway down and clean them. The odd
feeling is still there until I reach the end
and undo my skis, and realize I've skied the
whole way with my pipe in my mouth. That was a
year ago. Michel de Montaigne needed only to
lose a tooth to write about ageing; he wrote:
''Tis so I melt and steal away from myself.'
```

INTERROGATION I

A. What is your stance on force as a means of political struggle? There are people who wear glasses like you and avoid hand-to-hand combat but approve of the use of force in a political struggle.

B. —theoretically.

A. Do you think that societal change is possible without force, or do you condemn the use of force in principle—like Tolstoy, whom you're reading at the moment?

B. I'm a democrat.

A. I can see what you've underlined while reading. For example: 'The most dangerous people, according to the governing classes, have been hanged, or are in penal servitude, in fortresses and in prisons [. . .] One would think nothing more could be wanted! And yet it is just now, and just in Russia, that the collapse of the present organization of life draws nearer and nearer.'

B. Written in 1908.

A. Since you describe yourself as a democrat, I assume that you found the force exercised by the ruling class in tsarist Russia reprehensible.

B. Yes.

A. Would you consider the use of violence—that is, counter-violence—legitimate in such circumstances?

B. Tolstoy was against it.

A. I'm asking you.

B. We don't have the same circumstances. Is it even possible to speak of ruling classes, as Tolstoy does, and therefore of people the ruling classes regard as dangerous being violently persecuted, leading to counterviolence? Here and now, the situation is harmless compared with tsarist Russia, compared with Spain or Portugal or Greece, even compared with the USSR. People the majority consider to be dangerous are not hanged and rarely imprisoned, not unless they break the law, but not for the way they think. The only thing someone might suffer for their way of thinking are inconveniences, but no more than that; difficulties with their career, but not deportation to Siberia or Gyaros, not a denial of their rights. One person may lose his position as a teacher; dismissal, but not an employment ban. Or suffer vilification from the state-supporting press and, as a result, be subjected to condemnation in bars, but not punishment by public authorities. The freedom of speech enshrined in the constitution is upheld, as is the right to strike: workers can present their demands and there are negotiations; they aren't serfs. Someone who doesn't wish to work can laze about; there is no forced labour here. Someone who desires further change can speak out in public; he will not be appointed to a university post nor employed in television and his telephone might be tapped, but he can say whatever he likes.

He won't even have his passport confiscated. As I said before: there is no denial of rights. It is clear that such people are not considered for state patronage; that is bad luck, but not violence; they have nothing to fear when crossing the street. Those people the ruling majority considers dangerous even keep their right to vote; the majority decides. And everyone is equal before the law—the powerless and the powerful. Such a person is deluded if he thinks he can become a judge, but he won't be arrested, persecuted, etc. for it; in short: reprisals are very much within the bounds of the constitutional state.

A. Are you in favour of the constitutional state?

B. I am in favour of the constitutional state.

A. How do you define it?

B. No one is subjected to arbitrary decisions and violence from someone who happens to be more powerful; due legal process for all; a system ensuring that social conflicts are settled without recourse to violence.

A. And yet you mentioned reprisals . . .

B. There is, of course, force without violence, and that can look very similar to the constitutional state. It is, in a sense, a state of peace: in which, namely, conflicts are ignored and necessary debates are denied in the name of nonviolence. The ruling classes do not use force of the kind Tolstoy denounced in his pamphlets. That guarantees legal protection—protection from violence. That is why I am in favour of the constitutional state.

A. You already said that.

B. It cannot be said often enough.

A. How do you define reprisals?

B. They do not affect the law but only those concerned—not the constitutional state itself. Violence, on the other hand, breaks the law: bodily harm, damage to another person's property, etc. That is why the police, who are responsible for defending the constitutional state, only intervene when there is violence, not reprisals—which gives the impression that the police are only protecting the ruling classes. That is incorrect. They protect everyone from violence. The wrong impression arises entirely from the fact that the ruling classes are not violent. It is enough that they have the law protecting their rule; they don't need violence.

A. Why are you reading Tolstoy?

B. Because I'm interested in him.

A. You underlined this: 'I cannot and will not. First, because an exposure of these people who do not see the full criminality of their actions is necessary [. . .] And secondly because (I frankly confess it) I hope my exposure of those men will in one way or other evoke the expulsion I desire from the set in which I am now living, and in which I cannot but feel myself a participant in the crimes committed around me.'

B. He was writing about executions . . .

A. Of which there are none here.

B. And wars.

A. 'Strange as it seems to say that all this is done for me, and that I am a participator in these terrible deeds, I cannot but feel that there is an indubitable interdependence between my spacious room, my dinner, my clothing, my leisure, and the terrible crimes committed to get rid of those who would like to take from me what I have.'

B. That was the count speaking.

A. 'That is why I write this and will circulate it by all means in my power both in Russia and abroad—that one of two things may happen: either that these inhuman deeds may be stopped, or that my connexion with them may be snapped and I put in prison, where I may be clearly conscious that these horrors are not committed on my behalf; or still better (so good that I dare not even dream of such happiness) that they may put on me, as on those twelve or twenty peasants, a shroud and a cap and may push me also off a bench, so that by my own weight I may tighten the well-soaped noose round my old throat.' Why did you underline that?

B. I found it very bold.

A. And yet, as you said yourself, there are no such crimes in our country. A sentence like this one—'there is an indubitable interdependence between my spacious room, my dinner, my clothing, my leisure, and the terrible crimes'—could now only really refer to certain circumstances in the Third World.

B. Yes.

A. Did you think of that?

B. Maybe Tolstoy would have thought of it.

A. Here's another passage: 'Violent revolution has outlived its time. All it can give men it has already given them . . . '

B. I didn't understand that. It was written in 1905, and given the conditions Tolstoy just described, it's a claim I don't understand.

A. Looking at the places you've underlined, what strikes me is, firstly, that you are obviously exercised by the phenomenon of violence.

B. And counterviolence.

A. Tolstoy rejects both.

B. And secondly?

A. 'Every revolution begins when Society has outgrown the view of life on which the existing forms of social life were founded, when the contradiction between life such as it is and life such as it should be and might be, becomes so evident to the majority that they feel the impossibility of continuing existence under former conditions.'

B. That's a good quote.

A. Do you believe in revolution?

B. Where?

A. Here's another passage you underlined: 'The signification of the revolution beginning in Russia and hanging over all the world does not consist in the establishment of income tax or other taxes, nor in the separation of Church from State, nor in the acquirement by the State of social institutions, nor in the organisation of elections and the imaginary participation of the people in the ruling power, nor in the founding of the most democratic, or even socialistic republic with universal suffrage—it consists only in *actual freedom*.'

B. What is that?

A. 'Freedom not imaginary, but actual, is attained not by barricades nor murders, not by any kind of new institution coercively introduced, but only by the cessation of obedience to any human authority whatever.'

B. I don't believe in anarchy.

A. Then you would not agree with this other passage you underlined: 'To deliver men from the terrible and ever-increasing evils of armaments and wars, we want neither congresses nor conferences, nor treaties, nor courts of arbitration, but the destruction of those instruments of violence which are called Governments, and from which humanity's greatest evils flow.'

B. There are many sentences like that in Tolstoy, and I underlined them because they brought home to me how obedient I am, how much I trust the state.

A. Nevertheless, you are pondering change.

B. To my mind, the state of law does not exclude the possibility that the law underpinned by the State's measures should be changed if historical developments so require. Current laws, for example, protect property. Those with more property than everyone else do not have more rights, but power by the law. Why do the powerful love the state of law most? The necessity to change the law is always first and foremost a necessity for the weak, not for those who are allowed by the law to rule without apparent force, because their power is, after all, legal—through property.

A. You say 'without apparent force'.

B. The situation, here and now, is thoroughly peaceful. That is true. Power that is able to rely on our obedience is never or almost never violent, and as long as no one challenges the law giving one group power over the others, the weak are left alone.

A. How do you define power?

B. Capital.

A. You consider yourself a democrat, which means you acknowledge that the majority decides. What elections and votes show, however, is that the majority doesn't want change.

B. The majority are the weak, and so that doesn't surprise me because the weak want to be left alone. After all, they know they are weaker if those in power feel challenged or even threatened and turn violent. Those in power are in command of the army. If the weak, despite being in the majority, confirm the power of the minority, then the majority is dependent on this minority.

A. That's what you understand by democracy?

B. No.

A. Here's another passage from Tolstoy: 'The error at the root of all the political doctrines (the most Conservative, as well as the most advanced) which has brought men to their present wretched condition, is always one and the same. It is that people considered, and still consider, it possible so to unite men by force that they should all unresistingly submit to one and the same scheme of life, and to the guidance for conduct flowing therefrom.'

B. What's your question?

A. Do you support counterviolence?

B. Counterviolence in what circumstances? I would not have condemned a successful attempt on Hitler's life as common murder. For example.

A. I mean counterviolence in a democracy.

B. Reading about violence, my first thought is not of state violence nor of the violence of capital, not of war either but of cobblestones, shots fired at the police, arson, etc.—violence that shocks me. Reading at the same time about truncheons and tear gas and water cannons and gunshots not from the crowd but into the crowd, those shock me too, even though they are not violence but the use of state power to keep order. There is of course a difference between legal force and illegal force. The distinction in English is clear: violence, and power. Martin Luther King preaches nonviolence, not nonpower, in the Negroes' battle for civil rights; a bus strike in Alabama achieved something decades of petitions could not—without violence, but through a demonstration of potential power.

A. And you support that?

B. Sure.

A. How about violence?

B. I'm disgusted even by photos or TV news reports of acts of violence. That is why I love the theory that violence changes nothing. He who lives by the sword, etc.

A. Here you have underlined the following passage: 'However much they may assure themselves and others that the violation of all laws human and divine which they continually commit, is necessary for some higher consideration, they cannot hide either from themselves or from men of good will, the guilt, immorality and meanness of their conduct. For everybody now knows that murder of whatever kind is repulsive, criminal and bad. All the Tsars and Ministers and Generals know it, however they may hide behind the pretence of higher considerations.' New paragraph: 'It is the same with the Revolutionaries of whatever party, if they allow murder for the attainment of their aims.'

B. Tolstoy was a Christian.

A. If you think that social change is inevitable and have clearly come to the conclusion that people whose power depends on the constitutional state will oppose any change through legal avenues, would you then be in favour of using force?

B. What would be the alternative?

A. To do without change.

B. That isn't the alternative. The lesson of history is that it never stands still, or not for long. We can say that, I think, even if the phone has been tapped . . . I'm scared of violence, which is why I love the theory that reason can bring about change.

A. So your slogan would be: reform.

B. Although that places me in odd company; the powerful who stand in the way of any reform also say that violence never changes anything. You can understand their annoyance when there are riots; they can deal with them, but nonviolent repression, reprisals by law and order, are less dangerous for them too because there is always something infuriating and instructive about the state's use of force; it underscores the fact that the message of nonviolence is always addressed to the downtrodden.

A. Is that your argument in favour of counterviolence?

B. My horror of violence is not diminished by the fact that I have to understand it in certain circumstances—for example, the increasing violence of Negroes. They are in roughly the same position as the Russian peasants and soldiers and workers in Tolstoy's day; Tolstoy would have loved to help them, but he couldn't persuade the tsar; they had to help themselves.

A. So are you expecting a revolution?

B. I would probably have said the same before every revolution that has ever happened: I see no realistic chance of it happening. Which just goes to show that I'm not a revolutionary.

A. Don't you think that the extension of prosperity makes revolution unnecessary?

B. It makes it harder.

A. Are you sorry about that?

B. Reading Tolstoy, I wonder, for example, what would have happened if the tsars had extended some degree of prosperity, thereby making revolution unnecessary. We would still have tsars.

A. But of a different kind.

B. Tsars nonetheless.

A. You don't think that the threat of counterviolence could prove an impediment by inevitably hardening the attitude of those in power?

B. If Fidel Castro had gone to the American lobbies rather than conquering Cuban villages and expropriating foreign owners, Washington would doubtless have been more conciliatory (which would potentially have caused the whole experiment to fail) and the American exploiters would still be in Cuba.

A. Let's stay closer to home.

B. The questions are the same.

A. So you are in favour of change . . .

B. Yes.

A. But you think that those in power will oppose any change in the law and will do so with force, in the absence of an alternative, in the name of the constitutional state.

B. Naturally.

A. You are avoiding pronouncing the words: it can only be achieved by counterviolence. Are you avoiding them because, as you said, you're scared of any act of violence or because you still hope that social change is possible without the threat of counterviolence?

Late April
A military coup to prevent democratic elections in Greece. Having been fetched from his bed to approve the putsch in writing, King Constantine reportedly hesitated until the German-born Queen Mother urged the young

monarch to go through with it. Papandreou and other politicians arrested, deportations, dissolution of the rule of law with, as its rationale, the Communist threat. As usual: military junta for peace and order; a ban on elected parties for the fatherland. People are fleeing to Piraeus and placing their hopes in the 6th US Fleet lying at anchor within sight in the Mediterranean: no military interference in the domestic affairs of a country with American investments. (Our , also loath to interfere in the domestic affairs of a country with Swiss investments, notes that the imminent elections really could have produced a socialist majority; you have to understand the officers.) The result: a fascist dictatorship within NATO. Photos: helpless Greeks in front of NATO tanks with Greek insignia.

On Plays

There is always some satisfaction in a fable, which tries to create the impression that things could only ever have followed this one particular course, but it is untrue; all it satisfies is a dramatic form that weighs on our shoulders as a legacy of antiquity—a form of providence, a form of peripeteia. This great legacy does as much harm to our literary judgement as it does to our attitude to life. Essentially, we are always waiting for the classical situation in which a decision turns into fate, and then the situation doesn't happen. This may make for great performances, but not for peripeteia. Indeed, we see far more exciting things in real life: it is a series of actions that remain coincidental, things could always have turned out differently, and there is no action and no omission that fails to leave future alternatives open. The only event that leaves no alternative is death. Does a story become a model by ignoring coincidences? Something happens, and it can have various consequences or none, and something just as possible does not happen; a law applying to the majority of cases has a certain probability but no more than that, and what happens does not mean that with the same characters the play might not have followed a different course or path than the one that has become a story or gone down in history. It would be ridiculous to believe that the 20 July attempt to assassinate Hitler could not have succeeded. No playwright alive today could safely predict that the bomb, set down in the right place before being accidentally pushed a few metres to one side, would explode in vain. That is simply what happened, and the same applies to any story. Any attempt to present its course as the only possible one and as plausible on that basis, is fiction; unless, that is, you believe in providence and thus (among other examples) in Hitler. I don't. And so the only way to make a story convincing despite its arbitrariness is to employ a dramatic form that emphasizes that randomness—

5 June
Neighbours who went shopping in Locarno bring us the news: war in Israel. The radio confirms it. Fears for friends, no point in working, helplessness. Reports during the morning are vague, but nevertheless: WAR. I'm incapable of reaching a judgement. The familiar threats from Nasser, then the blockade of the Gulf of Aqaba, then the advance on Sinai. Who is the aggressor? In the paper: the relative strength of the two armies.

10 June
Waiting for a ceasefire. The risk that the superpowers will intervene, especially the Soviet Union, which has invested in the Arab side; the oil sheikhs' lands as socialist countries. It's all wrong. Frontline reports, frontline maps, frightening photos: all so factual. The men lying in the sand are dead; the ones holding up their hands are prisoners; the guards, with guns slung over their shoulders, are not berserkers, just young men in helmets. The sight of wrecked tanks always gladdens me. Israel is advancing farther towards Jordan and Syria. The precarious border. Memories of the highlands there——

16 June
Discussions. Is Israel planning on territorial expansion now? Rejoicing in the Federal Republic of Germany from the centre-right: blitzkrieg as a solution. Here too, some people think the matter is now settled.

25 June
A letter from the Hazorea kibbutz. I wonder how many voices like this are left; this one at least: We are alive and so is our son who is in Sinai, but please don't think we're celebrating here.

26 June
A transformation in anti-Semitism? In the unanimous support for Israel; now it is the Arabs who are categorized as subhumans.

On Plays

The only reality on the stage is the acting that goes on there. Acting allows things that life does not: it allows us to suspend the continuity of time; to be in two different places at once; it allows a plot to be interrupted (song, chorus, commentary, etc.) and only resume when we have grasped its cause and its possible consequences; to eliminate things that are mere repetition, etc. In the real world we can repair a mistake we have made with a subsequent act, but we cannot erase it, we cannot undo it; we cannot choose to behave differently on a particular day in the past. Life is historical, its every instant definitive; it brooks no variants. Acting does. An escape from reality? Theatre reflects reality; it doesn't imitate it. There is nothing more preposterous than imitating reality, nothing more superfluous; there is enough reality already. Imitative theatre (the label given by Martin Walser, as far as I know) misunderstands theatre; some directors are masters at it: theatre that puts the audience in the position of voyeurs and cheats them in this position. To slip into the position of the voyeur I have to switch off my conscious mind and forget that it is performance in front of me and if it doesn't work, it is doubly embarrassing. Original drama (with buskins, masks, verses, etc.) was of course not imitative theatre; the audiences of antiquity were always conscious that there were no real gods in the cast . . . Brecht employed deliberately alienating gestures from the actors against imitative theatre, and the well-known repertoire of songs and titles, etc. Friedrich Dürrenmatt opposes it with the grotesque, Samuel Beckett by paring everything back and Martin Walser speaks urgently of the theatre of consciousness, which means: representing not the world, but our consciousness of it. Whatever names they gave it, what they were searching for and finding in a variety of ways is a form of theatre that does not claim to portray reality (that can only be done through a certain kind of acting skill; the playwright's task is to dramaturgically rule out imitative theatre)—

VULPERA-TARASP

Everyone with numbered glasses in their hands. SAINT BONIFACIUS, help us not to grow old, SAINT LUCIUS, forgive us our years. Half an hour later, after a circumspect walk back to the spa building, everyone has a bowel movement and then breakfast, each on their own diet. During the day, a massage, a glance at the scales, in the afternoon a walk on neat paths through the woods, ozone, until it's time for the pump house again. SAINT BONIFACIUS, see how ascetic we are, SAINT LUCIUS, save us from calcification. The evening in the main hall: shipowners from Hamburg, holidaying diplomats, directors, manufacturers, professors, all still active. The band plays dance music, waiters take a shortcut across the empty dance floor. Gentlemen enter the hall with books in their hands. Konrad Adenauer's memoirs. The only young people here are the Italian waiters. No one actually looks ill; it seems that you can buy health. Everyone is suntanned. I am alone in the bridge room. The gentlemen all wear dark suits, the ladies, jewels; waiting for the lift, they study tomorrow's diet card.

At the Kurhaus spa they don't know, of course, what kind of club has booked 100 beds for the weekend. The management, obliging as ever and especially obliging towards the end of the season (it has already snowed up high), apologizes again for having only one masseur available—

Meeting place: the bridge room.

At the pump room this morning, I tried to rally a few more members. You have to be careful, of course, or you scare people off. An association for the rejuvenation of Western society, I say. They're open to talking about this. Rejuvenation: each thinks he will be rejuvenated. Former federal councillor Huber, taking the waters here for the eleventh time, will attend the conference; he is no longer in office, but he is a willing conference-goer and has a reputation as a tough negotiator. Another man I approached in the pump room, a famous pianist, declined because his doctor has prescribed him rest in bed. I'm under no illusion: not everyone who comes to the conference will join when they hear what is meant by the rejuvenation of Western society this afternoon. The only people who know so far are the chairman and myself.

Only six gents have turned up before lunch. They look no different from the other spa guests. Four of them are slightly overweight, three are bald, five don't appear to have any prosthetics; no one would say or even think they are elderly. Only one of them holds onto the banister as he comes down the stairs.

Casting my mind to the manuscript in my pocket, I am uncertain whether the premise ('Gentlemen, we have all noticed the symptoms of ageing in ourselves') is correct. Looking at these men in the lobby: sedate, maybe slightly weary from the journey, composed, one a little gloomy but quite spry, no longer spring chickens, they all sit there with their legs apart, probably wearing braces under their jackets, men with memories ('during the border occupation') and experiences ('I've been smoking a pipe for 40 years'), but all of them still up to date with events ('did you read the morning paper?') . . . It will be hard to tell them: 'Gentlemen, they can do without us!'

M., who used to be a well-regarded artist, comes with his latest bride, and I have to tell him it isn't allowed. (I will have to explain why not; all I know for the moment is that women have no place in this association or may even know about it.) The hotel concierge does his best, showing her some easy excursions on a map, the cable car to Naluns: fortunately, she has never seen a marmot before and is enthused by the idea.

Self-consciousness among the still-small group gathered in the bridge room; no one sits down, hoping that the other gentlemen might have got lost in the enormous spa building. My question to the concierge: might there be two bridge rooms? (The written invitation requested punctuality.) The concierge's answer: only one bridge room. I express another hope: maybe people have mixed up the Kurhaus and the Waldhaus; someone ought to ring the Waldhaus. I mean: the Kurhaus. Now I'm mixing things up . . . Maybe our invitation wasn't properly formulated. Too unclear, perhaps, to stir people's interest, or too clear; in any case, it wasn't an explicit invitation to suicide. It's a pity so many people who have stayed away didn't bother to cancel; this gives our little group the feeling that the world doesn't take them very seriously. Shouldn't we make a start anyway? I'm in favour of this. The chairman, who is incidentally my dentist and the true initiator ('When I notice one day that I'm going senile, etc.'), is determined to wait for the next bus. Meanwhile, a message regarding Kurhaus or Waldhaus: no one in the bridge room there. I'm in favour of sitting down.

16.00, the spa band strikes up outside.

There is little hope in the next bus bringing people from the railway station to the spa hotels; no trains arrive around this time. I don't really understand my dentist: is he counting on a special train? Former councillor Huber repeats (we already heard it in the pump room this morning) his praise of underwater massage; you feel born again, born again every time. Seventy and still fit.

The small bridge tables, covered with green baize, have been arranged to form one long table with chairs for 100 attendees; 11 men have taken their seats. We weren't expecting queues but still, we cannot mask a certain level of disappointment, even if we do tell ourselves that historic transformations are often initiated by small groups . . . Gentlemen, the chairman says, I would like to open our meeting—I am sorry to note—but something must nevertheless be done, as our ageing society—

A waiter interrupts him.

When one man after another orders mineral water, as if we were a dieting sect, I order a glass of white wine. Three order coffees, two of them instant. Only former councillor Huber, not always a friend of mine otherwise, also orders white wine.

Anyway:

But the chairman waits until the young waiter has finally closed the doors. Nothing can be done about the band playing outside. People are playing tennis opposite. I light a cigar, a Monte Cristo, so I'm relaxed when invited to speak.

The idea:

But first I read out the statistics, prepared for objections to statistics on principle: infant mortality at the time of Christ's birth . . . After some palaver, which the chairman unfortunately allows, we agree that a certain (I said: catastrophic) ageing of our society cannot necessarily be expressed in statistics but is nevertheless a fact. I say: Look out at the grounds! (There is a reason we chose to hold the conference here.) Look out at the grounds, gentlemen, and you will understand—

Interruption:

The young waiter brings in the drinks we ordered to general silence around the table, but since he cannot deliver them on one tray, he has to go out and come back again, so there is more palaver about the dubious merits of statistics until the young waiter, an Italian—which causes extra problems with understanding—has finally correctly distributed the three coffees, two of them instant, and the mineral water, four Henniez and two Passugger, and closed the doors.

The idea:

Given that the number of people living too long has risen catastrophically and is still rising—a question: do we need to get as old as modern medicine allows? . . . Deaths that cut off lives in their prime are becoming a rarity; a fear of death has been displaced into a fear of ageing, i.e. of going gaga . . . We control our entry into life, and it is now time to control our exit from it . . . Gentlemen! . . . without going into theological matters yet, the sanctity of life and so forth, although this in fact, as you know, refers primarily to the life of the White race and not necessarily to life in Africa or Asia, in particular to the lives of a specific class and not necessarily life in the slums . . . what I mean is that since, as statistics show, we can now extend the average human lifespan so that, unlike in previous eras, most people can expect to age, ageing has become a societal problem that it never used to be—it is not a matter of planning old people's homes, which would at most ensure a more humane treatment of our ageing society but does not contribute to its rejuvenation . . . it is also an individual problem: a problem of personality, which cannot be left to surgery and pharmacy, but must in future, I believe, elect its own ending—Gentlemen! . . . If the association we are determined to found aims to establish suicide as a societal and ethical postulate, then we are conscious of, first:— etc.

He was grateful, the chairman said, for these words of introduction and would now like to open the debate, requesting that the gentlemen might first give their opinions on the principle; the articles of association are not yet up for discussion.

Silence.

They sip their drinks.

The band plays outside.

As no one says anything—only old Hanselmann, the manager of the well-known import-export business HANSELMANN & SONS, would like to know what the association should be called; I suggest VEREINIGUNG FREITOD (the Association for Voluntary Death); (since no one takes him seriously any more, the painter thinks it is funny to make a counterproposal, which receives no backing: the HARAKIRI CLUB, which is reminiscent of the ROTARY CLUB)—as still no one says anything about the actual topic, the chairman explains how the proposal is to be construed: the association aims to contribute to the rejuvenation of Western society by campaigning for the novel idea of suicide as a duty not just in words but by example, i.e. that its members will commit to fulfilling the requirement at the relevant moment.

Silence.

Who, the chairman asks, would like to speak—or would you gentlemen like to take a short break?

My addendum:

The association would be international, open to anyone over 50, both politically and denominationally independent; the members will meet once or twice per year to inform one another of signs of ageing; any member culpable of living too long will be expelled; this is addressed at the annual general meeting, which incorporates a suite of examinations including a memory test, etc.; the annual general meeting will honour members who have opted to put an end to further ageing during the preceding year, etc.

TRAVELLING

If there were no newsstands where we could buy our daily grand overview of events, I really don't know how people like us would know about world affairs. People like us can barely see around the next corner, and hearing indirectly is enough to affect, confuse, upset or leave me indifferent, but first and foremost I have no overview. I am always relieved when I can read quality newspapers. Put simply, they know a great deal. However terrible the news from the teleprinters may be, I'm relieved by what the editors write about them, the masterly sobriety with which they put each newsworthy individual incident in a wider context. How naively sympathetic, confident or concerned, angered or powerless I had been, yet again! I tend to overestimate events. They think further ahead than people like us, and the fresher the paper, the more we sense it. Who reads an old newspaper? Some articles are boring and you skip them, but they do show that first-class newspapers do not surf on the spectacular; they report what is happening and how, whether it is boring or not. They feel a responsibility. I'm always a little ashamed of how random our concerns for the world are. Mainly, though: we lapse into personal opinions. For example, during the coup in Athens, I immediately suspected that the US had its finger in the pie, but I had no evidence. Quality papers, however, or those worthy of that description, remain objective. Not only do teleprinters keep them better informed, but they also have a way of thinking that stands or floats above mere opinions. We can expect something beyond the personal, whether the article is signed or not; something like the   that is confirmed, day after day, by that day's facts, as long as they are correct. If you happen to meet (in a Trans-European Express, for instance) the author of this or that article, you are not disappointed; he knows even more than he wrote—indeed, he knows much more. He usually personally believes in it, that is, he says very much the same things in private. The only difference is that you can now put a face to him, perhaps even a nice one; he cannot help the fact that I, as a reader of quality newspapers, almost made the silly mistake of believing that, unlike ours, their viewpoint is not coloured by personal opinion. I admit that my views are not as independent as theirs. If they were, people like me would stop going to newsstands. They can rely on our curiosity, our constant forgetfulness and our concern, guided by their judgement.

VEREINIGUNG FREITOD

It is of course impossible to demand that a member commit suicide. The annual general meeting can only note which member has broken the byelaws by carrying on living. A two-thirds majority in a secret ballot. Any member who continues to live is expelled from the organization; the association expresses its regrets. If any member feels unjustly treated by the two-thirds majority, there is a complaints procedure: the member must undergo an additional test, for example giving a speech on a topic of his choice, whereby the criterion is not oratory—old people are often good speakers—but his ability or inability to see a problem differently from yesterday and to challenge his own answers from the day before. A Marxist can, for example, have a good grasp of classical Marxism–Leninism; but if his speech doesn't contain even one idea that he previously regarded as unthinkable, he is considered to be an old man.

The annual general meeting:

The plans include hikes and also booze-ups, with the important thing for the assessment being the person's state the next day, which will begin with shorter hikes, followed by discussions, tests of quick wittedness, etc. and also a written exam to check if the members are still capable of using contemporary language. (We shall need to keep a catalogue of obsolete vocabulary and update it every year; even terms such as learning curve, transportation, consensus, polarization, denunciation, model, manipulation, efficiency, ritualization, elitist, relevance, etc. may one day be listed in this catalogue.) Convivial evening gatherings, recorded on tape: anyone telling the same anecdote from his youth more than three times will be noted.

Motion:

That in addition to full members (people over 50), we should let in people under 50 who are not required to take tests for the time being, but are involved in discussions and votes. This should avoid full members applying ever more lenient standards as they get older without realizing it.

Motion approved.

False teeth and dyed hair are allowed, as are wigs. Outward appearance ('You look fantastic!') plays no part in the assessment. No note is taken of a member who suddenly turns up with a crutch; slipped discs are permitted, as they tell us no more about a member's intellectual and psychological vitality than a bald head does. Nor does a drinker's nose affect a person's score. Conversely, the annual general meeting will, as mentioned before, not be deceived by a healthy appearance that can be achieved by spa visits or gardening; a relatively slim and suntanned member dressed for skiing or tennis ('sporty gaga') must do the tests too. What is relevant for the assessment are the persistence or regression of the person's deductive faculties, his responsiveness, openness to new experiences, willingness to discuss matters without citing past achievements and, most of all, spontaneity, which will be put to the test by means of certain happenings.

Motion:

That every member should report to the annual general meeting on what he has achieved professionally over the course of the year: building up a company, automation, setting up subsidiaries or, in intellectual and artistic professions, being appointed vice-chancellor or director of a theatre or festival, etc:

Motion rejected.

(This was seen as likely to offer an artificial incentive to members: a burst of activity made to look like youthfulness. It cannot be the goal of the association to increase old men's industriousness, for this is precisely what contributes to the ageing of society. Think of business, universities, government, the Vatican and the army general staff.)

PS

Since of the seven full members I am the only professional writer, I have been given the task of drawing up a register of symptoms of old age to be presented at the first AGM. It will not be a register of physical ailments which can be treated medically, but of intellectual and emotional signs of senility. A sort of handbook that will not be sold in bookshops but available to members only.

Venice, October

This time, St Mark's Square is not flooded, the pigeons go about their business, as do the black gondolas, but they are now rocked by the swell from the motorboats, which strips them of some of their dignity . . . Friedrich Dürrenmatt on his travels: he doesn't seem remotely bothered that we are in Venice, as his ideas are metaphysical and have nothing to do with where he is.

Interview answer

Listening to a biologist talk can make literature seem superfluous. Not music, but quite a portion of literary output. Musicians have never been deluded into thinking that their role puts them in competition with biology, sociology, physics, etc. Even painters and sculptors have rarely stood up as heralds with more to herald than art . . . The responsibility of literature? None of the discoveries made this century owes anything to literature. Anyone who expects literature to define our conception of the world cannot help but feel slightly inferior. Any literature worth its salt reflects changes in our consciousness, but it does nothing more than reflect them; the impulses for a different conception of the world come from elsewhere. Does this mean that literature is superfluous? Occasionally, you have to wonder whether it isn't this inferiority complex that drives writers into so-called activism. No one likes to be told that he or she lives in an ivory tower. This compels even writers with no political disposition to postulate that literature must have a social function. That is self-justification. Even if society is not convinced that it needs our activism, *we* need it. The biologist I listen to doesn't talk about activism; he cites discoveries . . . They say some authors think that literature is particularly unsuited to political matters and so they prefer direct action as a means to a political goal. That seems only right to me. Politics benefits and so does literature. The alternative is occasionally comical; literary works confer no authority in a field where someone hasn't earnt his or her spurs. I imagine that some writers may be more intelligent than some politicians, but that doesn't make them politicians. There are political authors, but more often there are politicizing authors . . . The domain of literature? I venture to say: the private sphere. The things that neither sociology nor biology records: the individual life, the ego, not *my* ego, but *an* ego, a person in the sum of his or her biological and social contingencies—that's what I think deserves to be described: a person contained in the statistics but without a voice and irrelevant within the larger whole, living with the knowledge that he or she is irrelevant. The domain of literature is all human experience: sex, technology, politics, but, unlike science, focused on the person who is doing the experiencing.

```
25 October
Accident on the road between Cadenazzo and
Giubiasco. The two cars are on the verge and
both drivers are still alive: they're lucky,
but so public—
```

VEREINIGUNG FREITOD

Statistics suggest that the rich live longer than the poor. The reasons for this are obvious. The consequence of this state of affairs is that senility is concentrated in positions of power, so the accusation that our association is primarily made up of wealthy individuals doesn't hold water. An old handyman who is reliant on his pension doesn't have the power to impose his calcified thinking on society; more dangerous is a calcified board director or judge. I'm happy that our members (now eight) come from the prosperous classes, who are more tempted than workers to outlive their usefulness, not only because they have enough money to alleviate their old-age ailments for longer (holidays on tap, service on tap, seaside spas, appropriate medical treatment, work on their own terms, comfortable homes, underwater massages, diets without regard to expense), but above all they believe that the power they derive from their wealth proves that society needs them. A waiter who is sacked because his hands tremble when he's serving is unlikely to succumb to such delusions.

VEREINIGUNG FREITOD

The first annual general meeting was held yesterday.

A speech by former federal councillor Huber. He still doesn't get it. He requests that we should have understanding for young people. No mention whatsoever that young people wouldn't require our understanding if we weren't still hanging around. It was boring: former councillor Huber with his hearing aid behind his ear, the spa band outside. All the members passed the tests. On Sunday a group excursion up into the mountains by cable car, followed by a walk down to Ftan, where we had a snack.

Annual report:

– – –

As before, there are eight full members. The actor sent his apologies, as he is currently filming in Yugoslavia; another full member, Dr J. Hauri, presented his excuses—he is on a round-the-world trip at the moment. No one should be misled by the number of applicants, which the annual report welcomes; it turns out that someone managed to persuade whole tables to sign up shortly before closing time at the Kronenhalle restaurant in Zurich. More than a few of those who actually made it to Vulpera were obviously surprised to discover that our association is a serious venture. Incidentally, it is not always easy to distinguish between applicants and full members. Applicants too show up at the pump room in the mornings, stand around with a numbered glass and sip lukewarm sulphurous water, even if they don't look as if they need it; most applicants are simply too fat. They do play tennis afterwards, however; I only play table tennis now. What the annual report does not mention, unfortunately, is that over the year a total of 11 applicants declared that they were leaving shortly before their 50th birthday, on which would have become full members; nine of them gave family as their reason. (One of these nine died in a plane crash not long afterwards.)

– – –

Lessons learnt from the first annual meeting:

1.
We need to change the testing procedure. An unforeseen phenomenon: quick-witted old men. Anyone over 60 has learnt to provide trenchant answers to questions no one asked, creating an impression of intellectual vivacity.

2.
The members are getting friendly. How can this be prevented? The export boss, the crystal collector and my dentist, whose standing within our group is beyond doubt, have no reason not to get on well. It also turns out that all our members (apart from me) used to be army officers, the only difference being their rank and type of weaponry, which is not enough to stoke controversy; on the contrary: it encourages chumminess. As soon as we get to like one another because there is no conflict of interest, we indulge in mutual deceit.

3.
Members who come without their wives are at an advantage. (Women are not allowed into the meetings but may take part in walks and meals.) Bachelors and widowers are not supervised at every turn ('Have you got your scarf?') and if ash falls on their belly, no one brushes it away; this makes them seem more independent and fit. However, the others who come with their wives always feel exposed when they try to act younger than they really are. On the other hand, you see how much the carers need their husbands. The result is pity for the women—or a temptation to protect the men from their wives. Both impede reaching a neutral assessment. It would be better without any women.

4.
Meals weaken discipline.

5.
Regarding the handbook on senility: I ask again for written contributions, but everyone acts as if they had nothing to share from their own experience.

ZURICH

Brecht's death mask hangs in Konrad Farner's large library. The lopsided nose is only recognizable from one angle. From the profile you might guess, for a second, that it is Friedrich Schiller. His irritating death smile; not a grin, but a harsh smile with a generous hint of general contempt. The eyes shut in their deep sockets; even when they were open, they were set far back under his forehead, as if in hiding . . . Our conversation in our coats (the library is impossible to heat) would bore the German police.

VEREINIGUNG FREITOD

The objection: why do you merely talk about it and not do it? I would respond: because we will have not achieved anything if a dozen people kill themselves before the doctrine of voluntary death has been disseminated. It only counts if at least 20 per cent of the population subscribe to the Freitod doctrine. It could be some time, however, before it gains a measure of acceptance because it is not a comfortable doctrine—my main concern is that the doctrine needs us, and so we, the advocates of the rejuvenation of Western society, could grow very old.

[1967]

I'm excited about the theatre again!—as long as they're rehearsing in some kind of public premises, this time an administrative building; the ground floor is busy processing residence permits, marriage declarations, polling cards, etc. and police wanted notices are posted by the entrance. The actors wear their own sweaters, have their own hairstyles when they enter the fictional situation, still holding their lines so, if need be, they can read them. Theatre devoid of illusion: and yet the fictional situation inadvertently takes over from the surroundings (administrative furniture). Question to the author: What does Antoinette mean when she says that? That's the director asking; the actress, on the other hand, asks in the first person: Do I love him this morning or not? It's hard to say before Antoinette comes into her own; she comes into her own the moment her voice and her movements make us believe that she loves the election official or doesn't. Later, after the performance, the actress asks: Is that how you imagined Antoinette? I'd be lying if I said I had; I didn't know her, I write dialogues as profiles, and then one day she's sitting there, a wanted notice in words, and so I gradually get to know her, from one staging to the next—each time a different person.

VEREINIGUNG FREITOD

Another year has passed, and nothing has happened, with the exception of one vexatious matter: the management of the Kurhaus in Vulpera (a waiter in the bar must have let the cat out of the bag) writes that they are no longer in a position to host our association. To protect the prestige of the mineral springs. We will have to abandon the idea of holding our annual general meeting in a spa, the intention of which was to provide a low-key demonstration of the ageing of Western society. Admittedly, it was noted that the Kurhaus and its grounds have had the opposite effect on the full members and particularly on the applicants: some of them suddenly feel youthful in comparison to the fossils around them. How about a venue where we are surrounded by lots of young people? a campsite (Locarno), for example. Among the cons: young people's activities don't always inspire envy. I have my reservations about another suggestion to hold the annual general meeting in a Tuscan villa: we always feel alive in a museum. A better venue would be an old people's home in a town or city; but they are jam packed.

PS

Eleven applicants have turned 50 and, in accordance with the byelaws, are now full members because they neglected to announce their departure in time; they had been informed.

PS

No full member has yet committed voluntary death. Our association is still young. However, one applicant, the painter Ettore Minelli, has died. It's the first time the association has to send a wreath; the text on the ribbon was written so as not to offend the next of kin, i.e. no congratulations. We sat in the back row. The protestant minister said the usual things: Dust to dust. As usual, he used the opportunity to do some advertising for the church. We chose not to advertise ourselves. A hot summer's day. Our members behaved fittingly at the graveside; some lapsed into cliches afterwards, though: so young.

PS

Vulpera will continue to host our meetings after all. The firm HANSELMANN & SONS has bought an old Grison house, something of a castello; renovations are already underway. We're all glad about this solution; we've become so accustomed to Vulpera, the countryside, the pump room; we've even got used to the spa band, which plays a new film tune every so often. Even if we no longer walk very far, if we sit in the spa grounds or go only as far as the third bench in the woods, we are familiar with the area and the local names: Laj Nair, Naluns, Ftan, Sent, Guarda, Il Fuorn, S-charl, etc. We can give applicants tips about the best walks.

STIFTUNG SANKT BONIFACIUS

Engraved in bronze on travertine.

1968

VEREINIGUNG FREITOD

Finally, a full member has committed voluntary death. The first name on our honours board: JAKOB HAURI. Absolutely no one expected it to be him; no one, even in a secret ballot, would have advised this man to do it. I remember our last conversation a year ago. He was a physicist, still working as a middle-school teacher at the age of 59, popular with his pupils. It was in the Engadine (on the way back from an annual meeting we both found pathetic) in Sils, where I said that it would be great to go gliding. That is how the ancients (our ancestors) imagined flying—Leonardo da Vinci. Hauri explained thermals to me. The warm air rises up from the valley in the evenings; but it's not quite as simple as I imagined. I can still remember his drawings on a serviette. The next day, we went to see gliders close up at Samedan's small airfield. When I enquired how many flying hours you needed, the flying instructor asked, 'How old is your son?' When Hauri explained that we were talking about doing it ourselves, the athletic young man in his blue overalls said, 'Why not!' He thought we were joking—

We now know that it was his 41st solo flight. Peak altitude: 2,900 metres. He was already descending when the accident happened below Piz Padela. According to the air rescue service: Herr Professor Hauri rode an upwind correctly near Muottas Muragl, glided over the lakes, second ascent near Marmore, crossed Corviglia at a good altitude later and was already flying towards Madulein where he turned and ascended again near Munt Gravatatscha and then crossed over again at high altitude towards Piz Padula. No föhn wind, no fog, a late afternoon with perfect visibility. According to eyewitnesses who were hiking near Trais Fluors, he flew straight into a rockface where his glider got stuck. One of the wings was torn off, the cabin wasn't smashed, and Hauri only suffered slight injuries. The postmortem examination concluded it was a heart attack. It is therefore debatable whether it was suicide. A letter in his car, already stamped and addressed, ordering a specialist journal from a bookshop, and a table reservation for that evening at the Restaurant Bernasconi all point to the fact that Hauri was intending to land on the plain in Samedan as he had done 40 times before. The flying instructor said the accident was avoidable and Hauri's piloting flawless until he steered his glider straight into the rockface. The association decided that his name should figure on the honours board. A man who takes gliding lessons at the age of 59 knows what he's doing.

PS

I will propose a motion that instead of becoming more antiquated from one annual general meeting to the next, the association should set up a gliding branch, a sauna branch, etc. These branches hold out the promise of fitness; the idea of suicide is implicit. We should also consider whether all full members, including those less courageous than Hauri, should be compelled to take a trip together every year—on a charter flight.

`Petitions always list as many prominent names as possible, Nobel Prize winners being particularly welcome, although the same names inevitably crop up again and again, each time more devalued. By now the public knows: he's also against the US invasion of Vietnam, against the military junta in Athens, against torture everywhere, for amnesties in Portugal and Spain and other places, no wonder he also objects to DOW CHEMICAL in Zurich because it produces napalm for Vietnam and yet doles out grants to artists; we know all these people petitioning:—We, the undersigned scientists and artists and writers, condemn this and that, we demand . . . Where do we think all this earnestness will get us? The constant naivety: as if morals were a factor in politics. The impact? Power responds only to power, which is what the signatories lack; their appeal proves it. It also leaves you with a vague sense of pompousness. I decide (not for the first time) not to sign any more petitions.`

VEREINIGUNG FREITOD

Seven years since its founding:

Our full members are now reaching the age that statistics suggest is the average life expectancy (in Europe)—67. One of them, former federal councillor Huber, is well past it. Some full members no longer come to the annual meeting because the trip is too demanding; they do receive the annual report, though. It cannot be said that the association is disintegrating. Our archives (which contain the speeches at the annual meeting, all the tests including the lists of questions and answers, also the results of votes, motions, plenary decisions, deaths with the medical reports and taped recordings of all our social interactions) are sufficient justification for the existence of our association; a German gerontologist is extremely interested in our archives, but we will not open them to others. Our honours board still has only one name on it: JAKOB HAURI. (The gliding branch I proposed at the time was never approved.) One striking fact: in those seven years a total of 19 applicants have died of natural causes, compared with only two full members; it would appear that the mortality rate actually declines after 50. Number of people who have left the Vereinigung Freitod: nine, one of them citing the sincere excuse that he no longer believed he had the willpower to kill himself. The two-thirds majority necessary to expel a full member on the basis of verifiable senility has not been reached once in those seven years. Accordingly, seven years after the association was founded, most of the full members are over 60 and some have already turned 70: their criteria are changing. No wonder, then, that the number of applicants is declining again; men under the age of 50, whose sense of social responsibility attracts them to our idea of conscious suicide, begin to wonder when they see and hear our annual meeting. Virtually none of the full members who raise their hands can speak for quarter of an hour without needing to ask: What's the name of this place again? It may not have reached the level of Lübke yet, but it's still embarrassing. The same during mealtime conversations: 'His name has slipped my mind, but you know who I mean, so it's fine!' and then ten minutes later, when everyone else has changed the subject, he pipes up, 'It's Jünger, Ernst Jünger, not the other one, that's his brother.' It's annoying. What holds the association together is age—an age at which you don't make any new friends. All of us now wear black ankle shoes. Only applicants sit on bar stools now. The group hikes have been discontinued. If someone goes on a hike on his own, afterwards he describes the whole route and then other members talk about hikes they did in the past and act as if these walks were only yesterday. My suggestion that we round off each annual general meeting with a trip in a chartered plane has been enacted only once; the association flew to Las Palmas; no one wishes to make a tradition of it, though, due to the high accident rate among charter airlines. They're all very attached to life. It is becoming a waste of time to tape our conversations; whatever might occur in the world, they knew all along that it would. They don't despair about the state of the world, however, as long as there are still people like them. They think each new incident (riots at universities) will blow over; they too were young once. They are all still anti-Hitler.

Ten years on: all seven founders are still alive. Only once did a two-thirds majority annual meeting indicate to a founder (not Hanselmann, to whom we owe the house between Vulpera and Tarasp) that his time had come. (I also voted in favour, but cannot hide that this would mean it was old Hanselmann's turn too.) The room was silent when the result of our secret ballot was read out. It was, as I said, the first time the agreed wording had to be pronounced: after a detailed assessment, the association has come to the conclusion, etc. in accordance with our byelaws, etc. it is left to the discretion of the named member, etc. the association reminds all members of their written undertaking, etc. and in advance expresses its gratitude to the named member. No one looked at the member concerned, of course; some sat there with their arms crossed, staring up at the fine wooden ceiling (mountain pine) or elsewhere, others flicked through the annual report. In response to the stipulated question: Does our member accept this majority decision?—more silence. The member concerned, whom I was sitting next to, was cutting a cigar; he hadn't heard his name being announced. When I alerted him, while offering him a light, to the fact that the chairman was still waiting for his answer, he showed no sign of being shocked and, his watery little eyes grinning in his permanently flushed face, said, 'Mind your own business!' and finally started to smoke his cigar, which was as wet as a lolly by now. He was informed in writing. When his appeal was considered the next day, including an expanded test, it was mainly the younger full members, those in their early fifties, who demonstrated the most leniency. Why them? I don't know. His appeal was successful, maybe because he was one of the founders. One thing is clear: people vote more objectively in the first round when the outcome is entirely unpredictable; then, at the appeal, humane concerns prevail. An applicant holding my coat for me commented correctly: He's still a human being! Incidentally, that was our first annual general meeting in the new place, which means this happened many years ago.

Anyway, yesterday was our tenth anniversary.

When one of the founders says: Picasso was 80 when he—and so was Theodor Fontane, as we were once told—and when Baltensperger adds: Just think of Titian!—I counter: Gentlemen, our association is in danger of turning into a society of elderly peers. (The younger members, those in their early fifties, cheerfully protest.) I'm 67, but I think I can safely say—(A heckler: Get to the point!)—and if not a society of elderly peers, then an old men's club. (No dissent, which causes me to lose my train of thought, which makes me angry): I respect your import and export business, Hanselmann, but if you, Hanselmann, cite Theodor Fontane as an excuse, and if you, Baltensberger, cite Titian as an excuse, then I have to say. (A heckler: Bertrand Russell!) Pray tell (I shout to those in the back rows), have you seen Bertrand Russell recently? (A heckler at the front: Where would France be without General de Gaulle?) Gentlemen, (I say calmly, to more heckling: What about Albert Einstein? To a chorus of: Einstein, Albert Einstein! I say even more calmly): You are in your early fifties. Among us older men you see no Einstein, not even a Bertrand Russell, and I find it repellent that we should start to console ourselves with famous exceptions. Is that the purpose of our association? (Silence.) You all know the rules and not one of you has followed them, gentlemen, not one of you. (A heckler: What about you?) Gentlemen. (A heckler: What about you?) I meant to say: not one of us. If it continues like this, gentlemen, we shall still be sitting here in our nineties, promising the rejuvenation of Western society. (Some of the 50-year-olds giggle.) Gentlemen, this is nothing to giggle about—nor shake your head about, ex-councillor Huber, even though you still look like a 60-year-old. (A murmur of acquiescence.) But that is not the point. (Heckling from ex-councillor Huber: What is?) I know, gentlemen, we have reached the point, and not just in this small gathering, we have reached the point in general, when a 75-year-old is credited with looking like a 60-year-old, and if a 90-year-old looks like a 75-year-old we act as if the problem had again been solved—by the way, gentlemen, I think that yesterday's slide show was mistaken: if the Georgians live to 110 or 120, that's their business! It is not enough (I say soberly again) that the number of full members is increasing. Incidentally, I can tell you that there are no longer 43, as the annual report states, but 45, since two more gentlemen enrolled as full members this morning in the pump room: Sir Ralph Emerson, former consul in Bombay, whom I welcome as the first foreigner to join our association, which was always planned as an international organization. (The British man stands up.) And Herr Peider Caflisch, a former tennis instructor and now waiter in the pump room, as you all know. (No one stands up.) Herr Caflisch has requested to be excused as he is currently working in the pump room, but I also welcome Herr Caflisch on behalf of the Vereinigung Frcitod. (Nods of approval all round.) What I wanted to say is this: it is not enough, gentlemen, to sit around here, smoking Churchill cigars to show one another what we're still capable of, or for others to preserve their health. You are getting older from year to year regardless. The purpose of our association is, as always, the rejuvenation of Western society—

Etc.

Etc.

Etc.

8 February

Performances of the play —
four victories (Zurich, Munich, Frankfurt,
Düsseldorf) for the stage over the author; he
challenges fate, the stage confirms it—
effortlessly.

Joy

The happy news that it is evidently not cancer is relayed only in passing; it affects no one but him. On the other hand, the news that someone has died of cancer or will do so in the coming months seems to concern us all, even if we have reason to be joyful right now. It often requires only the right weather conditions, the feel of a city (Berlin, for instance) or feeling healthy somewhere, an awareness of your own existence, a meal, a chance encounter in the street, a letter, etc.: there are countless reasons to feel private joy. Why don't I note them down? The songs of joy that have been passed down to us were always related to a reason for collective joy; we no longer seem to have those reasons today. A landing on the moon or on Mars won't provide it. Revolutionaries promise justice, not joy. Only those who believe in drugs talk of joy; they mean the ecstasy to be found in escaping from a world devoid of happy news.

FEBRUARY

It cannot be the goal to expropriate and disempower the few whose freedom comes at the expense of working people if this does not lead to freedom for working people. The new men in Prague speak soberly, but theirs is a bold attempt to develop socialism towards its promise. Will they be allowed to achieve this? It would be a mistake to suspect that this attempt signals nothing but a repentant return to capitalism; all support for this interpretation would also be a disservice, insofar as it is precisely the one that the enemies of democratization would like so that they could crush it. A larger part of this

```
hypocritical applause for Dubček is
denunciation—but not innocent. 'Socialism
with a human face' is not something our
leaders wish to see.
```

RETURNING TO CHAPLIN

'Every reviewer pretends he will fall by the wayside and die of thirst if the cup of social relevance is not held to his lips at every step,' one man says. 'Returning to Chaplin,' says the other. 'Millions and millions of people have seen his films, his class-driven buffoonery, and what do you think Chaplin has achieved?' a third man says. 'You think you are politically minded because you wonder about the political impact of literature,' the first says, but in fact everything has already been said. 'Politics as a literary fad,' someone says. 'Returning to Chaplin,' the first man says again. 'Or Brecht,' someone says. 'Literature has lost if it needs to justify itself by its social relevance; its contribution to society is the irritation that despite everything it continues to exist,' the one man says. '*L'art pour l'art*?' the other asks. 'Now you'll cite Jean-Paul Sartre's famous saying that faced with a starving child and so forth,' the former says. 'Sartre was right,' the latter says. 'What if Chaplin didn't achieve anything, even though millions and millions of people still laugh at his films,' the one man says again. 'You're right, I do think I'm politically minded, which is precisely why I refuse to accept politics as a literary fad,' the latter says. 'I'm reading Neruda at the moment,' someone says. 'Philosophy for philosophy's sake—would you condemn that?' this latter asks. 'I'm asking you,' says the former. 'What

Sartre forgot to say was that faced with a starving child or a napalm victim, even a simple meal is obscene,' someone says. 'Chaplin was great as long as he was silent,' but everyone knows that. 'Any literature worth its salt is fundamentally subversive,' someone says. 'Proust, for example?' someone asks. 'So why don't you go into practical politics if, as you claim, you are politically minded? someone asks. 'We'll take action one day,' one man says. 'When?' the other says, laughing. 'Do you think the news that literature is dead is accurate?' one man asks. '*I've* been active for years,' the other says. 'I know the people spreading the news that literature is dead; one of them writes poems that he won't publish yet, and the other does admit that Samuel Beckett is important,' someone says. 'Seriously, to return to Chaplin,' the man says again. 'Fame has abandoned poetry, it is the province of scientists and acrobats; Apollinaire said that,' someone says. 'When speaking about Peter Weiss and Jean-Paul Sartre, shouldn't you distinguish (let's say) between an author who produces ideology of his own and an author who transforms an existing ideology into literature?' someone asks. 'And what is it *you* do?' a student asks. 'Do you think that Chaplin was a trained Marxist or a Marxist *par génie*?' asks someone who has not spoken before. 'What do you mean?' his female companion asks. 'Whatever works,' a man says. 'There's little enough of that.' By now it is midnight. 'I really only wanted to talk about Chaplin,' I say out in the street. 'I watched *The Circus* again today—'

BERZONA, March

Spoke to two SDS people in Canero. Their names are Wetzel and Amendt; one is very smartly dressed and happy, the other blond and serious, but also cosmopolitan. Luckily, I have read quite a bit about this subject. Late, but just in time—if not, the two men would not have been able to express themselves freely. Their blinkered intelligence. Someone around the table didn't stick to the proper terminology while asking questions and arguing, so he was out. The correct consciousness has its own vocabulary now. The revolutionary masses, the workers, will have to learn a lot to realize that it is salvation that is meant, and that they are essential to their own salvation. Very frank about the establishment: for now they have a use for us, but later of course they won't. In the evening, a long meal of spaghetti with Chianti by the fireside. Enlighteners who are willing to use violence, with the magic formula: violence against things, not people. And what if people are guarding those things? People will die.

Handbook for Members

> ''Tis so I melt and steal away from myself'
>
> Michel de Montaigne

None of us wants to know what old age has in store for him. We witness it at close quarters in our daily lives, and yet for our own protection we turn ageing into a taboo: the marked man himself must hide the vileness of old age. This taboo, which is only superficially for the sake of the ageing, prevents him from avowing it to himself and delays voluntary death until he no longer has enough strength to do that either.

[1968]

The commandment to venerate old age has been passed down to us from times when old age was the exception. (See statistics.) Any praise of an old person nowadays comes with an assurance that he is still relatively young, still youthful in fact. We always qualify our respect with the word STILL. ('still tireless', 'still cuts a figure', 'still quick witted', 'still capable', etc.) In truth, it is not age that commands our respect but its explicit opposite: that, for all his years, the person is not yet senile.

The outward signs of the geriatric are familiar. He shuffles, his heels barely leave the floor now; he takes only tiny steps, as if he were constantly walking on ice; when he sits down in an armchair, he spreads his legs in a vaguely indecent way. All his movements, both casual and urgent, proceed at the same pace. If he drinks beer, he cannot hold it in for long. He isn't bothered if he can't hear what people are saying at the table around him. We don't just have to speak louder so he understands but also simplify our speech, and what he eventually understands merely reinforces his impression that he didn't miss anything. His chewing puts us off eating the same food. If he still smokes, he sucks; his cigar is always wet, and the ash falls onto his tummy or his thigh. His head may look fine, especially if he is lean; but even then, he tends to have an inflated belly, which explains why he spreads his legs when seated. When several of his kind sit together, we are reminded of amphibians; they are totally unlike us. It makes us uncomfortable to help a geriatric in the street or up some steps; we would rather not touch his body. He looks like a dead man when asleep—the one time we do not pity him. He is not in our way on a park bench. If we knew him before, we are distracted when talking to him; we only see his outward appearance now: the veins in his hand, the watery eyes, the lips—

Since ageing is a taboo in our society and is therefore barely ever spoken about as a personal experience despite being publicly evident with all its physical signs, it is these physical signs that we tend to fear above all else—the familiar evidence of old age: missing teeth, baldness, bags under the eyes, wrinkles, ailments, etc., all the things that, in spite of the taboo, are now visible to those around the person. If it is possible to cure these by medical or cosmetic interventions, the marked man yields to the illusion that youth can be prolonged. By its very nature, senility is not a physical ailment but a process of mental degeneration.

Senility can set at an earlier or later stage. Its onset is not determined by the year of one's birth. The only certainty is that senility is inevitable.

Self-deception is possible for a while. Other people may gradually notice a person's decline, but they don't usually let on; on the contrary, they encourage this self-deception in a variety of ways (birthday speeches, election as honorary president, etc.), partly out of compassion, partly because a marked man is easier to deal with, as long as he is compelled to conceal his ageing. Should he be forced to avow that he is an old man—which he has been for years—he will discover that no one is surprised by his avowal; they are merely embarrassed.

The marked man begins to say things like: 'After all, we've seen before that / We too used to / One day you'll see what it means / In my day / In our day / Nowadays everyone thinks / You know, I would've been ashamed at your age / In my experience there's only one thing / We must give youth a chance / etc.

The marked man recognizes himself as such by the fact that no one envies him, even if he enjoys esteem or is wealthy and therefore has possibilities that they, his youngers, do not have; no one would trade places with him though.

If someone mentions a person who has achieved extraordinary things or shows signs of achieving them soon, the marked man immediately enquires about the person's age. (Very early stage.) The marked man begins to admire his contemporaries less for their achievements than for their date of birth: for their remaining future.

The marked man may or may not notice that his presence inhibits other people; they shake his hand when he arrives, and it doesn't have to be a wasted evening, it is simply a different evening; the effect is immediate when a marked man is present: there is something strained about it—he doesn't want special treatment, but it only works with special treatment.

The marked man finds himself entertaining new sporting ambitions: a victory in a physical game (ping pong, badminton, etc.) satisfies him more than a victory at chess.

The visible change that irritates him most is not his changing hair colour—he is well aware that hair, including his, turns grey. The only slight shock now is at the barber's: his hair on the linoleum, where it is later swept together, is greyer than on his head; in fact there are dirty white clumps, no trace of blond or brown; he can barely believe it, but it can only be his *hair lying there on the linoleum, and then when the barber brings the handheld mirror and holds it up so that the customer can see himself from behind (as others see him) and give thanks for the onset of baldness (something his shaving mirror at home doesn't reveal), he gets up as if in a rush . . . The most irritating visible change: wherever he goes for work or a social engagement, most of his contemporaries are younger than him; not everyone is younger than him, but the contemporaries he's interested in are.*

His need to give advice.

The marked man's obsession with immediately comparing current events with the past; whether this comparison is fertile or not, the old days must be mentioned so that the marked man can show he is up to the conversational mark.

If someone makes a dirty joke, he laughs with a slight delay, as if to check he isn't the butt of it; then he laughs a little too hard and gives himself away.

The marked man goes on and on about his achievements—

The marked man recognizes himself as such by feeling a new kind of boredom. If he was bored in the past, it was generally due to the circumstances: at school, at work, in the army, etc. . . . He was always able, at any time (earlier), to imagine a situation in which he wouldn't be bored at all. What is new: he's starting to get bored of his wishes being realized—

In company, he often feigns overcheerfulness so as not to feel bored; the marked man dresses up wittiness as mental acuity.

Having his wishes realized is not the only thing that bores him; the marked man knows which of his wishes are unrealizable. He calls this experience. *What bores him: seeing his experience confirmed—the future as déjà-vu . . .*

Dwindling curiosity.

The marked man becomes compassionate. (Intermediate stage.) At every opportunity he enquires about what others, his youngers, are currently doing. People already know what he has done. It is now his duty to ask. It is touching to see how he immediately shows empathy or at least endeavours to do so. Despite possessing all his critical faculties, the marked man shows an increasing propensity to dispense praise. It is earnest praise, after all, that still enables him to stay in touch with the younger generation. Or so he thinks. (It is a well-known fact that old men are reluctant to acknowledge that which comes after them; he must therefore demonstrate that he is not an old man—through praise.) He occasionally ventures criticism, but only criticism that offers hope. What the marked man always steers clear of is showing overt indifference to his youngers . . . He is deluding himself: his praise carries little weight; those he praises sense that the marked man is offering it as bait.

Anyone can make the odd joke that falls flat; the marked man is shocked when this happens. (Early stage.)

When it comes to opinions, it hasn't escaped the marked man that people argue with him less and less. This makes him feel like an authority—while the others, his youngers, stare at the ashtray or stroke a dog under the table as he talks. Opinions interest people only in so far as the person airing them has a future. After a polite pause to show him reverence, someone cracks a joke to change the subject. Realizing that he won't make any new friends and wishing on no account to inspire pity, the marked man likes to speak of a dead friend, elevating their friendship to legendary status; the dead man cannot contradict him (unless their correspondence has been published), and the younger people can only marvel that such magnificent and genuine friendships as then ('Bauhaus', etc.) are rare nowadays.

If he has grounds for pleasure, the marked man knows how much more pleasure he would have if it had happened earlier—

If, against all expectation, he experiences something new, he says less about it than he used to. Long before he tires of thinking, the marked man wearies of content; he wants pure essence. (Aphorisms as a senior device.) Only later, when he is also tired of thinking, does he become talkative.

A sense of family and senility. There is little argument, at least, that one's sense of family increases with senility. So does one's sense of home. (Returning from abroad in later years.) In his fear of isolation, the marked man stresses any kind of belonging he need not create since it already exists.

A need for tradition.

A fear of one day being dependent on assistance expresses itself in conflicting ways: the marked man's obsession with binding his loved ones to him through kindness—on the other hand, the marked man has a tendency to decide everything alone and assert his authority, for as long as possible, over those on whose help he will soon rely.

The marked man needs less food than he could enjoy and is therefore inclined to obesity, which he fears because it betrays him at first sight—although there are thin people who are marked and, conversely, obesity is returning amongst the young . . . The marked man does indeed give himself away by attributing all of his conspicuous physical features to old age.

The marked man likes to complain about his poor memory—in circumstances where it would be astonishing if any human brain, even a 17-year-old one, did not fail. (During the early stages of senility, coquettishness is a general symptom.) Memory does not decline; it is simply full up. The marked man can remember verbatim a conversation during the Second World War, but has more trouble recalling a conversation he had last night.

A collapse of natural self-confidence in late middle age can lead his family to disenfranchise him even if he provides for them. At first he tries to ignore this. He knows from lifelong experience how to use a tin opener, but that doesn't prevent them from saying, 'Oh, leave that to me!'

He occasionally used to think it was Wednesday on a Thursday; now, though, he is dismayed when it happens—

The marked man is always concealing some anxiety or other. He feels exposed if his napkin falls under the table. His fellow diners notice. The closer people are to him, the more frequently they interrupt him; spouses in particular, even when they have nothing to add, convey so vividly that their husbands are marked.

Should the marked man know something, for example when Khrushchev was toppled, his loved ones doubt his memory. This date may in truth be unimportant, but the family vie to win the argument. If an encyclopaedia confirms that he was right, they let the date stand: he was lucky this time. Nonetheless, his eagerness to be proved right shows him up—

The marked man becomes fixated on his foibles as markers of his character, at least to himself; if those around him are unconvinced by something, he will do it anyway out of spite. (Late stage.) The obstinacy of old age.

A fear of going gaga—

The marked man increasingly wakes up before daybreak—execution hour; he wakes up because he isn't at all tired. He becomes an early riser—but for what?

A propensity to panic—mostly for trivial reasons; it occurs to him that he has not paid the fire insurance yet, or he imagines that his landlord might terminate the tenancy agreement, and for a second the situation appears utterly inextricable and unmanageable. He is struck by these panic attacks in broad daylight.

Although he has travelled a great deal over his lifetime, the marked man feels anxious at customs despite having long since given up smuggling. If there are spot checks, he can have a tantrum: 40 years answering the same old questions, and people still don't believe him.

Knowing how many times he has later made up with people who have been guilty of atrocious behaviour, the marked man now tends to show contempt in circumstances where he would once have flown off the handle.

The marked man has an amazing memory. Apparently. In actual fact, there is virtually no recollection involved. The marked man reproduces anecdotes he has dreamt up for himself. It is his spouse who is most likely to notice this: he repeats himself word for word. Occasionally, there is some additional material she has never heard before, but very rarely. His repertoire is sufficiently large for him to continue to mix socially: he regularly surprises his audience but barely ever himself. He has an album of precise memories at his fingertips: the wallpaper in his parents' house; a furious teacher's dentures on a waxed classroom floor; details of a prisoner-of-war camp or a fatal avalanche; outrageous statements by his first boss; the weather on the morning he got divorced, etc.; people are stunned by the accuracy of his accounts. He has a particularly incredible memory for punchlines that went down well in the past . . . The marked man recognizes himself as such by the fact that he does not actually remember his teacher's dentures on the waxed classroom floor or the idyllic weather on the morning he got divorced; he remembers his memory of them.

The marked man marvels at how little energy young people have. If they don't feel like doing something, then not much can be expected of them; the only thing that can inspire them to greater effort is an expectation of pleasure. The marked man is not mistaken in his belief that he has more energy than most young people. He does more and more things that need doing if he is to go on living, not only without pleasure but also with no expectation of pleasure; which is why he is aware of his energy (mistaking it for vitality)—

How can you, he thinks reproachfully, laze around all day. The marked man is incapable of this: one thing no longer gives him pleasure—the pursuit of pleasure.

He sits on the edge of his bed and for several minutes he realizes that it is only energy keeping him alive. Although many things are getting harder—not just carrying a suitcase and climbing stairs but sometimes even getting dressed, more fundamentally the certainty that this day and each day after it will bring no new experiences—there is no way he will stay in bed any longer and sleep the day away like youngsters do; the marked man reveals himself as such through his heightened sense of duty.

Prosperity accelerates senility.

Prosperity masks it for longer.

The marked man increasingly relies on indulgence; but by no means all his mistakes and errors come to light. Did he really lock the front door as he claims? He can no longer trust himself.

If he gives presents, they are increasingly swapped; his taste is outdated. The marked man's saving grace, however, are his lavish cash gifts.

Dignity: the marked man's last redoubt.

What becomes indispensable to a person with a reduced capacity for spontaneous communication: convictions. These function as a common denominator without any need for personal communication. Guilds, societies, academies, etc.

whose essential and secret function is to prevent the senile from feeling isolated. The marked man reveals himself as such not through a particular conviction (Left or Right), but by his increasing need for convictions.

Once in a while (usually around daybreak) the marked man enjoys moments of great lucidity; he thinks as he used to think in his prime—he recognizes this because suddenly, for no apparent reason, he sees his future with absolute horror.

Fear of having a stroke.

If he cannot stop appearing at social events, or feels obliged to, the marked man recognizes himself as such by the fact that he is afforded more room than is necessary—it perhaps escapes his attention that the people who talk to him take turns as if by rota, but he does catch himself realizing that there's no one he actually misses . . .

The likelihood that the train will derail, the ship sink or a jet crash obviously doesn't increase with a passenger's age; and yet the marked man increasingly feels the urge to put his affairs in order before travelling.

We often feel embarrassed when we finally see an old person in their coffin; the dead person's face almost always shows that this individual must once have been more than what he seemed in his final decades.

Our first reaction is of course relief: from now on, no farmers will be killed in their fields in North Vietnam and no children at school . . . It is no wonder, however, that genocide is abandoned once it no longer pays. It pays neither militarily or politically. It is also easy to figure out that the daily loss of prestige worldwide, since the world has been informed, is too high a price to pay for destroying Vietnamese villages. They miscalculated and have learnt their lesson, that is all. Saigon is waiting for the next attack; the number of losing battles where we pity the American soldiers is increasing; President Johnson's decision is patriotic: his partial capitulation, dressed up as a peace offer, is designed to maintain imperialist power as it goes about its business elsewhere, e.g. in Latin America, without too much open warfare. A cessation of bombing against the North, for which the Americans expect gratitude: in return, the American occupation of the South is to continue unchallenged. The Vietnamese will continue to intervene in their own affairs regardless. Peace will not come until the invading army is back on its ships.

But who will rebuild this Vietnam that has come at too high a cost for United States? Given that the invasion of Vietnam was the result not of any personal failing by Kennedy or Johnson but rather the consequence of a system of domination that depends on the oppression of other peoples for its continued existence, Johnson's withdrawal changes very little; a system has been exposed, and the revolutions against this system will only grow.

'*C'est pire qu'un crime, c'est une faute*,' said Talleyrand, and what he meant is presumably this: mistakes come back to haunt you, but not necessarily crimes. Today's news proves that the war was a mistake, the escalation of an inherent flaw in the system . . . Our relief will be fleeting.

Published as part of a *Weltwoche* survey on 5 April 1968

[1968]

PARIS

Paris is always a bit like a former lover; more precisely: a potential lover, but you passed each other by at the time. She was everyone's lover, and full of literature. You give her a nod, as if you knew each other, but that is completely untrue. She has never engaged with barbarians, and anyone who cannot speak proper French will always be a barbarian—as any waiter makes us feel after three words. Your silent aspiration makes you as ridiculous as if you were in front of a lady who cannot know that you have dreamt of her. Why do I bother looking! I would be better off not nodding and just open a foreign newspaper, the ,
instead, like a white flag. Even if you know the names of her boulevards, the lady's monuments, her Seine in every season, this or that restaurant, her galleries, the dirty facades with their bouquets of tricolours, her metro, etc. this city is convinced she never had anything to do with you. I can sit there as long as I like, even conjure up memories: that Bastille Day after the war, that awkward perfume purchase on Place Vendôme, rehearsals at the theatre, my meeting with Samuel Beckett, that night at Les Halles when the two of us wandered among the morning butchers with their blood-soaked aprons; none of this matters to Paris, this city of youthful faces, weary of reminders of her grandeur. Incidentally, I have generally been happy in this city—but that is my business. It is still Place des Vosges, Jardin du Luxembourg, Seine, Arc de Triomphe, Goya at the Louvre, Café de Flore, etc., centre of the world.

Murder as a Political Weapon

The great man of nonviolent opposition, a militant against poverty in the richest country in the world and for the civil rights of American Negroes, has been shot dead by a White man. It would be reckless to suggest or even suspect that this murder was organized by the US government. For one thing it looks different when the state murders; for another, the state could not possibly have wished for the murder of this man, the prophet of nonviolence; never have they been more reliant on nonviolence by the oppressed inside their own country; we know the cost of waging the Vietnam war, and poor folk back home are going to have to be patient right now, as always. The Poor People's March that Martin Luther King wanted to lead this spring was going to be as peaceful as all his previous speeches and acts. His death will not end the poverty of the American Negroes, but it might end their patience, their hope of a peaceful entrance into the Promised Land, as the steadfastly gentle Dr Martin Luther King used to preach. What are Negroes to do? They should not lose their nerve just because a White man—one individual—fired a gun. A man who had already attempted to assassinate Martin Luther King: who hurled those stones in Chicago; who sent threats all over this huge country so that every pilot was scared that if the pastor was on the plane, this time the time bomb would be on board; who phoned the other leaders of the civil rights movement to tell them they would be next; was this not always the same individual from Memphis, such a hard man to find in a country that keeps deploying its impressive police force during race riots? Only one man can have fired the gun they found; but the theory that it was a lone wolf who killed Martin Luther King would still be a lie. They knew about the threats in Memphis. 40 men from this police force, hardened by operations against unruly Negroes, were guarding the endangered pastor's motel, but apparently not the building opposite. The shot was audible, but the sniper 70 metres away couldn't be caught: the back exits weren't being watched. A good country for murderers. The White House tells the nation: violence will achieve nothing. It has, though: Martin Luther King is silent.

I read in the *Neue Zürcher Zeitung*:

> *Having waited in vain for the implementation of the Supreme Court's historic decision to abolish racial segregation in schools, to which many places merely paid lip service, King, who was a preacher at the time, organized a bus boycott by Negroes in the late '50s in Montgomery, Alabama. This asserted their right to sit in any unoccupied seat on the city's public buses. Until then the regulation throughout the South had been that Negroes were only allowed to sit at the back of the bus, even when seats at the front were free.*

That is progress. Once, at a party here in Zurich, I heard a woman say, 'Give them a finger and they'll take off your whole hand.' There's something to that. Even Martin Luther King, it would seem, bit off too much when, instead of preaching in Atlanta, he got involved in the problems of northern ghettos like Harlem, Chicago and Baltimore, and Los Angeles . . .

I read in the *Neue Zürcher Zeitung*:

> [. . .] *the problem of the northern ghettos is much harder to solve because it is an economic and social problem manifesting as a racial problem* [. . .] *The*

successes [of Martin Luther King] are becoming increasingly rare. And it was increasingly the radical Negro leaders who began to exploit the festering misery in the ghettos.

This points out who the exploiters in these ghettos are: not those who exploit the labour of the Negroes in a way that produces the festering misery of the ghettos, but the Negro leaders who are trying to rid them of this misery.

In Memphis the garbage collectors—all Black—have been on strike for a long time, and not just for a pay rise from the council but also because they want to organize in trade unions.

The report admits that:

A second protest march was scheduled for the next morning, even though a local judge had issued an injunction against it. The paths of all American social reform movements, especially unions, are paved with these injunctions. They have been repeatedly violated.

So Memphis is not an exception but a model: rights are suppressed, and because the oppressed, with Dr King's enlightenment, violate the violation of their rights, there is resentment among the oppressors.

Amid the mood of deep unease that has swept the land, a climate of hatred and resentment, King's defiance of Memphis's white 'establishment' has now led to his murder.

Our source in Washington, hardly to be suspected of a tendentious, left-wing portrayal of events, writes the following about the trade union movement in the United States as a whole:

> *It was a road paved with sacrifices. It brought prison and often worse, all too often death, to those who participated in its operations.*

That is not only true of the Negroes. In the '20s two Italian immigrants, Sacco and Vanzetti, were arrested on suspicion of having murdered employees transporting wages. A number of eyewitnesses spoke at the trial in Boston, which lasted for 63 days. They had seen Vanzetti with a barrowload of fish 32 miles from the scene of the crime. The death sentence was pronounced anyway. Sacco and Vanzetti were members of the political opposition, a workers' movement. The civilized world protested, but Sacco and Vanzetti were still sent to the electric chair. Politics by murder and politics by judicial murder are not restricted to the American mode of government; Stalinism has employed this method to perfection. Judicial murder is always a test; it is a spectacular illustration of what the dominant class most fears and which must therefore be destroyed: in the United States it has always been social reformers, the attorneys of the workers. Joe Hill, whose real surname was Hillström, came to the UN from Sweden in 1907 and soon became the most popular songwriter for the American trade union movement, the Industrial Workers of the World. In January 1914 he was arrested in Utah, a state with the largest copper mines, still worth visiting as a tourist, and Hill was sentenced to death for a murder he didn't commit. After spending 22 months in jail amid a worldwide clamour of protest, the sentence demanded by the owners of the copper mines was carried out on 19 November 1915. There are a variety of different methods. On 24 April 1963 mailman William Moore was on Highway 11. Mississippi-born Moore was on his way to present a personal petition in favour of recognizing the rights of Negroes to the governor, Ross Barnett. Moore was White. He was shot in the back by an unknown killer.

Oh, Bill Moore walked the lonesome highway,
He dared to walk there by himself,
None one of us here were walking with him,
He walked the highway by himself.
Yes, he walked to Alabama,
He walked the road for you and me,
In his life there was the purpose
That Black and White might both be free.
They shot him down in cold-blood murder,
Two bullet holes were in his head,
His body lay upon the roadway,
Where lynchers left him cold and dead.

In Talladega, Alabama 200 college students marched on the town hall. They were protesting against the riots and police brutality targeting supporters of the civil rights movement. The peaceful march was halted by 40 state police officers firing tear gas; the students stood and sang:

We shall not, we shall not be moved,
We shall not, we shall not be moved.
Just like a tree, planted by the water,
We shall not be moved.
We are fighting for our freedom,
We shall not be moved,
We are Black and White together,
We shall not be moved,
We shall stand and fight together,
We shall not be moved.

These songs were not a battle cry, not even an accusation; the protest consists purely of a song of hope and belief; it is also appropriate that the tunes were often adopted from spirituals.

On the occasion of a strike in Charleston in 1945 by the Black Food and Tobacco Union Workers, a song for the decades was born, with a sound of quiet determination:

We shall overcome, we shall overcome,
We shall overcome someday.
Oh, deep in my heart, I know that,
I do believe, oh, we shall overcome someday.

What happened after the murder of Martin Luther King? To reassure the world President Johnson immediately sent his justice secretary, Ramsey Clark, to Memphis to investigate the murder. We shall remain sceptical. Not only because we know the Warren Commission's report; not only because the police report on the serious riots in 1966 in Watts, a Negro ghetto in Los Angeles, contradicts eyewitness reports—but because the report by the US race committee set up by President Johnson, after questioning 1,200 witnesses, comes to this conclusion:

> *Our nation is moving towards two societies, one Black, one White—separate and unequal. What White Americans have never fully understood—but what the Negroes can never fully forget—is that White society is deeply implicated in the ghetto. White institutions created it, White institutions maintain it, and White society condones it.*

According to official statistics, 14,000 babies and small children were bitten by rats in American slums in 1966. A proposal that allocated $40 million to rat control in slums was slashed. One day of war in Vietnam costs $79,795 million. In 1964 Congress approved significant civil rights legislation in Washington, guaranteeing equal rights to Negroes at the ballot box. Current practice in the South looks like this: in order to vote, Negroes must pay $30; or they have to pass a test, and the people who decide on their level of education are White; they might need to take a bus to the polling location, and those who oversee public buses are White. However, Negroes are of course free to walk for a day if they want to vote. And what about the level of education? In 1966, 12 years after a landmark decision by the Supreme Court in Washington, only 10 per cent of 3 million Negro children go to a desegregated school. In 1965 President Johnson announced at the signing of the Voting Rights Act:

> *Today is a triumph for freedom as huge as any victory that has ever been won on any battlefield . . . And today we strike away the last major shackle of those fierce and ancient bonds.*

What followed this solemn signing? In the next year, numerous Coloured and White supporters of the civil rights movement are murdered in the Southern states; the trials of the murderers, if they are ever found, are short and generally end in acquittal.

(Police Inspector Kurras, who shot dead a student called Ohnesorg in Berlin, has also been acquitted.)

What hope is there for the Negro?

SAN BERNARDINO

We take this route seven times a year and every time at the wheel I feel a lust for life. It's a grand landscape. Especially in the bends: your body embraces the landscape through motion, the same harmony as while dancing.

Notes for a Handbook for Applicants

When someone at a party asks us to guess how old he is and seems to delight in the wait for our guesses—I guess: late thirties. His smile betrays slight disappointment; he was clearly hoping for my guess to be wider of the mark. Someone indulges him: 35. The man acts as if it's an auction: 35, going, going . . . ? We could of course work it out, but our curiosity doesn't stretch that far, and for most people late thirties would suffice. He's wearing horn-rimmed glasses, which perhaps make him look a little older; he takes them off. A middle-aged woman flatters him: 39. He has to do it now before someone bids higher; he has to come out with it: 40! He announces it with an exclamation mark . . . The pre-marked man is pleased that we think him younger than he is, even if it's only by a year, and yet he's not so *pleased. He is 40 after all.*

The pre-marked man gives himself away by saying more often than he used to about one or other of his peers: 'He's gone senile!' He finds dealing with old men more troublesome than before; he no longer finds them so amusing—

If he goes in for sport (skiing, for example), the pre-marked man will catch himself going faster than he would actually like to if younger people are around—

He's not happy having to say hello to people the same age as him, former classmates with bellies and balding heads; he is a little embarrassed at such moments, especially if he has brought along a girlfriend, and also at other times.

A clear symptom: alcoholism—

Intellectuals notice that their initial reactions to their own ageing are more primitive than their usual behaviour: an intellectual will suddenly find himself casually taking two steps at a time on public stairs rather than one.

The pre-marked man finds it harder than the marked man to acknowledge his younger and youngest peers who join his profession. He catches himself considering every proposal by his youngers as a fad—although for him this term covers any area where he can't keep up despite his best efforts to adapt.

PS

The marked man is once again inclined to do the opposite: he sometimes scents the momentous in what is nothing but a fad, and poses as a trailblazer.

Early-onset senility in former prodigies.

An inclination to hypochondria: the pre-marked man still hopes, in all seriousness, that this or that shocking sign of senility is merely a sign of disease—curable or incurable, it is in any case purely physical.

Since no one around him mentions his age yet (unlike later, when no waiter makes a secret of who the old man at the table is when it comes to settling the bill), the pre-marked man considers his ageing to be a top-secret fact—excuses for his depression include that the political situation depresses him, the culture industry, the impotence of intelligence in a regulated society, etc.

A 40-year-old always on the lookout for exquisite cuisine (if he can afford it) who talks about dining even as he dines: a gourmet—a pre-marked man.

His fear of no longer having any impulses—whereas he has as many impulses as ever, it is simply that he doesn't easily surrender to them: the pre-marked man knows what kind of impulses he has.

He refuses to let anyone help him into his coat. If there's a shortage of seats at a gathering of friends, he is one of those who sit on the floor. On no account does he use the ladder at a swimming pool; he jumps in. At black-tie events, he strikes a boyish pose, hands in pockets. On bikes with people younger than him, it is he who carries the rucksack, etc.—at the same time, he points out his first grey or white hairs: as if what is completely natural were something of a curiosity in his case.

The relationship between a marked man and a pre-marked man is easier for the marked man than for the pre-marked man, who is allergic to any attempts at rapprochement by a geriatric, however eminent—the pre-marked man likes to emphasize the distance between them through modesty.

He cannot stand the jokes old men crack. That is nothing new. The problem is that they now pop into his own mind.

If he goes to a bullfight for the first time in ages, he gets carried away: the matador is down, the crowd in the arena is screaming—the pre-marked man has leapt to his feet like everyone else, but sitting down again he says: 'I saw a matador in Bilbao once', etc.

His stimulant: activity.

The future . . . For a young man it is a sum of vague possibilities (one day he will get married, later, maybe never, maybe he'll emigrate somewhere.) . . . For the pre-marked man the future is just as uncertain, but it is a time he can foresee, not without hope, a sum of measurable possibilities (he can still be elected to the federal council, but it will have to happen soon) . . . For the marked man, the future encompasses everything that no longer concerns him, a sum of definite impossibilities (he will no longer go gliding, he will not see the Mars landing, nor even Zurich's new main station, etc.) . . . The pre-marked man speaks primarily about the future and his plans.

He sometimes gives himself away through a lack of tact; in the presence of people decades older than him, he stresses that he is no longer so young himself—whereas to young people he likes to stress how much he has achieved. The pre-marked man is always the first to bring up the subject of age.

He has a keen eye for age-related changes in others. Until now he could only ever imagine an old person as an old person; more recently, he thinks he can guess quite well from looking at an old person what this face looked like 30 years ago . . . He doesn't like looking at himself in a photo album: as a student, as an apprentice, during his military service, etc.

Long before there can be any talk of senility, the pre-marked man identifies himself as such by his interest in how he will be remembered. Until now he couldn't care less what people might one day say about him. The artist who incorporates his posthumous reputation into his work is a pre-marked man.

Professionally he is more capable than he used to be, knows more and has opportunities he didn't use to have; he is promoted. At the same time, he identifies himself as a pre-marked man by the fact that he has things to learn from his youngers. He didn't expect this; until now he has always learnt from his elders, which is easier . . . The pre-marked man does not resist new things; but they don't come from him.

If he comes through a serious accident (a total write-off, but miraculously he survived) he recounts the precise course of his near-death experience; the pre-marked man knows that it will not be the same a few years from now—our chances of a tragic death are time limited.

The pre-senile phase of most people's lives is the period of our greatest professional achievements. ('Maturity', 'control of resources', 'mastery', 'authority', etc.)

He makes a discovery. During a conversation in the street or at a party where there's dancing later, or during the announcement of some bad news, he suddenly recalls old O., long since deceased: how old O. didn't say a word when some bad news was announced but went on seamlessly with the conversation (which at the time impressed him, the younger man); how when people were dancing at a party, old O. would tie someone down with special sympathy so that he did not have to sit there on his own, offering his full support (which seemed very generous to him, the younger man, at the time); how old O. would often stop to make his point as they talked in the street . . . His discovery: that what he took for the characteristics of any person are the characteristics of an old person. He does exactly the same himself.

As a father, the pre-marked man knows that his children are adults and hence his peers—he therefore expects them to treat him as their peery too, and no longer (what else can he do) behaves like an educator and a know-all but as a friend, until he realizes that they regard him not as a peer but as their father.

If he is in good health, the pre-marked man is easily tempted to believe in miracles when they are confirmed by a doctor: that you do not go senile if you stay healthy.

Given that his wife is also getting on (something he doesn't notice at home, only in company), the pre-marked man likes to socialize alone—he feels freer, free of ageing . . . She may dye her hair (which he doesn't) and she is a livelier conversationalist than he is, but she invariably brings up their son-in-law or how they met (during the Second World War) or that time they were in Cairo, etc. and she does this especially when younger women are around—unconsciously, perhaps.

When he turns 50, a moment he has dreaded for years, he is surprised: he always thought a 50-year-old was an elderly man. He doesn't feel that way at all. It's a joke how all his friends let themselves be fooled by a number. HAPPY BIRTHDAY TO YOU—but he makes a point of seeming unaffected by the whole thing. In the past, maybe, you were an elderly man at 50. He still has a good grip on himself (unlike Michel de Montaigne: ''Tis so I melt and steal away from myself.'), which is worth celebrating . . . Despite all his secret anxieties he still hasn't learnt to deal with ageing in a conscious way; he just resists any form of resignation.

[1968]

BERZONA

During a game of boccia, a wife says to her husband: You're as bad as ever. Later he says: There's only one thing to do: I'm going to get shot of my wife. He means her ball in the court, of course. All in a very cheery voice. After he has taken his go and missed, she laughs: You can try! . . . There are two options: a couple on the same team, or we mix things up so that husband and wife play against each other with other partners. As the host, I leave it up to them. Most couples, married or not, would rather not be on the same team, particularly couples who have seen each other in action before. They are genuinely less happy playing together; even a glass of wine between games doesn't help. Then he says: Listen to me for once. Or: Sorry, I shouldn't have said that. And when she doesn't respond he repeats, Sorry. We are adults and educated people, so of course it's not about winning. She says: Watch how   does it! She means the man on the opposing team. He says: You married a loser, too bad. Sometimes a couple who were in the best of moods moments earlier don't talk to each other for a long time until she says: Your turn. Just don't mess it up again—all in a cheery tone of voice. It isn't possible to have a serious conversation while playing. He wants to get it right. She says: Good, very good! To which he says: Don't you go and mess it all up now. You almost get the feeling they would rather lose; in any case, winning brings them no shared joy . . . When they play against each other, with different partners, everything is more light hearted, more fun. She says to her male teammate: We're winning! He says to his female teammate, Brilliant! or if she misses: An unlucky bounce. But husband and wife keep up the chatter on their opposing teams; he says: Give up, Helene, there's nothing you can do now. All in a cheery tone of voice. She tells her teammate: Come on, knock him out of the way! and he does, but no one's feelings are hurt—it's a game. They're only teasing each other. She says: See! or now she says nothing because her ball is exactly where it should be; he asks: Did you take your throw? Of course she threw that ball; he's just checking. Her teammate encourages her when he hands her the ball (her husband doesn't even do that): Right, now win us another point! Her husband says, What a fluke! It really isn't about winning. She says à propos of nothing: Leo can't stand losing. He doesn't react, but to his teammate he says: Your husband is unbeatable. Now and then, there's the odd opportunity to chat about children, the traffic, the Zurich Schauspielhaus, etc. but not to get on to university matters; he or she says: Come on, take your go! . . . Anyway, one team does end up winning, which is immediately beside the point, a nice evening and more conversation: at some point later on they leave as they arrived: a happy couple, a good marriage.

INTERROGATION II

A. You saw the news on TV.

B. The burning cars, the phalanx of students, the smoke over the boulevard, etc. The images make me angry of course, but I must admit they don't shock me.

A. Watching it on TV from home.

B. I wasn't at the scene, that's true, but when I see footage from real war zones, I'm still shocked: watching it on TV.

A. How do you explain the difference?

B. What's happening in Paris right now is chaos and rioting, violence as part of a revolt. But there is something normal about pictures of war zones in Vietnam or the Middle East for example. *A la guerre comme à la guerre*. Bombed-out ruins, corpses here and there, prisoners being interrogated with their arms tied together and in their bare feet, surrounded by uniforms and helmets and machine guns—it all obeys familiar rules.

A. Leaving war aside . . .

B. Why?

A. Students and others who cannot achieve their demands by legal means are perpetrating violence against the state, occupying the Sorbonne, destroying anything in their path and forcing the police to use violence. Whose side do you take when you see street battles like these?

B. Uniforms make a big difference. I can identify more easily with an individual than with a unit, even if a unit is made up of individuals too, but only really when they are wounded . . . I don't know how I'd have behaved if I had been there.

A: Do you identify with the students?

B. I'm too old for that.

A. Even at your age people take sides. I assume you didn't see yourself in the police ranks.

B. I'm a civilian.

A. What outcome did you hope for?

B. I admit that this question wasn't in my mind when I saw the water cannons, then the hail of cobblestones, the truncheons, the stretchers; the outcome was clear from the start—to the demonstrators themselves too. They demonstrated that there is no point in hoping.

A. Do you think the police are brutal?

B. There's something professional about their violence. Something practised. By the way, they weren't on horseback today, which makes a real difference; when they're mounted, civilians are immediately degraded . . . Maybe I laughed because the police officers with their round shields reminded me of Shakespeare productions in which the battle becomes a joke: so decorative. It is of course no laughing matter. Violence scares me.

A. Describe your impressions.

B. A boulevard packed with students all of a sudden . . .

A. When those students suddenly started to attack, did you think of the Bastille or did you have an intermittent feeling that this is how fascism begins?

B. On which side?

A. Among the students.

B. That didn't occur to me. Fascists are better at it; they do it with the military, not against them. That is no criticism of the students; the military are to blame.

A. The fact is that students, or whoever it was packing the boulevard and claiming to be progressives, started by disrupting the traffic, occupying the Sorbonne, putting up emblems as if they already had a victory to celebrate, then there were assaults on the guardians of the constitution, violence. Do you condemn it or not?

B. I noticed that it all began in a generally good-natured atmosphere, young people singing arm in arm, fun and slogans, enthusiasm without any tactics, etc. A certain amount of merriment in any case: not at all like a battalion before a mission in the Mekong delta. You didn't get the sense these people were bent on killing.

A. They did throw cobblestones though.

B. Most of them look very young and also tired; you get the impression they don't know what to do with their youthful energy in this society.

A. They have just about everything.

B. Everything their fathers hold dear.

A. What do they still need?

B. For instance, the guy in the leather jacket who ran towards the water cannon, I don't know what he hopes for apart from excitement. Once, I wondered what would actually happen if there were no police.

A. What's your response to damage to property?

B. As I said before: different to the traces of actual war. We saw considerable damage to property, but it is also slightly ironic. Why shouldn't people be allowed to destroy the work of human hands in their own country? I find the damage less shocking, to be honest, than in the daily images of war. In fact, there's something mischievous about it all, even when blood was shed—like when I imagine shooting at a crystal chandelier or driving a steamroller through a department store. It is genuinely serious, which makes it funny because the police could in fact immediately take control of the situation with machine guns and flame throwers, but they come across as fiercer than the weaker demonstrators and frustrated. They clearly have orders as the repository of state authority to rein in their violence for as long as possible. They present themselves as protectors, but those they are protecting remain invisible. Suddenly the police cordon off a boulevard. Why? To make it clear where the state begins—precisely where the police units are now standing. If they're going to start hitting people, they need disobedience, and that can be provoked by cordoning off a boulevard. But the police themselves seem dismayed. Every operation they carry out takes a bit of the shine off their aura of protectors. It turns out that paratroopers are not only better trained in using violence, they are also better equipped than the students and whoever else is out on the boulevard; each and every one, it struck me, was superior to a whole student union: he acts on orders. This creates a natural relationship to violence; he isn't beating or shooting someone as an individual, and the state can always deal with matters of conscience.

A. So you *are* taking sides?

B. Theorists of revolution say this one isn't rooted in the masses, etc. and is therefore a misplaced enterprise; it's no way to lead a revolution.

A. They appear to be right.

B. But perhaps the enterprise is still important for the society in power; it realizes that it can only sustain itself through violence—which is what ordinary citizens would rather forget.

ROME, June

The man at the newsstand on PIAZZA DI SPAGNA doesn't recognize me any more. The waiter does: ? The snot-nosed old beggar woman with a cigarette in her mouth is still there. VIA GIULIA. As with every return to a former home: you start to doubt yourself. In VIA CORONARI they are still upholstering and polishing antiques, Settecento chairs, chests from Abruzzo, tables from Tuscany. VIA MARGUTTA now has beat shops. VIA DELLA CROCE hasn't changed: fruit, eggs, vegetables, wine, pasta, flowers. One Roman friend still has his eagle owl. Another, a Sicilian, is still a professor. SPERLONGA: the sea cannot be expected to have changed, but I still feel slightly stunned that it hasn't. The same waves. We sit down on the same chairs, eat the same fish: . CERVETERI: the Etruscans are still every bit as dead. PIAZZA VENEZIA: only the policemen get younger, the traffic even busier. GIANICOLO, view of the city: we stay for too long everywhere . . .

Questionnaire

1.
Do you feel sorry for women?

2.
Why? (Why not?)

3.
When a woman's hands and eyes and lips show arousal, desire, etc. because you've touched them, do you attribute this to yourself?

4.
What do you think about men:

a. when you come after them?

b. when you come before them?

c. when you both love the same woman at the same time?

5.
Did you choose your partner?

6.
If you happen to meet up again in friendly circumstances with ex-partners many years later, does it reassure you about your past relationship, or are you surprised, i.e. do you get the feeling that your professional life and your political views actually interested them, or do you now feel that you could have spared yourselves all the related conversations?

7.
Does a clever lesbian unsettle you?

8.
Do you think you know how to win a woman's love, and if you were to learn how you really earnt a woman's love, would you doubt your love?

9.
What do you consider masculine?

10.
Do you have sufficient evidence to support the view that women are particularly well suited to specific tasks that men regard as beneath them?

11.
Which of these has seduced you most often:

a. motherliness?
b. feeling admired?
c. alcohol?
d. anxiety about not being a proper man?
e. beauty?
f. the premature certainty that you will play the dominant role, even if it is as a loving protector?

12.
Who invented the castration complex?

13.
In which of these two situations do you speak more fondly of a past relationship: when you left a woman, or when the woman left you?

14.
Do you learn your lessons from one relationship for the next?

15.
If you keep having the same experience with women, do you put it down to the women, i.e. do you think it has taught you to be a connoisseur of women?

16.
Would you like to be your wife?

17.
What has taught you more about intimate relationships between the sexes: conversations with other men, or conversations with women? Or do you learn most from things other than conversations: from women's reactions, i.e. by noting what women are accustomed to and what they are not, what they expect from a man, fear in him, etc.?

18.
If you find a conversation with a woman stimulating: how long do you manage to have the conversation without thoughts popping into your mind which you keep to yourself because they're irrelevant?

19.
Can you imagine a world dominated by women?

20.
Do you believe women incapable of:

a. philosophy?

b. organization?

c. art?

d. technology?

e. politics?

and do you therefore consider a woman who does not conform to your male prejudice to be unfeminine?

21.
What do you admire about women?

22.
Would you like to be kept by a woman:

a. on her inherited wealth?

b. on her professional income?

23.
And why not?

24.
Do you believe in biology, i.e. that current relations between men and women are immutable, or do you think, for example, that it is a legacy of millennia that women have no grammar of their own to express their thinking and rely instead on male linguistic conventions, and are subject to them?

25.
Why do we not need to understand women?

BERZONA

A hippie invasion: he is 19, she has just turned 15, and they have both extricated themselves from a repressive system by dropping out of school—years ago in his case. He doesn't accept any money from his father (that's what he says anyway), and there's no question of studying or doing an apprenticeship: all repressive institutions. Favourite topic of conversation: how stupid the police are. And how stupid teachers are. And everything else too. Everything's based on performance. Frustration due to taboos breeds aggressivity, etc. we have to denounce it, change society, destroy it first. Lots of jargon, nothing but jargon in fact, third-hand terms; all translated into comfortable

```
positions. They revel in their lazy protest
posturing. The young man promises me hash; to
pay me back and all. He wears a wreath of
little flowers over his crotch. Their
knowledge is confined to LSD. The 15-year-old,
otherwise as silent as the grave, tells us
what it's like: colours that make it worth
being alive. They're probably on a trip . . .
```

Moscow, 17 June

A stroll around Red Square on my own. A summer's night. Lots of people out for a walk in one of the world's great cities; country folk. Skyscrapers as in the West now. Girls in not very short skirts but still shorter than two years ago; men wearing white shirts without jackets. Sunday. I don't find a single outdoor cafe. All you can do is wander. From time to time a couple of lovers on a public bench; they hold hands in silence. No neon adverts, but the streets are bright; it's a pity I'm thirsty. Once there's a barrel on two wheels drawn by a donkey; people queuing up for a drink of kvass. Smartly uniformed soldiers with Asian features; they aren't at home here either.

18 June

L. has been expelled from the Party for protesting against the trials of authors, and has been relieved of his teaching post and reprimanded by the Union of Soviet Writers. K. too. Another crackdown: a reaction to Prague? We eat out publicly in a restaurant where the two censured writers are known, and we talk in German.

Hotel Rossiya:

View of the Kremlin. HILTON-style comfort, except that the fitted carpets are crinkled. Breakfast: I sit down at a table; I am not with a delegation and the waiters give no instructions on what to do if you're not with a delegation. I'm not bothered. After all, I haven't come to Moscow to have breakfast.

Sofiya:

Her German is impeccable and she takes care of everything; I can see how powerful a Writers' Union pass is as we don't have to queue. What not even Sofiya can manage is to get the people at the counters to be helpful—not obsequious but maybe polite or at least not sullen. Sofiya doesn't seem to find it unusual. She doesn't ask who I met in Moscow yesterday. I'm completely free, of course. We drink beer—when it finally comes; I praise Russian beer. Topics that are off limits: Paris, the situation after the street battles and the general strike. As soon as conversation turns to other countries, a curtain comes down. So I ask her about tipping practices in the Soviet Union. Sofiya confirms that there are no tips; people here don't live from alms dispensed at a master's whim. An hour later, when my friend gets into an argument with the taxi driver, I discover that the taxi driver wasn't happy with the tip. Dinner in the kitchen: what does it take to get expelled from the Party? No jail sentence this time; he calls this progress. No great acrimony; patience.

I hold up the piece of paper with the address of the Swiss embassy on it in Russian script, but the taxi driver: *Nyet.* I don't know. The second: *Nyet.* The third: *Nyet.* Only the fourth deigns, with a long-suffering sigh, to look it up in the A to Z.

Hotel lobby:

It could be in Milan, in Hamburg or Geneva, the same architecture, but instead of middle-class men coming out of the lift there are workers. It's natural for them to walk on marble, bourgeois ostentation as their ambition: we can do it too! Their architecture has no style of its own—

Embarkation for Gorky:

A ship full of authors, but: a ship is always lovely, and this is the first time I've ever travelled by ship on a river. A hot summer's evening. I don't know anyone on board apart from Günther Weisenborn. I say hello to Christa Wolf (East Germany) and sense distrust. The speaker plays music from a French film. Gulls. We glide across the water—

VOLGA, 19–20 June

Sharing a cabin with a Finnish writer who speaks Russian; no common language. He wakes me up and points up into the air and then into his open mouth: breakfast.

The Volga—

Writers from all over the world, but no one famous apart from Alberti. There's no list, unfortunately. I ask my way slowly through the group. No one from France. An Italian translator of Gorky; no Moravia, no Pasolini, no Sanguinetti. Some old factotum from the US, another from Norway. No young writers. No one from England; a poet from Iceland who doesn't say anything. No Czechoslovakian authors; a happy female translator of Gorky and an elderly gentleman from Prague—a critic, I think. Indians in their wonderful traditional outfits; their dignity, the earnestness of their dark eyes. An author from Australia who joins up with me because I understand English. A man from Uruguay; a small group that speak Spanish, stick together and seem very lively. Hungarians invite me to Hungary, Bulgarians to Bulgaria. The loudspeaker announcements are in Russian only. Sofiya arranges contacts with Soviet writers; they are Party officials. None of the Soviet authors whose names are familiar back home are here . . . A work outing; the firm encourages us to make personal contacts, but this is impossible due to the lack of a common language, and people gather in language groups. The chairman of the Weimar Writers' Union only speaks German but is still happy to be here; he hands his camera to someone to take a picture of him sitting with Indians, and I have to join them: writers from around the world.

An evening of vodka.

The Volga is brown and slow and wide, its banks sparsely inhabited, fields, plains, forests, the occasional cluster of wooden houses; I enjoy the space. Once, a reservoir, no banks in sight for hours; then a lock, then more banks that look deserted, the flat emptiness with churches from sunrise to sunset, many disused churches, land under sky, our almost silent gliding across the brown water, gulls; it isn't boring when you sit on deck and watch.

Conversation:

Mikhalkov (total copies published: 75 million) tells me how Soviet writers are paid. What I understand is: Soviet literature is not manipulated by capitalist profit motives; it isn't demand but the authorities that determine the print run. In the West, he says, writers are always dependent on the public; here they aren't. Mikhalkov is an affable man. Not a single Soviet child grows up without his books. He also writes for the stage and for television. To occupy position like his as well is a strain of course, but Soviet writers submit to it; service to society. Mikhalkov speaks German. Paper is still too scarce to publish a large number of copies of every book. Soviet writers are paid according to print run, which is, as previously mentioned, set in advance by the authorities; they would suffer no loss if the public preferred a different book. I understand. Mikhalkov is chairman of the Moscow Writers' Union. I do a lot of nodding . . . There's no point in arguing with him. I praise only what is praise worthy, and some things are. I answer no differently than I would elsewhere. Lying begins with silence. Of course, as a foreigner I can say whatever I want, but gradually I stop. The right comments are the official comments. It is known in advance, so there is nothing to discuss. The best thing is simply to like Russia. I praise the great breadth of the Volga; I refrain from relating my memories of the Mississippi; comparisons irritate them. Seated between bureaucrats at lunch, I praise the Georgian wine, which is very good; I make a constant show of being happy. I am not asked: what do you think of the riots in Berlin, the situation in Paris, the incidents in Rome? People are not after information. I praise Soviet cucumbers. It is also possible to praise the old icons. If you don't get there first, they praise their own cucumbers, and that too is tedious. Of course, I keep to myself the things I miss; I haven't come here to offend people. My poor Sofiya: she shortens my questions while translating them to tone down their unseemly aspects and suffers in front of her superiors like a mother with an accident-prone child. It doesn't really matter who answers my question; they never contradict one another. The only criticism they know is criticism of the West, and it is uninhibited and simple, unconcerned with facts; no one is allowed to criticize Soviet conditions—no one practises it, least of all bureaucrats.

PLENARY SESSION on deck:

We sit there with headphones on; gulls; every speaker says the same things about Maxim Gorky, translations into 13 languages are superfluous; Maxim Gorky as a proletarian writer, a master of socialist realism, gradually I understand it in Spanish, Romanian, Portuguese, Finnish and even when I can't make out what the language is. Of Maxim Gorky and his conflict with Lenin, his exile after the revolution, Maxim Gorky and Stalin, the writer and the state, not a word. When I leave for the front deck, I am not alone in skipping the plenary session; even bureaucrats find it boring, but the firm demands it.

Another evening of vodka.

Talk to Christa Wolf and her husband until four in the morning, outside the night is bright above the Volga and the land. Refreshing to agree to differ. A Soviet comrade sat with us for a long time, listening in but without disturbing me. He seems to have filed his report: my bureaucrats know today that we had a very interesting conversation.

Reception in Gorky:

Children are lining the quayside with gay white flowers with red ribbons. Each progressive writer from all over the world receives a bunch, and I get one too, peonies and angina.

GORKY, 20 June

At our arrival yesterday a waiting Russian student was looking for some personal advice for her exam; a childish, slightly too big face with spherical, very light-coloured eyes. She came here from Moscow. Her arduous trip was full of expectation; I stood there shivering and holding peonies. Why didn't I at least give her the peonies? Sofiya packed her off to Moscow; the girl isn't part of the programme.

21 June

I now have three Russian mothers: the fat maid and a nurse on the hotel staff and then the doctor who sits down on my bed and pats my chest and back; all three of them are tender in their concern, a room full of chubby mothers. No shared language They wash the back of my neck, and all I need to do is stretch out my leg to have my feet washed. Later on, the maid brings me a present: three Russian dolls. The Union of Soviet Writers is maternal too; my Party official says, You won't be missing anything if you miss the plenary session. Sofiya also drops in frequently with greetings from others. The chubby maid tells a long story of which I don't understand a word, but she doesn't get annoyed. Herr Wolf brings me something to read, a magazine called *Sinn und Form* in which I read a piece of prose by Christa Wolf. A Soviet critic (the man who listened in on that night-time conversation with Christa Wolf) pays me a visit with a woman: both are very well informed about the literature of the capitalist world. Suddenly, a more open conversation. I should visit Novosibirsk, he says, the city of scientists, progressive Russia. He speaks German, she on the other hand speaks English; he pretends he doesn't understand English, and she pretends she doesn't understand German; so she speaks and he speaks as if in private with me: off the record. They stay for a long time, and I get the feeling that they're glad to have an hour away from the Union. When Sofiya arrives, the conversation turns official again; I cannot deny that, unfortunately, I find swallowing painful.

22 June

A tour of the city with the chief architect of Gorky. There's lots of building work going on, but I would have some questions. Instead, I'm shown the same thing, over and over again. I see: one block of flats next to the other like boxes for bees, all of them five-storey buildings, a gigantic wasteland. I ask: What is your experience with high-rise buildings? Oh yes, oh sure, oh of course: high-rise very good. Why don't I see any? As a concession I admit that I live in a high-rise building and am not happy there; it doesn't alleviate the suspicion that I, a guest from a capitalist country, don't believe socialism capable of high-rise construction. Hence: lots of high-rise buildings in the Soviet Union, yes of course, high-rise buildings lots. In between a project by our chief architect: a school; he is still using pilasters and Baalbek columns. More lecturing: high-rise buildings have the advantage of providing unobstructed views with the same residential density. I know this, and it's the same back home, but I don't say anything. What's the use? A nice view of the Volga as he uses the fourth specimen to explain what everyone grasped decades ago: prefabricated elements. It's annoying. I nodded at the first specimen so as not to spoil the man's fun; I nodded at the second specimen featuring an identical explanation so as to spare him a third; at the third specimen I remind the interpreter that I studied architecture. Incidentally, what the chief architect shows are not variations on the familiar construction design but exact replications—as a socialist achievement. Presented with the fourth specimen, I look the other way, towards the Volga: I nod, I nod. I'm not a huge fan of old churches, but here is one, and I'm shown around inside too; they are proud of the beautiful old Russian churches. Rightly so. We carry on driving: more estates, estates under construction; I look and look, as expected, and stay silent and should really say something from time to time. I'm sweating. The buildings I see unfortunately deserve no praise: stolid and horrible and devoid of imagination, not good enough for even a dissertation, but finished. I praise the trees along the roadside and hear that they were planted, all planted. Once, a large factory: this is where Volga cars are built. Someone points to a building: laboratory! and since I am not astonished, once more: laboratory! I find out that before a car goes into mass production, Soviet engineers do lots of tests and calculations and so forth. When on the way back they repeat, laboratory, I feel uncomfortable; silence is interpreted as mistrust, if not stubborn envy. I ask how much a Volga costs. 5,200 roubles. Since they expect me to be amazed at how much cheaper cars are here than in the capitalist West, I do the sums. According to the black-market rate: 6,000 Swiss francs, enough for a Volkswagen. But I know this rate is impossible. According to the official exchange rate: 22,000 francs, the price of a Porsche; but I know what a Volga car is like, we're driving in a Volga, and I confess my amazement at how expensive it is when I consider the wages here: 100 to 170 roubles per month. Instead, I am told that petrol is four times cheaper here than in the West—

Attempt to initiate a discussion:

Garden cities have been held up as an ideal since the beginning of the century and several have been realized around the world; are they the right path, or do they lead to a disintegration of cities? The liveliness of earlier cities: workplace—living place—after-work place as a unified space; nowadays, on the other hand, there is a geographical separation between residential city and cultural city. What do Soviet sociologists think of this? Satellite towns, even if they are equipped with cinemas and schools and the rest, will never be a social hotspot; on the other hand, the city centre, no longer inhabited, only visited, necessarily loses its intensity. That is our experience, which gives rise to the question: are cities even possible in an industrialized society where workplaces can no longer be in the city centre or living places next to workplaces? If not, what replaces the city as a social hotspot? I ask them. No discussion. Here, there are only solutions; what has been built is the solution.

In the evening a large banquet with long tables, bottles always within easy reach, toasts no one can hear despite the loudspeakers, everyone immediately starts drinking, the city of Gorky and the Gorky City Writers' Union welcome authors from around the world. It's hot in the hall, everyone takes off their jackets, caviar, melting aspic, approximately 500 people in backslapping mood; I sit with the Germans, who are quieter, while the Georgians buzz with life, embracing one another, and an officious Romanian reminds everyone over the loudspeakers that Maxim Gorky was and is and always will be a proletarian author, the elderly gentleman from Prague assures us of the same thing and an Indian confirms it; self-service buffet, a band plays fin-de-siècle Viennese music, my Party official raises a glass to my recovery. Applause for the Indian, lots of people walk around clinking glasses, the man from Weimar wants his turn at the microphone too, greetings to the sister peoples, but he has to wait, the dogsbody from the United States first, the Georgians sing among themselves, a Hungarian sits down next to me, but neither of us can understand a word the other is saying, so we clink glasses, the Weimar guy gets to the microphone, greetings to the sister peoples, no one can understand a word, but he returns to our table satisfied, he has spoken in the city of Gorky's birth. My handler drinks, Weisenborn secretly replaces vodka with water, I observe Christa Wolf, who occasionally slumps but then she makes an effort again, and we raise our glasses at a distance without draining them—a children's party, but these aren't children, they're bears, toast after toast, vodka good, humans taking a holiday from their state, you a human being, me a human being; this isn't boozing but time off from Sunday school, lots of good people, then suddenly the question: What is a good person? I suggest that a good person is a brave person, who is loyal to himself and to others; here, in this country, that is a good person. Agreement all round, we knock back our drinks, and a bureaucrat immediately fills them again, comes around the table while the others carry on chatting and says the name of a person, yes, we both know him; the bureaucrat says: A good person! We drink to a man who is disgraced because he spoke up for Daniel and Sinyavsky, and was expelled from the Party and dismissed from his teaching post and from the Union of Writers, which is celebrating here today, with a severe reprimand; the bureaucrat: Your friend is my friend! . . . It's unsettling. I travel back to Moscow ahead of schedule to see a performance. Sofiya puts her arm through mine. An older comrade travelling on the same night train handles my handler; she takes the tipsy younger woman off to her compartment and tops her up with vodka.

MOSCOW, 23–26 June

A rumour: a Soviet physicist has written to the Kremlin, criticizing the status quo, warning of neo-Stalinism. A need for cooperation between East and West, the obstruction of science and of intellectual life in general by Party bureaucrats, the madness of the nuclear arms race, etc. the need for reform.

Performance at the Satirical Theatre: *Don Juan or the Love of Geometry*, without any major misunderstandings. Mirinov is a first-rate actor. Thirty-five degrees Celsius in the full theatre; an overwhelmingly young audience. Spent time afterwards with the director and three of the main actors; unlike the Party officials, these people are avid for information. The performance has been in the repertory for a year and a half, but is frowned upon by officialdom.

Elections in France, but no news here. Only in the three or four large hotels are there newsstands with foreign press; I buy *L'Humanité* and *Paese Sera*: they are respectively nine and eleven days old.

Trip to Siberia approved.

The student who came to Gorky has reappeared; she has taught herself German and read a lot, her questions are precise and intelligent and therefore difficult. Unfortunately, Sofiya is there too, but it doesn't put the student out at all when Sofiya interprets with a disapproving look on her face; Sofiya is not naturally stupid, just trained to be: questions about Kierkegaard or the Second Commandment regarding graven images or Pirandello do not fit into her frame of reference, and Sartre is not a name to her liking. The student obviously keeps hearing that I'm in a hurry, which is clearly not true. On the contrary: we could have some tea together. But where? With her fitted dress, Natasha (the student's name) could be in a Chekhov play: one of his Russian souls, waiting and withering away.

Gorky Institute:
German literature scholars ask questions until I ask questions of myself—others, the kind that are really relevant to writers. They won't be provoked, though. A heretical statement they listen to attentively is shot down with a Mayakovsky quote. What if a comrade were to say it today?

Afterwards, a visit to the museum: documents from Maxim Gorky's life. The miseries of tsarist Russia; this sheds more light on the revolution than comparisons with the modern West; the revolution's necessity, and also its horror.

A rest in a park: you can't tell from the trees and the clouds where you happen to be, so you can recover from feeling somehow haunted—

A library of foreign literature. Women heads of the various departments. A random sample within my field: not a Potemkin village. (Sadly, that's how mistrustful you become.)

A banquet at the Swiss embassy: three literature officials and three disgraced men shake hands; those in disgrace seem more free and more relaxed. Only Lyublinov, who has just heard that his theatre (they are putting on Brecht) is to be closed, has trouble being sociable. A reunion with Tamara, my translator. The melancholy Aksyonov; I later find out: a broken heart. My Party official: We always feel at home in these rooms. I can't wriggle out of a toast this time, so I thank not least my friend who has been expelled from the Party, and Party officials raise their glasses: almost emotionally, in a case without any animosity. They like him; I know they do. Even if they have to pronounce or approve an even harsher sentence against a comrade, they only pronounce a life-destroying one if they have to. I ask Andrey Voznesensky why he didn't come on the Volga trip; he smiles without innuendo and asks in English: How did you enjoy it? A young man of the world, a touch too elegant; then a conversation about Beckett's play *Endgame*. Afterwards, alone with Ambassador Lindt. 'Bring your glass. It's better we talk out in the garden.'

Question to my handler as to why Voznesensky and Yevtushenko are in disgrace. Her answer: they aren't disgraced, they were simply abroad too often and must learn to love their homeland properly again:

Evils: fascism, Maoism.

My impressions from my first trip (1966: Moscow, Leningrad, Odessa) have barely been disproved so far. There is little point to this trip without any proficiency in the Russian language; a silent film with title cards provided by Party officials. Ultimately you rely on what you see and you know that it is only the surface, and you are annoyed with yourself; this annoyance then rubs off on the country. You judge more than absorb. Given that they immediately attribute all the pleasant aspects to their system, you silently commit the converse mistake of immediately attributing anything nasty to the system too.

Departure for Siberia. Travelling alone with my handler.

Flying is very cheap for Russians: five hours in a jet costs 48 roubles. Lots of people in the large hall; workers, farmers. Officially sanctioned trips.

NOVOSIBIRSK, 27–29 June

The Siberian writer who picks me up at the airport, despite it being very early in the morning, is hard of hearing, which is why he talks too loud without ever looking at me, while providing information about western Siberia: size, length and width of the rivers, height of the mountains, winter temperature, summer temperature, population growth, mineral deposits, length and width and depth and contents of a reservoir, etc. Everything is incredibly enormous. The width of the Ob in the north: 28 miles. My response to an incidental question about the width of rivers in Switzerland does not require Sofiya to translate: the smile of a beaten man. At some stage we cross two unremarkable sets of tracks, but here they are: the tracks of the Trans-Siberian Railway. The lecture resumes, and it is welcome; the emphasis is on quantity, as in all pioneer lands. A hotel room like a ballroom. Breakfast (I fight off sleepiness) with vodka and a replacement of my escort, then a drive out to the city of Soviet scientists. An industrial landscape on the banks of the Ob; a sense of the sky here being even wider than on the Volga. My new escort of colleagues: two Siberian poets, one older man, one younger, clearly still delighted by voluntary work, both in dark suits, white shirts, and ties, the young man with a blond birdy face, always completely upright, whether he's sitting or walking, always cheerful and kindly taciturn. A reservoir (length: 124 miles) in the pale blue of morning, shores with birches or pines; how I imagine Scandinavian landscapes to be. Military trucks. The older poet asks how long military service lasts in my country. He's the first person to ask what life is like at home—

A campus amid birch forests. Houses for academics, complete with garden fences. Blocks of flats with kindergartens. Quiet—few cars. City centre with cinema and restaurant, hotel, department store, etc. lots of low buildings. No university here, just research. Most of the people I see are between 20 and 30. No rushing, a monastic feel. Before we can visit a couple of institutes, a stroll down to the big lake: swimmers, the mere sight of them makes me shiver, ball games on the beach, girls too, a bespectacled runner in a blue tracksuit in the woods.

No portraits of Lenin here.

Lunch at a sort of cafeteria or snack bar; for the first time, Russian waitresses who do not take it amiss when you order something. The two poets: not a word of propaganda for the Soviet system. There's no need here. Institute for Genetics. Information about genetic research. In English; there's immediately a different level of trust when you can talk without an interpreter. Information about a new antiviral drug; despite being a layman, I think I at least grasp the principle.

No East–West hysteria here.

Evening stroll through the old town with my handler, but there are hardly any old wooden houses left. The opera house on a square that is far too big. Arc-lit emptiness. A wall of portrait photos: male and female workers who have received awards. Theatre posters: a touring company from Moscow; photos of one of the local productions: clearly a Hitler play. Actors in uniforms with swastikas, Hitler himself, realistically melodramatic. People in the park. Still light at midnight.

Institute for Geology.

Siberia's natural resources: coal, oil, gas, copper, silver, gold, diamonds, etc. The problem: transport.

Institute for Mathematics.

How they select talent. Pupils in every Soviet republic can take part in a competition every year, solving mathematical tasks which are then sent to the teacher in Novosibirsk; they are also printed in the newspapers. It is not about the correct result but how the pupils get to it—or don't. Those who show an aptitude come to Novosibirsk, where they are set new tasks; they have to defend their solutions in an auditorium; discussion with the other aspiring mathematicians and with the scientists. Those who show their mettle here enter the elite school in Novosibirsk and then university; the best are taken on by the research institute.

Vodka accident at the hotel:

East German road-building machine reps get me to join them at their table; I don't know what I said; Sofiya takes me to my room, she doesn't like these people—

MOSCOW, 30 June

Farewells to friends.

> BERZONA
>
> Someone tells me the story of an actual meeting between Robert Walser and Lenin in Spiegelgasse in Zurich in 1917, during which Robert Walser asked Lenin just one question: 'Do you like pear bread from Glarus too?' In my dream I have no doubts of the story's authenticity and defend Robert Walser, until it wakes me up—I am still defending Robert Walser as I shave.

THE ZURICH MANIFESTO (signed)

WE NOTE:

That there has been fighting between young people and the police in Zurich. The kind of conflicts that are happening in both East and West have also broken out in our city.

WE CONCLUDE:

That the incidents in Zurich should not be judged in isolation. They are a result of failing social structures. It is superficial to discount them as riots and portray the participants purely as rampaging idlers and gawkers.

WE ARE CONVINCED:

That one of the causes of the crisis is the inflexibility of our institutions. This inflexibility is detrimental to our citizens. It prevents necessary adjustments to people's changing needs and also hinders the development of creative minorities.

[1968]

WE REMIND EVERYONE:

That essential change has always been sparked by minorities. Liberalism found passionate supporters among young people in 1848. This minority, despite being branded revolutionaries at the time, preserved Switzerland's independence and established our federal state.

WE WARN EVERYONE:

That a culture conflict will be solved neither by brawls and bans nor by patronizing appeasement. 'Charity is the drowning of the law in the cesspit of mercy.' (Pestalozzi). Suppressing conflicts drives young people to the barricades.

WE DEMAND:

1. The establishment of a centrally located and autonomously run discussion forum for young and old.
2. No imposition of sanctions such as the expulsion of students or pupils, the withdrawal of grants, the deportation of foreigners, and dismissals in the absence of evidence of serious crimes.
3. The restoration of the constitutional right to demonstrate. (This demand has since been met.)
4. The resumption of discussions with all minorities.
5. Invitations from the press, radio and television to allow all parties in the conflict to express their opinions.
6. The immediate establishment of a scientific working group to examine the deeper causes of the conflict and come up with practical proposals.

For the Record

My youngest daughter was there but was neither beaten up nor arrested. She says it was great fun, everyone in a good mood, sitting in the middle of the street (Bellevue)—that was the best bit.

'One, two, three, make Globus free!' cry the young people gathered outside the empty GLOBUS department store. An official notice: 'Anyone who enters this building illegally or encourages others to do so will be prosecuted.' There are no plans to enter the building, but there is a demonstration outside, a protest because there has been no progress on the YOUTH CENTRE promised by the authorities. Police on standby. What the demonstrators could not have foreseen is that the police would block the pavement in front of the building where they wanted to assemble, forcing the demonstrators into the street. Disrupted traffic. The police (Dr R. Bertschi) order them to leave within a few minutes, and the demonstration's own security cannot make themselves heard over the police's louder PA system. People are not pleased. A planned police operation, use of water cannon, defence with cobbles and beer bottles and bits of wood, use of truncheons, arrests, injuries on both sides. Those arrested are taken down into the GLOBUS basement where they are beaten up again with truncheons, even if they haven't put up a fight; unconscious men are kicked in the testicles. One policeman thinks they need to get an injured demonstrator to hospital; his uniformed colleague says, 'Let the bastard croak.' Later at the main police station, those arrested are greeted once more with truncheons. They go through the police judicial system.

A dead child. First headlines and reports immediately blame the demonstrators for the fact that a six-year-old boy has died in an ambulance due to the disruption to traffic. Only three days later does councillor A. Holenstein feel the need to pacify the widespread anger a little: 'The descriptions we saw on television and in various newspapers were in fact inaccurate . . . The driver said that the detour delayed him by between five and eight minutes . . . But I would like to stress once again that the child's death cannot be directly attributed to the demonstrators.'

At the first extraordinary meeting of the city council, Mayor Dr Sigmund Widmer weighs up whether to send in the army.

The young people (students, middle school pupils, apprentices) want to call a general meeting to discuss the situation. The council won't give them a room. Publicans who own these kinds of premises refuse to let the pariahs meet there. Eventually they are allowed to use the VOLKSHAUS on one condition: a 10,000-franc deposit to cover any potential damage. We provide the guarantee in three cheques. They hold a teach-in, sitting on the floor, debating until midnight with breaks for guitar music, then clean the room and go home. So do the council's detectives. Not even a broken chair leg to pay for.

Young men (with beards) say that police officers told them a week before the rioting: Wait until next Saturday—you're in for it! Their riot was orchestrated.

A student named Thomas Held, known as a spokesperson for the PROGRESSIVE STUDENTS OF ZURICH isn't arrested because he is guilty of no actual or alleged trespassing, but he is dismissed from his teaching post with immediate effect. An anonymous death threat has forced him into temporary hiding.

Collecting signatures (ZURICH MANIFESTO) people often answer: I completely agree, but I can't afford to sign as I'm a civil servant / I'm an assistant professor / I'm a newspaper editor / I work in TV, etc.

The police have taken to turning up in plain clothes. When five people are standing together on the bridge by the main station, a detective tells them what to do: clear off. A small group promising not to offer any resistance tries to march through an area where they're not disrupting the traffic in any way; they immediately hand over their banners to detectives.

A civilian taken to the main police station is beaten to the ground with a truncheon; afterwards, he presents his credentials as a lawyer and car driver who was coming to pay his parking fine.

An apprentice who didn't even take part is told to cut his long hair if he wants to keep his job.

People who have been arrested and questioned are not entitled to give their version of events; they are only allowed to answer questions: if they belong to a society, a club, etc.

A young set designer arrived from Frankfurt and had no idea what was going on when she got caught by water cannon outside the main station, walked away, was beaten up by three policemen and dragged down into the GLOBUS basement, where she was struck between her legs with a truncheon.

One foreign student is immediately deported: with no investigation into what he might have done.

Doctors confirm that many injuries they have to treat were 'definitely not a result of close fighting', but can only be explained by 'systematic beatings'. The head of the criminal investigation department, Dr Hubatka, denies eyewitness reports that he stood by during police abuse and did not intervene.

An adult civilian (wearing shorts because he had just come off his sailing boat) intervened on the Quaibrücke because a young demonstrator was being kicked all over after being hurled to the ground; he asked for the names of the police officers involved and was beaten with truncheons and taken to the main police station, where he later turned out to be a doctor.

NEUE ZÜRCHER ZEITUNG: 'Huge disruption to traffic and damage to property, along with incalculable loss of trust in the city's young people by the people of Zurich' / 'The rioters were real warring scum' / AN APPEAL FROM THE MAYOR: 'The vast majority of people in Zurich are angry about last night's youth riots. I am angry too . . . If need be, the law enforcement forces will be reinforced . . . In conclusion: young people will not achieve their goals by defiance and violence . . . ' *NEUE ZÜRCHER ZEITUNG*, Issue 395: 'A hard but legitimate police operation.' / *VATERLAND*, Lucerne: 'In our opinion, the Zurich police had every justification for intervening as vigorously as they did, and let the rioters who got hit cry and gnash their teeth now . . . Watch your step! Now we know the methods of these fellows who constantly talk about rights and reforms, but are basically no more than nasty rabble rousers and brutal anarchists.' / *ZÜRCHER WOCHE*: 'We cannot ban this group, but we can ostracize them.' / *Die freisinnige Partei*:

'The Liberal Party demands that the authorities take the following steps: . . . The full force of the law should be brought to bear on the rioters and their ringleaders . . . Students and middle school pupils who are convicted by a court should be expelled from educational institutions in Zurich . . . Foreigners who participated in the riots should be deported.' / ANNOUNCEMENT BY THE CITY COUNCIL: 'There is an investigation into allegations that individual officers committed abuse. The city council is responsible for law and order, without discrimination.' / POLICE REPORT: '— Forty-one people were injured during the street battles on the night of Saturday to Sunday, namely 15 police officers, 7 firefighters and 19 demonstrators. All of the injured, except for one firefighter and one police officer, have been discharged from hospital. A total of 169 arrests were made. Fifty-five of these demonstrators are under the age of 20. Nineteen of the detained youngsters are still in custody.' / STATE OF EMERGENCY: Zurich city council has banned demonstrations 'until further notice'. Any infringements of these rules will be punished in accordance with the Swiss penal code. / *NEUE ZÜRCHER ZEITUNG*: 'Mob rule in the streets of Zurich.' Caption under a photo of a young man: 'The powerful water jet prevents further acts of heroism.' Under a different photo: 'An injured police officer is carried from the square by his comrades.' / THE GOVERNMENT: 'The governing council received guidance from the head of the relevant department at its 4 July meeting on the situation following on from the riots in Zurich. Federal and district prosecutors have launched a number of investigations to bring the guilty to trial. The border police have been instructed to deport any foreigners who played an active role in the riots. The university and middle-school authorities will take disciplinary action against any students and pupils who have committed crimes. The governing council will work with the authorities of the canton of Zurich to take all necessary measures to maintain public order and guarantee the security of their citizens.

The cantonal police have been placed on standby.' / *NEUE ZÜRCHER ZEITUNG*: 'Nip it in the bud!' / 'The positive effects of the demonstration ban' / 'The rules of democracy' / 'a tiny minority and an overwhelming majority' / 'young people and the masterminds behind them' / 'their foreign manipulators' / 'Errant youth' / 'The task of assessing the facts is the responsibility of judges, who must give their verdicts with total independence and unaffected by pressure from the streets.' / 'It is worth noting here that all the relevant bodies have come out in recent days against a referendum on the higher education system.' / 'We must hope that the judicial system can look beyond those throwing stones and bottles and take action against the intellectual instigators, whose full names are well documented.' / 'A show of support for the city police. A girl delivered a bar of chocolate to police headquarters. A farmer from Herrliberg offered to mobilize all the famers in the region to fight the demonstrators. An academic applied to join the police athletics club. A male choir in Zurich's fourth district announced that its members would all rush to help if asked. A caller vouched that he and his fellow butchers would come forwards as volunteers.'

PS

A special edition of the *NEUE ZÜRCHER ZEITUNG* from 24 September 1933 with the headline: 'Torchlit procession by patriotic parties falls victim to organized Marxist assault. Nighttime battles in the streets of Zurich. Social Democrats and Communists provoke and attack the centre-right torchlit march. Bombardments with stones. An appeal for calm.' The slogan of the patriotic rally in 1933: 'In this time of need, we must take back our city from a social democratic clique intent on class war and its own interests.' Speakers at the rally: Niklaus Rappold, LIBERAL PARTY. Robert Tobler, NATIONAL FRONT, which supported Hitler. 'The Battle for Patriotic Zurich.'

Reminiscence

Back in 1936, when I wanted to marry a Jewish student from Berlin and went to pick up the necessary papers (birth certificate, certificate of family origin, etc.) from Zurich city hall, I was given an official Aryan identity card with the stamp of my hometown without requesting it. I tore up the document on the spot, unfortunately. Switzerland was not occupied by Hitler; it was what it is today: independent, neutral, free, etc.

Handbook for Members

The marked man sees more desirable women than he used to, switching the focus of his attraction several times a day. He no longer confines himself to a specific type. A tendency to pan-eroticism. (Early through to late stage.) The number of women to whom he is attracted is inversely proportional to his real chances.

The pre-marked man recognizes himself as such by the fact that he even tries to please women he doesn't like, and that he follows up on his successes—at least up to the point where he thinks he can be sure that his virility has been acknowledged.

He goes to bed with women merely to confirm that he is not a marked man; he knows in advance that it's a bad move, but he had to make it—

If the pre-marked man genuinely does fall in love again: he is ruthless towards anything that prevents its fulfilment—he cannot deny himself this miracle . . .

The marked man does not understand how these creatures could once have been so important. And yet he still looks at every one and is angered by his obsession: he can hardly look at a woman now without wondering, for a second at least, what it might be like—

Nostalgic for desire . . .

However, the marked man goes through long periods when he is not remotely interested in going to bed with anyone; in fact, (when he does think of it) he considers it an absurd act.

The marked man catches himself feeling particularly bored when film characters embrace; he always finds these parts a drag—

In social situations he is so courteous towards young women in particular that (if they saw it) his former partners would be amazed: the marked man as a perfect gentleman. They can be sure of his attention, even if their conversation is silly. The marked man treats them socially the way they would like to be treated by the men they sleep with.

Long before his chances drop to zero (the marked man sometimes underestimates them because it would be embarrassing for him to get it wrong), he refrains from flirting even in favourable circumstances . . . He can see that the tennis player who flicks her hair out of her eyes or shakes her head a bit too much after a double fault is aware of him. He watches for a while, not for the first time. He fancies her. Once, he tosses a ball back over the high fence before going on his way. He knows which button to press in the lift for her floor but he doesn't speak to her. If she's sitting in the bar in the evening, he sits down a long way from her; he has seen what she's reading, though—an obvious ice breaker. The marked man knows the long conversations it would take to discover shared interests and he shies away from these long conversations because his own lines would bore him. The marked man would prefer to sleep with a barmaid once in a while. (Middle stage.) *If he falls in love, he recognizes that he's a marked man by the fact that he still has a choice; he packs his stuff and leaves.*

If the pre-marked man's flirting fails, he immediately attributes it to his age—as if he would never have failed in the past, when he was young.

The pre-marked man is a better lover than he used to be; he knows that physical passion is not enough and is grateful for this; it makes him more tender . . .

Unlike the pre-marked man, who is scared of the moment when he will completely cease to be virile, the marked man knows that it never ceases completely. He would be happy if it did . . .

Bachelors stay in shape for longer.

Members who hope that widely available compounds might delay ageing merely stoke their fear of ageing. The bed as a place to prove themselves. They seem to be trying too hard.

He realizes he's bored during sex—

The marked man recognizes himself as such from the fact that he suddenly thinks of women he could have seduced 30 or even 10 years ago; he now regrets every missed opportunity—and it strikes him that there were many; but the marked man forgets what stopped him in most of these cases: his discernment.

Masturbating to memories. (*Early to intermediate stage.*) *He no longer believes himself capable of conquests or the mere idea of them strikes him as too much effort.*

Why the marked man feels many things are becoming a drag (a walk in the city, shopping, parties, bus journeys, waiting at the airport, etc.): his appearance triggers no female reactions: it's as if he's not there . . . If a young woman comes walking towards him along the pavement, she doesn't act as she did in the past, as if she were looking a hand's breadth past him; she genuinely doesn't see the marked man. No flirtation. He can look round at her, but she doesn't notice; he can tell from the way she walks that she doesn't notice. At the newsstand he is treated purely as a buyer; the person looks at the newspapers he has picked out and then at the money. Nothing else. Things change on planes too; he starts to like the air hostesses' stereotypical smiles, but he can't even count on that for very long: if he enquires about their arrival time, they become motherly, even nurse-like. If the marked man happens to sit in the same train compartment as a younger woman, there's no sense of discomfort; they used to stare fixedly out of the window or hide behind an open magazine so he wouldn't talk to them. Nowadays they just sit there, as if he were merely a piece of inoffensive luggage. If he bends down in the bus to pick up a woman's gloves from the floor, she is astonished to find someone opposite her. A waitress, when she has finally noticed him, comes over to the table to empty the ashtray and casually takes his order: without a glance; when she puts down the beer, she stares over his head; later, she takes his money: without a glance. The marked man wonders what he was expecting other than beer. If he happens to look in the mirror as he's drying his hands in the toilets, he can understand why and he puts his coin in the dish . . .

If a woman (actress) says to a man (director) that he is gaga:— the man has no comeback. ('Cow' or 'bitch' aren't comebacks, given that cows and bitches can be young.) The use of gaga as a signal that he has defined women as sexual beings, and she is now judging him from this position; and rightly so.

The marked man already refrains from kissing his daughter or kisses her ironically; he is also shy of kissing young women even when the social event (birthday, New Year's Eve, etc.) would entitle him to do so. He feels that his lips are an impertinence. If it turns out at one of these events that younger women give him the same innocent kiss they give everyone else, the marked man recognizes himself as such by his embarrassment—

An old man's charm—sometimes a younger man is jealous despite having nothing to fear; for the marked man it's enough to see that the younger man is jealous.

In discovering that he is more attractive to women now that he is afraid of failing, the pre-marked man discovers his mistake up to this point: he thinks he is a connoisseur of women—but he was simply ascribing to women an expectation he thought he could satisfy, whereas he now has an idea of all the other things they expect of a man, i.e. all the things he failed to be for women; this idea alone makes him more attractive.

The marked man as a connoisseur of women . . . By no longer seeing himself as a man in company but simply as a participant in a conversation, the marked man often comes to the conclusion that most women are not only superfluous to a conversation but actually obstruct a fruitful conversation; he prefers the company of men (clubs, pubs, teams of experts, etc.). If he still has his wits about him, the marked man recognizes himself as marked by the fact that younger men will talk to him about anything, with this one exception. Their discretion is perfect: they don't want to hear a word from him on that subject.

Taking a taxi with a young woman, he is wary of putting a hand on her arm or shoulder on any pretext. This is wise of him. Yet his very wariness means he's thinking about it. And thinking about it makes him tense. If she senses it, she moves away, even though the marked man is being wary. The marked man is free insofar as he is not in love; he simply finds her nice to look at. He is irritated by his awareness that he would make an unsatisfactory bed fellow, especially as there is no reason to believe he has any chance. If she glances at him, the marked man feels embarrassed: like an impostor caught red handed. He's always already thinking of bed. And yet, actually, he is quite happy sitting in a taxi with her. He knows that his hand wouldn't electrify her. It is not imperative for him either (he realizes as he stares out of the window). (Intermediate stage.) He is glad when the taxi journey is over . . . Not long ago the marked man would have found himself impelled to put his hand on her shoulder; occasionally, he has even suddenly found her head against his chest, although his experience then was that her touch dissolved his anticipation. (Early stage.) Later, the marked man is no longer even wary of this experience. (Final stage: they should tie his paws behind his back.)

Senility does not protect you from sexual dependence.

Lovers seem strange to him.

In his memories of a particular fling—house, scenery, weather, season, a specific meal, her clothes less, her body only vaguely—the marked man catches himself primarily remembering the circumstances, often in minute detail: the lumberjacks who stumbled upon the couple and the exact spot in the woods . . . The rest is myth.

21 August

The rucksack's packed, the white wine cooled, everything's ready for the hike. Our behaviour reminds me of a different day, another unmistakably historic day: Hitler's invasion of Czechoslovakia. The news reached a friend and me at the swimming baths: we were just getting undressed. A quarter of an hour later we went swimming anyway—not oblivious, just helpless. Golo Mann wanted to show us the Valle Verzasca today, and it wouldn't have taken much for us to have set out unsuspectingly on the hike: I don't start the day by listening to the radio; a friend rang me up. How much do we know right now? He told me: overnight Soviet invasion of the CSSR, a few details of the plan of attack, occupation of the airport, etc. Dubček arrested and taken away by the Soviets. We know nothing about our friends in Prague; it doesn't occur to me to phone them. It would still have been possible.

Our long-scheduled hike seems to be the only thing we can do on such a day; hiking with the small transistor tucked under one arm. The qualified historian refuses to speculate; he tells me he recently went to the CSSR for documents about Wallenstein. I see the Valle Verzasca: rocks, stream, flora, butterflies, a whole load of unforgettable

```
trivialities. The small transistor is no use;
it produces only a crackle.
```

```
PS
```

```
Reading Kafka's diaries again: '2nd August
(1914). Germany declares war on Russia—
Afternoon: swimming lesson.'
```

Questionnaire

1.
Do you usually know what you're hoping for?

2.
How often must a particular hope (e.g. in politics) fail to be fulfilled for you to give up on that hope, and can you do so without immediately latching on to a new one?

3.
Do you occasionally envy animals, e.g. fish in an aquarium, which seem to get by without hope?

4.
When one of your private hopes has finally been fulfilled, how long do you usually go on thinking that you were right to hold that hope, i.e. that its fulfilment meant as much as you had spent decades believing it would?

5.
What hope have you abandoned?

6.
For how many hours per day or how many days per year do you feel satisfied by a reduced hope—that spring will come around again, that your headache will go away, that a secret will never come out, that your guests will leave, etc.?

7.
Can hatred breed hope?

8.
Regarding the state of the world, do you place your hope in:

a. reason?

b. a miracle?

c. things continuing as they are?

9.
Can you think without hope?

10.
Can you love a person who will sooner or later believe they have got to know you and place little hope in you?

11.
What fills you with hope?

a. nature

b. art

c. science

d. human history

12.
Are private hopes enough for you?

13.
Suppose you were to distinguish between your own hopes and the hopes other people (parents, teachers, friends, lovers) invest in you: what upsets you more—disappointing the former or the latter?

14.
What do you hope for from travel?

15.
If you know someone has an incurable disease, do you get their hopes up, even if you realize they're unfounded?

16.
What would you expect if the roles were reversed?

17.
What reinforces your own hopes:

a. encouragement?

b. recognition of your mistakes?

c. alcohol?

d. honours?

e. luck at gambling?

f. a horoscope?

g. someone falling in love with you?

18.
Suppose you harbour the Ultimate Hope ('that man can aid his fellow man') but have friends who cannot subscribe to the same hope: does this diminish your friendship or your great hope?

19.
How do you behave when the roles are reversed, i.e. if you don't share a friend's hope? Do you feel smarter than him each time he is left disappointed?

20.
For you to pursue a hope in thought and deed, does there need to be a high probability of its being fulfilled?

21.
No revolution has ever wholly fulfilled the hopes of those who instigated it. Do you deduce from this that having one great hope is absurd, that revolutions are pointless, that only the hopeless spare themselves disappointment, etc., and what do you hope for by sparing yourself?

22.
Do you hope for an afterlife?

23.
What determines your everyday actions, decisions, plans, considerations, etc., if not some specific or vague hope?

24.
Have you ever spent a day or even an hour without hope, without even the hope that, for you at least, this will all be over one day?

25.
When you see a dead person, which of their hopes strike you as inconsequential—those that were fulfilled, or those left unfulfilled?

Seven weeks ago there was talk in Moscow of a message a scientist had addressed to those in power in the Kremlin: it wasn't published but it was apparently circulating among intellectuals. Now the detailed text, whose contents were only rumoured before, has appeared in various translations (*The New York Times*, *Die Zeit*): its author, Andrei D. Sakharov, a Soviet physicist, a member of the Academy of Sciences and the 1958 Nobel Prize winner, is a Communist. His message denounces the Stalinist era which he estimates claimed at least 10 million victims, and considers the legacy of that era, the situation today. Sakharov describes the sterile bureaucracy posing as socialism and therefore taboo; he speaks openly about the idiotic dogmatism of Party officials, which is incapable of solving the problems of the future and is therefore a fatal threat to the Communist countries themselves and to the whole world. As an insider, Sakharov's critique, which he can back up, rings serious alarm bells and is a sober warning that both camps, East and West, need to shed their ossified modes of thinking and unite in global cooperation (which is more than simple coexistence, as people see it today: an agreement between the global superpowers, which negotiate their power interests at the expense of other countries) as the sole chance for the future of humanity. Sakharov points to Prague; his hopes are the same as ours: that socialism will finally evolve to realize its great promise.

Has this experiment failed?

People say that the Soviet tanks remind us of 17 July 1953 in Berlin and of Hungary in 1956, but this parallel is wrong: there was no uprising in Prague; it was the Communist Party itself that experimented with making socialism more democratic, and the Czechoslovak government didn't lose control of this experiment for a single day. The Soviet troops are not defending socialism against a counter-revolution as claimed; what they are doing is defending the present Soviet establishment, which is afraid of an evolution of socialism, though this is inevitable in the long term and inevitable for the Soviet Union too; their show of military force is evidence of this fear, which is not the fear of the Russian people but Party officials' fear of their own people. Czechoslovakia's experiment did not fail; it was crushed.

Die Weltwoche, Zurich, 30 August 1968

Handbook for Members

When, at the age of 71, Friedrich Hölderlin heard Goethe's name mentioned, he said: 'Oh—Herr von Goethe!' He immediately recalled his visit to Goethe's home on 22 August 1797, 44 years earlier; Friedrich Hölderlin let out his reported sigh in 1841 . . . The marked man recognizes himself as marked not only by his forgetfulness but equally by his inability to forget certain events.

Hispano-Suiza is selling to Africa artillery that Hitler ordered but never collected as well as defect ammunition. Switzerland is offering its services: Ambassador August Lindt from Moscow. The papers are reporting that Bührle-Oerlikon has been making illicit arms deals. The headlines: Federal Council calls for inquiry. It is originally quoted as 10 million, then 90 million for weapons shipments to Nigeria, Israel, Egypt and South Africa. Falsified documents to get official approval for the arms exports; Dr Dietrich Bührle was completely in the dark, but two deputy directors are charged. The federal council and Bührle, a colonel in the Swiss army, which he also supplies, agree on one point: that the Swiss arms industry depends on weapons exports. A few weeks after the scandal, which distresses the public, as if nothing of this kind had ever happened before, the federal council orders 490 million francs' worth of military material from Bührle-Oerlikon. Who else could they order it from? No question, however, of nationalizing the arms industry; nationalization would spell the end of the freedom our army is there to defend. Posters appeal for aid for Biafra. The federal council donates one million francs for Biafra. Children shake collection tins in the street for Biafra.

HANDBOOK FOR MEMBERS

(Correspondence)

Dr U. B., 53, Berne
The kinds of visual representations of the age pyramid found in old books ('A child at 10', etc., 'In the grave at 100') should be treated with caution. If such pictures show you in your prime, this is entirely due to the artist's naive penchant for symmetry.

A. W., 55, Lucerne
The photo you enclose is plausible; we can but salute the sight of you water skiing behind a motor boat . . . Nowhere does our handbook claim that physical exercise is not advisable; the healthier the marked man is, the better he feels.

G. U., 76, Ascona
Death is a possibility at any age, i.e. the marked man is not necessarily identifiable by a growing fear of death—which tends to diminish in an old people's home. (Late stage.)

M. S., 43, Zurich
You are not the first person to be preoccupied with the fact that he is already 10 years older than Mozart was when he died—that has nothing to do with senility. You'll see: senility is upon you when you feel reassured that there is a genius 10 years older than you.

Professor O. P., 65, Basel
The fact that you are now retired and have time to write a great work is (you note) a cause for celebration. This handbook has never denied that we are grateful for every reason for celebration as we age.

O. Sch., 63, Melbourne
Our handbook has never suggested that love of your native country (you are a Swiss expat) is a symptom of senility. There must be some misunderstanding. It's true that young people display patriotism and chauvinism too; conversely, we know of cases in which natural patriotism declines with age . . . You have lived in Melbourne for 40 years; your unbroken love of your country has less to do with age than with the fact that you live in Melbourne.

H. H., 37, Stuttgart
Your objections as a vicar are irrefutable. ('I give guidance in an old people's home and I do not deny that there is mental enfeeblement, but I guide these people in the certain belief that they will not appear mentally enfeebled before our Maker on the day of His resurrection.')

Frau Dr A. St. (-), Constance
It is not true that I was referring to you and your husband in the passage you mentioned; not every husband who allows his wife to emasculate him in company is necessarily a marked man. In your case there must be other factors at work. As far as I can tell, although you may be older than him, you are quite simply what is known as a 'character', and I do not get the impression that your esteemed husband feels emasculated; maybe he thinks you would get on our nerves, but that is not true, believe me! The passage you highlight refers to an industrialist from Pittsburgh (USA), whose wife said, Don't speak but think, honey! and she is not wrong either. I repeat: I respect your quiet husband, believe me!

A. G., 5, Herrliberg
SENILE and SENILITY are not terms of abuse but descriptions; it is merely because the facts they describe are still taboo for you that you react as if they were terms of abuse. People also use them colloquially for that very reason.

Prof. Ch. V., 47, Princeton, USA
Your comments are extremely valuable. A scientific handbook would undoubtedly be of great use to our members; most of the relevant publications I know are by sociologists, and although they are largely intelligible to some readers, I have noticed that none of the members feels personally affected by sociological presentations, more so by medical texts, although our members merely conclude that they should avoid over-exerting themselves.

V. O., 68, Berlin/Vienna
Research is needed into the symptoms of senility by profession. I haven't seen you on stage of late. You say that confronting the public every evening keeps you young; the evidence you give for this is that you still get stage fright before every performance. Nowhere in our handbook do we claim that the marked man will not suffer stage fright, or cease to, when his profession compels him to make public appearances.

H. P., 23, Frankfurt
Experience breeds stupidity . . . That is a slogan often heard among students, and it is accurate in some senses; it is based on experience.

Frau Ch. G., 50, Kilchberg
Of course I believe that women deserve equal rights. The reason that this handbook does not refer to ageing women has nothing to do with carelessness or tactfulness, but because my experience of women is as beings whose reference point is men (not necessarily those they share their lives with, but men in general) as sexual partners. Men are therefore afflicted by a vague sense of failure insofar as not only does the camouflage effect of women's makeup fade but her sense of her own identity, which she previously sacrificed to her husband, increases. Her belated sense of identity puts him to shame—it may be that at times she reminds him of the girl she once was, but he now feels ambushed by an asexual partner who no longer responds to his attempts to impress her, or not much: intelligence being equal, she now has the upper hand. Women age better.

PS

But not always.

PS

If we say that women age more quickly, we mean that they are released from their sexuality more quickly—whereas men still need (or try) to imagine themselves as sexual beings, and age like them; an old man is more ridiculous than an old woman. (Intermediate to late stage.) The power of the matron over the permanent mannikin.

Monsignore G. C., 69, Rome
You will find Michel de Montaigne's motto in his essay 'Of Experience' not in the essay 'Of Age', although the latter's first lines would also have been appropriate: 'I cannot allow of the way in which we settle for ourselves the duration of our life. I see that the sages contract it very much in comparison of the common opinion: "What," said the younger Cato to those who would stay his hand from killing himself, "am I now of an age to be reproached that I go out of the world too soon?" And yet he was but eight-and-forty years.' (Montaigne lived to the age of 59.)

H. Z., 81, presently in Bad Ragaz
Of course, there are always exceptions.

> Manifestos, graffiti at the Sorbonne, posters, caricatures in chalk and ballpoint pen, slogans coined by the French students in May, pamphlets—now published in book form, I can leaf through them at home in peace and enjoy them in colour, disconnected from the scene of the events, art. BOURGEOIS VOUS N'AVEZ RIEN COMPRIS. I read with my legs crossed: FEU LA CULTURE. Or: L'ART C'EST DE LA MERDE.

Tovarich

'It isn't possible,' I say to the interpreter. 'It would be ridiculous. Ask him if it's really him.' I of course understand her hesitancy to translate my question; if it is him, then he used to be one of the world's two most powerful men. 'Why won't you ask?' I say, thinking that it might actually be possible. 'I think,' she says, 'we should carry on.' Always mothering me, and then she presumably also told the old tovarich that we don't have any time. Nevertheless, her cold respect for him refutes her words to me: 'I'm telling you, he's just an ordinary farmer. Lots of people here look like him.' The only certainty is that he doesn't have any petrol and doesn't know where we might get some nearby . . . A few days ago in Moscow, I mentioned his name once and was told by Sofiya that respect was unwanted, indecent even, every mention of his name a grave lack of tact. I realize that this encounter by a garden fence, if the old man really is him, is very uncomfortable for my interpreter, and indeed cannot be true. I can't do anything about that. If it is him, then he looks great; he must have noticed straight away that I'd recognized him and he also understands Sofiya and doesn't want to embarrass her, this straight-laced, diligent modern-day comrade who is now probably telling the old man about our mishap for the second time. 'He doesn't know where to get petrol, he says, but it is available somewhere,' Sofiya says, then stresses: 'Of course there's petrol!' as if I might doubt it. He doesn't understand German, but he still nods. He is still leaning on his rake with his sleeves rolled up—an old pensioner. Once again, it's too bad that I don't understand any Russian. I would promise him not to tell anyone outside Russia, not a word; I don't have a camera with me either, just an empty jerrycan in my hand. I've no idea why Sofiya is laughing, but I'm happy. When we came up to the garden fence and the old man saw how sweaty we were from hunting for petrol, he offered us a drink; Sofiya immediately declined. Why? Well, at least she's laughing now; I see the old man looking at me. The Russian word for 'stranger' is (as far as I know) 'the mute man'. The way he looks at me—almost as if he's touched. 'He asked where you come from,' Sofiya says dutifully. 'I told him you're a writer.' I never find out why she burst out laughing after this. I smile anyway. Sofiya doesn't translate a question the old man now asks the mute man (she often does this) and so he doesn't get an answer. I don't find out if he understands English; in any case, he doesn't respond to my tentative question: 'Do you have many visitors?' God knows it's a clumsy question; luckily, Sofiya doesn't understand English. You get the feeling that he is not under surveillance here, not dissatisfied with his surroundings and in rude health despite his age. I'm wondering when the Cuban crisis was, the missile threat, while he's obviously still asking himself what business a Western writer has being around here. 'He has a lot of respect for writers,' Sofiya says, then to make sure I don't get any wrong ideas: 'Our farmers have a lot of respect for writers.' She generally chooses her words carefully. When he appears to ask what she just told the stranger, she doesn't answer him either and glances at her watch instead, and the two of us look at each other, the old man and I—two powerless men. Now I praise the flat land, his splendid lettuces, a birch tree, etc. in order to persuade Sofiya to start translating again. He is actually shorter than expected, not fat but squat, his round head almost bald. The more convinced I become that it really is him (in the first instant I was just trying to tease my dear Sofiya), the shier I feel too. 'Sofiya, tell him I'm a guest of the Union of Soviet Writers,' I say, so that, if it really is him, he doesn't take me for a spy. 'Please tell him that.' It doesn't appear to surprise him, disappoint him or please him; whether he is a farmer or an insider remains a mystery. 'We have to go now,' Sofiya says again, and the old man who might once have decided on war and peace doesn't seem particularly bothered whether Miss Intourist, whose job is to protect the Soviet Union, and the foreigner with the empty jerrycan in his hand stand around outside his fence for a little longer or not. He doesn't have a filling station. He allowed Solzhenitsyn to publish; *Novy Mir*; he moved Stalin's corpse out of the mausoleum. You wouldn't think it possible from the way he stands before us with his hefty hands on the handle of his rake. 'Tell him,' I say, 'that we unfortunately lost our way.' We don't have permission to be here, yet here we are; I feel sorry for Sofiya. Her eyes are like a bird's; I can't always tell which way she's looking. She sometimes translates even when the tovarish didn't say anything. 'He asks if you've been to the Soviet Union before,' Sofiya says, 'but I already told him.' I say anyway: 'My third time!', which isn't true. Why did I say it? Sofiya doesn't translate this either, merely points to her watch, and I get the message. When we arrived and spoke to the old tovarich, we shook hands, a nation of brothers; it's harder now. 'Go on, ask him,' I say, 'if he is Nikita Khrushchev.' He must have understood the name, really, despite my pronunciation. A difficult moment for straightlaced Sofiya; she pretends she didn't understand the name either. I guess she's in her mid-thirties, which would mean that when she went to whichever school she went to, she would have waved peonies at this man without any doubts. 'Why don't you ask him?' I say quietly; Sofiya can't help it if it's him. The old man looks at me, and I'm hesitant to offer him my hand. 'Tell him we're grateful,' I say. 'We're bound to find a petrol station.' Sofiya looks confused now: 'Is there anything else you'd like to know?' she asks instead of translating. The old man must know (whether it's him or not) about the measures in Czechoslovakia and about Vietnam as he tends his lettuces here; he doesn't look senile, or—if it really is Nikita Khrushchev—bitter that he is unlikely to receive a state funeral. 'What did he just say?' I ask Sofiya; but she finds it unimportant, undeserving of translation, a chat over a garden fence. 'Let's go,' she says, 'he can't help us.' The fact that we still don't have any petrol is making her more and more anxious. 'Tovarich,' she says to the old man with a peasant's bald round head, but that's all I can understand. He laughs as he used to on pictures in the world press: with little eyes. As we shake hands, I think it probably isn't him after all.

BERZONA

Swiss TV asks for a comment on the Higher Education Act, sends a crew and films me for no fee, but is then unable to broadcast the report: unless, that is, the federal councillor I criticize would care to answer, and the federal councillor—a social democrat incidentally—would rather not. So they send me 100 francs instead . . .

REMINISCENCE

One of our senior architecture lecturers, a Swiss man, was an avowed Nazi supporter. He only ever mentioned Le Corbusier as a proponent of 'cultural bolshevism'. Switzerland, he declared, was a natural part of the Reich, and where the Jews were concerned, Jesus cannot have been a Jew; read the Testament again, the New Testament, and you'll see how profound and wise it is, and Jesus was blond, a carpenter's son, probably from the north. This sentimental man, Professor Friedrich Hess, was not intolerable; this was the decision of the federal council on the request of the higher education council, which is appointed by the federal council. At the same time another lecturer, Professor Hans Bernoulli, was teaching urban planning, which famously causes sociological and economic problems; at the time he advocated the Freigeld theory and was critical of the federal council once. This man was seen as intolerable and was sacked.

22 December
Apollo 8 on television: three people on a flight to the Moon. They are currently some 125,000 miles from the Earth. A picture: our Earth as a brightly coloured ball, albeit unfortunately blurred. At one moment, a pack of small meteorites, accompanied by the voice of Borman, who is speaking with the people in Houston (Texas). No reason not to carry on smoking my pipe here. Their slow, fish-like movements in a state of zero gravity. One of them, who looks like a white embryo, waves. They clearly cannot tell which way is up or down, and this makes viewers in front of the television feel slightly dizzy, precisely because they have their feet on the ground. There have been no technical problems so far. One of them is feeling sick; his doctor gives him advice from down here on Earth. After the broadcast, we all say to ourselves: For the first time in the history of humanity, etc. and then switch over to the Sunday sports coverage.

23 December
Good pictures of the Earth today. Just as we could have imagined: our Earth is a planet.

24 December
They are travelling on their ellipse around the Moon. Very clear pictures of the nearby Moon; craters in the oblique light, their shadows clearly visible, slide slowly across the TV screen, more and more until you admit to yourself that it's pretty bleak. The only cause for excitement is imagining being there. What you see merely confirms what you imagine.

25 December
The ignition that pulls them free of the Moon's gravitational field after their orbit and puts them back on a flight path to Earth has now happened. More pictures of the Moon, which seems familiar now. Everyone at home and our neighbours are watching; no one has much to say about it. Relief that the enterprise has been a success, but we don't know what promises it holds. Prestige for the US. Again we tell ourselves: For the first time in the history of humanity, etc., but we've seen it now.

26 December
Company at home, winter outside; I sit looking at the year's unanswered letters and declare an amnesty.

27 December

Apollo 8. A happy return to Earth today, the three White men looking well on television. They walk along a red carpet on the aircraft carrier; watching them, we think of science and technology, of computers which made the undertaking a success, but not heroes. The TV newsreader (Monte Ceneri) tries emphatically to plant the three names firmly in our memories and in the memories of our children's children: Borman–Anders–Lovell. No human has ever flown as far as these three tough men; we now wish them some rest and good health and a promotion. There's a difference between Borman–Anders–Lovell and Nansen, for example. The enterprise that kept us all in suspense is out of all proportion with their personalities. The three White men do not act at all like heroes, incidentally; they just look happy to be out of that capsule again at long last: three technicians who took on the most dangerous job in an anonymous adventure; it could have gone wrong, in which case they would now be starving as they orbited the Sun; but since it succeeded, it is not they who orbited the Moon but (as the newsreader correctly said): Mankind!

The Locarno Pharmacist's Dream

'It's a scandal,' he says calmly but loud enough to wake himself up and just hear his voice from the outside: 'A scandal!' and only now in Italian: 'UNA VERGOGNA! È UNA VERGOGNA!' . . . What he can recall of his dream right now is: a doddery old bishop, limping on both legs, maybe a comic actor playing a bishop while being an actual cripple, and the whole thing in a gymnasium.

. . .

At the time, he is a country doctor, IL DOTTORE, as if no one knows his name; everyone in the village simply says IL DOTTORE, even though his name has been in the phone book for years, on his letterbox, etc. IL DOTTORE, whereas he of course is expected to know their names, even their children's first names.

. . .

The scandal must be something else.

. . .

After his own voice has woken him, though still exhausted, he sits upright on the edge of his bed in the dark so the dream won't start again, and when he switches on the light, he is no longer a country doctor and for a while he is unsure whether he ever was one; but shortly afterwards (each of these things only takes a few minutes), everything is cleared up.

. . .

A scandal in the village, nothing to worry about, virtually nothing ever happens, not a murder in decades. They seem friendly enough by day. Everyone playing scandalous tricks on everyone else are what bind the place together, other than the land, which receives very little sunshine in winter. But you have nothing to worry about if you were born here. The village doesn't have a gymnasium, by the way.

. . .

Il DOTTORE! It sounds gently mocking.

. . .

He's a drinker, as he knows each time he wakes up and has forgotten what is not clear, whereas only moments earlier it was clear, so very clear. A happy dream, actually.

The doddery bishop, who takes no interest in him, and the gymnasium bear no relation to him, they're a kind of joke, an incident; this slovenly bishop is of no interest to him; a bishop who limps on both legs is spooky and risible, a disturbance, and therefore a dirty trick.

. . .

He is a lapsed Catholic.

. . .

The evening before, he thought they had cheated him—the villagers have been cheating him for years, starting with the water bill. He always trusts the green forms, out of laziness. They're incomprehensible but probably fair and accurate, as accurate as punch cards are, and they have his name on them.

. . .

She is no longer a girl, of course. Her cheekbones, her hairstyle as dour as it was 20 years ago. She looks happier than usual, which means she has something planned. She isn't scared. She's talking, but they are not alone, there's a mess all around them, and he apologizes for it; there are children lying around. Lots of children, not her children or his.

. . .

He only slept with her twice.

She seems to know what he has become, a country doctor, but it's not important. She's very trusting. She's saying something, but it has nothing to do with him. They could be anywhere. He doesn't recognize the place, the unfamiliar flat. It makes no sense to apologize for the mess. They do not touch, however.

. . .

He wakes up with a headache.

. . .

The village is aware of what he really does, IL DOTTORE. Maybe they're talking about him behind his back. But what do they say? He is, for instance, campaigning for the factory (a tannery) to be forced to finally build a water treatment plant—so far without success. It still stinks. Maybe they are lying, but he doesn't worry about that. That is not the real scandal.

. . .

When the doddery bishop suddenly limps into the gymnasium and sits down in a splendid armchair, she has vanished. Pity, that. He wanted to ask her something that only she could know and that relates to him, no one but him.

. . .

As always, his headache is from drinking grappa.

. . .

He hasn't seen her for many years and has never thought about her. All he knows is that she and her husband once had a stillborn child. Nothing else. He met her years ago in Bahnhofstrasse in Zurich: a lady, bourgeois by birth and now simply bourgeois.

. . .

She enters his dream for the first time.

. . .

As usual when he wakes up, he can only remember the stupid outline of his dream; for a while he is like a beaten man. Later, he goes about his day's work, IL DOTTORE, who has become a drinker, of which the village is also aware.

. . .

Why was it a happy dream?

. . .

In the pharmacy during the day, when he wears his thick horn-rimmed glasses on his narrow face, he remembers the facts that the dream made use of but which are not relevant. The gymnasium, for instance; they once put on a play in a gymnasium when he was at high school, that's all.

. . .

The water bill is probably accurate.

. . .

He has never been a country doctor in his life; it worries him that he should have thought for a while after waking up that he used to be a country doctor. It simply isn't true.

. . .

What is true, though, is that he has been campaigning for ages for a water treatment plant, IL DOTTORE has; it's not only the village that knows about this but people in Bellinzona too—they know him and his clumsy Italian. He's from Winterthur.

. . .

The tannery didn't feature in his dream.

. . .

'UNA VERGOGNA!' he says only when he can hear the sound of his own voice. The villagers only speak Italian.

. . .

He later remembers a walk with Leny, or to be more precise: he remembers a memory he has already recounted about how a woman came by, pulling a wobbly handcart, and sitting in the cart was a crippled, retarded child, and the student laughed at him when he told her very gravely that the child's face was his own or might have been. What he has never told anyone: he seduced the student afterwards in the woods, and it was ridiculous.

. . .

In the daytime everything goes back to normal.

. . .

It is a nice dream until the bishop arrives, displacing everything else, this purple-clad doddery old man, this old comic with the crosier and the audience, tourists from Locarno, his clients.

. . .

He has long known, though, that he won't get anywhere with the tannery, even if it is polluting the small river; IL DOTTORE has requested expert reports, but it is clear without any reports; children swim in the river. Why should he bother? His children don't swim in the river.

. . .

It's a sunny day in winter.

. . .

It's all linked to something different or to nothing at all; it's only clear when he's dreaming, completely clear. The way he thinks about it after he wakes up is wrong; everything is different and truer than any thoughts he has in his pharmacy.

. . .

In fact, when he sees the doddery bishop, limping with both legs, he knows it's all a dream. That was the scandal.

. . .

When he has stopped thinking about it (in the meantime he has gone to Locarno by car and needed to speak to his employees; before that he had breakfast with his family; now he's dictating orders), he suddenly thinks of E., whom he hasn't seen for a long time. This is how it must have begun: E. is sitting on asphalt, meaning on the ground in public, his legs tucked under each other like a Buddhist, clever and funny as always but naked, a lot smaller than any normal person and sadly without arms. It's moving rather than grisly: the famous revolutionary, still smiling, a little cripple.

. . .

Around noon it all dissolves into meaning.

. . .

When his wife asks what the scandal in his dream was (she heard his loud exclamation), he says, 'They're crooks, the whole village are crooks.'

. . .

E. doesn't believe in reform. That was always the cause of their arguments. But the way he sits there on the asphalt with his missing arms—without any self-righteousness, naked and endearing.

. . .

The middle of his dream is always empty.

. . .

When it's time for the children to start school they will leave the village—they more or less decided this some time ago, though it isn't urgent; still, he brings it up at breakfast, saying there's no life here.

. . .

He loves the student, who is now a woman, for the first time in his dream; now she knows everything. No signs of affection, as mentioned. Yet it is not the first time he has had a secret love affair in his dreams, but every time he wakes up, it has never happened. The thing he would like to ask her: if she remembers it. If so, it was her.

. . .

IL DOTTORE is what they call anyone with a job requiring a university diploma; if he was a doctor they would say: IL MEDICO.

. . .

Everything is slowly on the slide.

. . .

For example, it now occurs to him who the real crooks are: the accident insurance company, who simply haven't paid up in all this time. But that wasn't in his dream.

. . .

There's still the student with the cheekbones and the austere hairstyle. Pug faced, to be honest. She's sitting at a long table (grotto) in a brown silk dress—a city woman, sun tanned incidentally; only later is she in a flat with other people's children on chests of drawers, messy but bourgeois; she has nothing to do with any of it. She only speaks to him. It doesn't matter that he's married. She assumes that it's his friends who wander in and out. They don't bother her. They are his friends, except he doesn't know them. She says that she is very strong now, very strong.

. . .

He thinks he remembers corridors.

. . .

Their affair had long gone stale.

. . .

Animals in the corridor, but undefined.

. . .

A few days earlier, he had told people in a local bar why he wouldn't pursue the case against the tannery. Something like: you can't change the world, well, he can't anyway, it isn't his job, etc. he's not an idiot.

. . .

He doesn't actually like the Danish woman.

. . .

E. is aware of it all too, and there's nothing more to be said. A good reunion, an unexpected reunion. It doesn't seem to trouble E. that he has no arms, barely any arms. Not an accident; it's just the first time anyone's seen him naked. The way he sits there grinning on the asphalt (a sit-in) invites you to caress him. He isn't actually grinning, or hardly. He's like a child, that's all; he's endearing.

. . .

Maybe the television has intruded.

. . .

It isn't as if the next day is overshadowed by the dream, so to speak; he doesn't need to forget any of it; it just cannot compete with the day (or not the day at the pharmacy anyway) and merely fades away into something private and trivial—happiness that does not hold up to daylight.

Why isn't he a country doctor?

. . .

The bishop alone is still repellent.

. . .

Sometimes he has a drink towards the evening (although he tells himself every morning that this must stop), first wine, then grappa, because all he knows is that everything he thinks, says, does and knows is wrong.

1969

NEW YEAR'S DAY

The Zurich police thugs whose wrongdoing (abuse of people under arrest) is beyond doubt have still not been investigated seven months later. They will never be investigated. The police force has closed ranks. A film that would identify the thugs has vanished. The men responsible for developing this esprit de corps are still in office.

BERZONA

Once I thought I spotted the house from a plane: a grey block in a side valley. It made me sad: it is often uninhabited. But then it holds our books, civil documents, letters, notes, crockery and wine too. Each time we return, it looks so impersonal. Everything is still there. It tells no stories. The phone has presumably rung every now and then. It hasn't collapsed, and after an hour it seems credible again: this is where we live. Winter on the south side of the Alps: slush runs over granite, which turns purple-black in the wet; amid this withered bracken, birch trunks, snow on the peaks, beyond them the Mediterranean. You meet no humans out walking these days, a few goats now and then; the streams are iced up, but it's warm in the sun. Nowhere could possibly be more beautiful right now. Without the guests who have eaten at our granite table or slept in our house, this would not be our place; it would still be countryside—very beautiful on a day like this.

READERS' LETTERS ABOUT ARTICLES

'Do you really believe the Viet Cong didn't murder anyone?' / 'If you feel the need to criticize the US, why don't you finally go and live in a Communist country if you think it's so wonderful there?' / 'Are you even Swiss?' / 'Is the author of this article willing to enlighten us neutrals on the real conditions and goings-on over on the other side?' / ' . . . I only know one of Lenin's phrases, but it's true: useful idiots. That's precisely what you are. For how much longer?' / 'These are the so-called youths who support you and your kind: criminals, ex-convicts, homosexuals, antisocial elements, malingerers. That's where our taxes go.' / 'After everything else, it was only to be expected that you would put in a good word for conscientious objectors too.' / 'Your whole article is filth, but you earned a load of money for it and that's all that matters to you.' / 'Bastard! You're a fucking bastard! They should feed your prick to the gulls outside Globus! You're a loathsome idiot, but any day now your hut is going to go up in flames! You bastard!' / 'Why do you do nothing but criticize?' / 'The American soldiers in Vietnam are dying for you too, Herr Frisch, you seem to forget that, and so as neutrals we have absolutely no right . . . ' / 'It's impossible to resist the impression that you are an intellectual scoundrel, even if one would really like to resist that impression because of your good qualities. Such a corrosive and negative message is highly irresponsible in times like these and in a world like this . . . The repugnant, perfidious and subversive nature you reveal points to a vile character, the unavoidable feeling being that it's impossible to discuss things with this man.'

HATRED

If I had to take stock, then right now there's no one I hate; only a few people I don't wish to meet, as that might well inspire me to hate again. It's not uncommon for me to hate, but it's always shortlived. Maybe it's just anger, mainly. No instances of lifelong hatred. Above all, I'm pretty sure that my hatred has harmed me more than it has harmed the people I hated. Hatred like a jet of flame that suddenly illuminates things but then dulls my mind. Maybe that's because the hater is more inclined to reconciliation than the person he hates. If I realize someone hates me, it's easier for me to avoid them; I'll stick to those who don't hate me. Despite possessing my natural quantum of self-loathing, when I find out that someone hates me (although I've never put a spoke in his wheel) my first response is irritation. Did I expect kindness? Not really. What's irritating is the unexpected intensity of a one-sided relationship, my reflex reaction being not hatred in return but possibly confusion or, more commonly, wariness. My sense is that it is stimulating (to a certain degree), or else I simply forget about the person who hates me. It's not the same the other way around: my hatred binds me to the person I hate, and it doesn't help for him to avoid me. Quite the opposite, in fact: the less I see of him or hear from him, the more all-consuming my hatred and thus my self-harm. Moreover, I observe that hating a person obliges me to strive for a degree of righteousness that I never achieve, and this wears me down. Usually, no reconciliation is even required; my hatred proves too costly over time, that's all; over time it loses any relation to the actual person, to whom, whatever he or she might have done to me, I have actually grown indifferent . . . It's a different matter with hatred that isn't directed at an individual but at a group or perhaps a person representing a group. My only undying hatred is for certain institutions; hatred itself becomes an institution. But even then, hatred harms me more than anyone else, yet I remain loyal to my self-harm, because this hatred is now a principle that precludes both indifference and reconciliation—

```
We're moved, we help, we give advice and
furniture and money; our awareness of our own
powerlessness in the face of current events
means that whenever we can do something, we
seize the chance; we answer the phone and make
magical arrangements, actually achieving
something, promising no miracles. But we're
here—that always fools refugees at first. Now
they have an apartment, maybe even a job, but
half a year passes and they feel alone; their
problem is not our problem for long.
```

Premiere of *Turandot or the Whitewashers' Congress*, directed by Benno Besson. Why in Zurich? The parable doesn't properly apply to the East or the West, but, like any parable, it pretends to hit some kind of nail on the head. Where Brecht goes wrong in his critique of the West: we are not summoned to congresses to approve the Vietnam war, for example, and we can even protest without being beheaded—it's just that our protests don't achieve anything; on the contrary, our protests famously prove to those in power how tolerant they are. How true for the East is this parable of parakeets having to line up to ideologically applaud the invasion of Czechoslovakia? It is well known that when Brecht started writing the play, he was talking about intellectuals under fascist rule; why didn't he complete it and develop it on stage? His China/Chicago is, as always, set in the immediately pre-socialist era and is therefore as innocent as the old farmer with the child who has understood what is in the little book through shrewdness and common sense. (It is supposed be a little red book, but that isn't possible nowadays . . .) The play leaves no doubt that the truth is coming and the truth will triumph, the curtain comes down—as if intellectuals would have no further trouble with the truth after the curtain comes down. Unfortunately, now the audience knows too much. The proverbial bread basket that flies up into the air, swoosh, if you don't worship those in power: how true, how true!—then confiscation of your passport, expulsion from the Party, banishment to a labour camp or admission to a psychiatric institution (because you don't worship those in power) wouldn't be so easy to portray as allegory. Overly simplistic. When I see the severed heads on the battlements, I naturally know whose heads they are *not*; but they still come to mind. And it is no use projecting a Matterhorn poster, as Benno Besson does, to prevent misunderstandings. But Zurich cheered; that doesn't happen when a society sees itself unmasked. It was terrible—a theatrical happening. Even the confidence that under socialism there will no longer be a problem with intellectuals seems thoroughly outdated. That's the problem with parables—

ZURICH, February

Arson at the Hottingen telephone exchange. The perpetrator, a man called Hürlimann, a longstanding telecommunications employee familiar with the facility, laid fires in different places so the firefighters couldn't really do all that much to stop them; the building has been saved, but most of the switchboards were gutted. The headlines report huge damage; above all, it is going to be weeks before the main telephone exchange is up and running again. The perpetrator handed himself into the police immediately and seems satisfied with his act; a first psychiatric assessment describes him as a hitherto normal mechanic, an elderly father and socially isolated. He confesses that his work bored him; also, he recently felt slighted because

```
he wasn't promoted; he was placed under a
younger mechanic, which closed off all avenues
to change. The psychiatric assessment cannot
judge whether the existing working conditions
are tolerable or not, and its simple
conclusion is: psychopath. The technical
consequences of his precision technological
strike: 30,000 phones have been muted. My
conversation with people in a restaurant: even
those who have been inconvenienced are not
without sympathy for this man Hürlimann.
```

Questionnaire

1.

If you cause someone to lose his sense of humour (e.g. because you have hurt his pride) and then realize that the person doesn't have a sense of humour: do you see your laughing at him as proof that you have a sense of humour?

2.

What is the difference between wit and humour?

3.

If you sense that someone has taken a dislike to you, what do you consider a more successful response—wit or humour?

4.

Do you think it is humorous to:

a. laugh at another person?

b. laugh at yourself?

c. make someone laugh at him- or herself without feeling ashamed?

5.

If you subtract all the laughter at other people's expense, do you think you're often humorous?

6.
What is the telltale sign that you have squandered all goodwill at a social gathering: do people ignore your serious argumentation, your knowledge, etc., or does your particular brand of humour simply not land, i.e. you become humourless?

7.
Do you have a sense of humour when you're alone?

8.
If you say someone has a sense of humour, do you mean they make you laugh or that you make them laugh?

9.
Do you know of any animals with a sense of humour?

10.
What is it that unexpectedly makes you confident that you might be able to be intimate with a woman: her appearance, her past, her beliefs, etc. or the first sign that you share a sense of humour, if not the same opinions?

11.
What does a similar sense of humour reveal:

a. a convergence in intellectual matters?

b. that two or more people can be alike in their imagination?

c. a similar sense of shame?

12.
If you become aware in a particular situation that you lack a sense of humour, does the sense of humour you sometimes show seem like a superficial act?

13.
Can you imagine a humourless marriage?

14.
What makes you more jealous: that the person you love kisses, hugs, etc. another person, or that this other person manages to provoke an unsuspected sense of humour in your partner?

15.
Why are revolutionaries so allergic to humour?

16.
Can you look at a person or a social group you hate for political reasons with humour (and not just with wit) without this blunting your hatred?

17.
Is there such a thing as classless humour?

18.
If you are subordinate to someone in your job, do you think it is humorous when your superior smiles at your serious complaints and demands, i.e. do you see it as humourless if you don't smile along, or do you laugh until your superior stops smiling, and which has worse results?

19.
Do you sometimes find that your sense of humour shows you to be a different person than you would like to be, i.e. that you are shocked at your own sense of humour?

20.
Does humour come only with resignation?

21.
Suppose you have a gift for making everyone laugh and you show this gift in social situations, acquiring a reputation as a humourist—what do you hope to gain from this?

a. communication?

b. to avoid spoiling any relationships?
c. to insult someone and later pass it off as a joke that the person concerned didn't get, etc.?
d. that you will never bore yourself?
e. that people will laugh along with you on a subject that cannot be resolved with arguments?

22.
What can you bear only with humour?

23.
If you live abroad and find your natural humour impossible to convey, can you get used to only getting on with people seriously, or do you start to feel foreign to yourself?

24.
Does someone's sense of humour change as they get older?

25.
Does your sense of humour make you:

a. conciliatory?
b. modest?
c. fearless?
d. averse to moralizing?
e. surpass yourself?
f. bolder than usual?
g. free of self-pity?
h. more candid than usual?
i. grateful to be alive?

26.
Assuming you believe in God, do you know of any evidence that he has a sense of humour?

5 March

Spent the whole day watching German television. The German presidential election. Frozen faces on camera: after the first round; after the second round. The conservative CDU politicians try to look relaxed and cheerful, like men on holiday together, as if there were really more important things to be getting on with than this ballot business, but it must be done for the sake of democracy; a melee in the lobbies, but don't forget in the melee that TV voters might just be watching, the procedural complexity doesn't get on their nerves, a game with a foregone conclusion, God willing, and they haven't heard anything to the contrary from God; they get through the first round as expected (though it's a little tight), Chancellor Kiesinger, as usual the grinning chief, Minister Heck and the other gentlemen from the CDU show palpable compliance when running in elections. The results, at last, towards evening: it is the Social Democrat Heinemann after all. After this defeat, which Chancellor Kiesinger explicitly declares he is willing to accept as a democratic outcome, a democrat for as long as anyone can remember and to his core, even if democracy has once more revealed its failings, the embittered Minister Strauss declares concisely: 'Not a glorious election.'

Sketch of an Accident

It was his right of way, and therefore none of his fault. The articulated lorry joined the avenue from the left just outside Montpellier. It was noon, sunny, the traffic light—

. . .

She wears her blonde hair short, trousers with a brass buckle atop a wide belt, and a pair of purple poppy glasses. She's 35, from Basel, witty. They've known each other for a year.

Her question—'Or shall I drive now?'—are not her last words before the accident (as he might later believe); she had said it a number of times before on this trip.

. . .

In Avignon, alone in the bathroom, whose door he locks even though she's still asleep, he decides: This can't go on! He wants to tell her over breakfast (without arguing): 'Let's go back! It'd be better.'

. . .

She met him at the hospital in Basel where he was the doctor to whom she owes her life, so to speak; she's divorcing for him.

. . .

Nights in bed followed by visits to Romanesque and Gothic sites, every day like an exam: the history of the popes, purely because they're in Avignon—she delights in asking things he doesn't know or only vaguely knows, and this discomfits him. She could read up on why the pope moved to Avignon in the fourteenth century if she really wanted to know. But this isn't about the popes. Later, in bed, she restores his self-confidence.

. . .

He's a bachelor.

. . .

She thinks the trip has been a success. She's been saying so since Genoa, where it poured with rain. Then the weather improved. She says, 'You're not even looking!' Provence is the biggest thrill for her; she occasionally bursts into song as they drive along.

. . .

He's balding, and he knows it.

. . .

Aix-en-Provence: of course he thinks it's pretty—very pretty in fact. But she doesn't trust him because he looks at different things than she does.

. . .

It isn't called CAVILLION—it's CAVAILLON, famous for its asparagus. Incidentally, she told him that yesterday. She's right. It *is* called CAVAILLON; soon afterwards there's a signpost marked CAVAILLON. He falls silent, and soon after he drives through a red light.

. . .

A hotel room with a *grand lit*, where she later reads the newspaper, *Le Figaro littéraire*, of which he, as they both know, doesn't understand a word. She has a doctorate in Romance Studies.

. . .

In Nice they have dinner with friends, a nice evening although she tells him afterwards that he spent the whole meal (bouillabaisse) talking about food. You're surely allowed to say that to your partner. He has sworn to himself that he will never talk about food again and overdoes it now, remaining doggedly silent when Marlis talks about food, which is particularly normal in France.

. . .

This isn't their first trip together. He used to have a sense of humour, which he drew on as long as she still admired him as a doctor. Their first trip after she recovered was to Alsace.

. . .

He has never had a serious accident, but he would still be grateful if Marlis would put her seatbelt on. She doesn't because she fears he'll only drive even faster if she does. He promised to stick to his promise. And he has. Since Cannes. When he notices that she's still silently keeping an eye on the line at the side of the road, he forgets what he was about to say. He's boring and he knows it.

. . .

In Avignon, after using the bathroom, he says, 'I'll wait downstairs.' 'What's wrong?' she asks. She really doesn't know. Maybe he's been working too hard.

. . .

She admires clever people, especially men because she considers men to be cleverer than women. She will say of someone: 'He's very clever.' Or: 'He's not exactly clever.' She doesn't let someone know if she thinks he isn't clever, though. She regards it as a sign of her love that it pains her if he, Viktor, doesn't say cleverer things than she does when they're in company.

. . .

He isn't minded to marry.

. . .

'You're doing 140!' He's been expecting this. 'Please don't shout!' Firstly, he isn't shouting, merely saying that that he'd been expecting this. She never takes her eyes off the speedometer. Secondly, as the speedometer shows, he's doing exactly 140. Which is what she said. Yesterday he drove 160 (on the motorway between Cannes and Saint-Raphaël) and 180 once, which resulted in Marlis losing her headscarf. They agreed on maximum 140. Now she says, 'It's simply too fast for me.' Even though every single Volkswagen is overtaking them. She says, 'I just feel scared.' He tries a joke: 'Yesterday 140 max, today 120 max, at this rate it'll be 30 max by Bilbao. Happy?' Since he himself thinks it's a stupid joke, he doesn't need Marlis to find it stupid too. She has stopped singing, he has stopped overtaking; they sit there in silence.

. . .

Her husband—her first husband—was (is) a chemist.

. . .

She isn't upset that she didn't buy those shoes in Marseilles because of his impatience; she merely says that her shoes are too tight and that there are no shoes for her in Arles, where he shows patience.

. . .

He'd actually rather have breakfast on his own. He doesn't know what's wrong with him either. He doesn't know any woman he'd rather have breakfast with than Marlis. And she knows that.

. . .

How clever is Marlis?

. . .

He knows it's his fault.

. . .

He might think later that he woke up with a feeling that the day would end in an accident; under the plane trees in Avignon he was almost certain.

. . .

The childlike joy she takes in shopping: even when she doesn't need anything, she'll stop in front of a shop window in the middle of a conversation. It wasn't much different with other women.

. . .

He's from Chur, the son of a train driver, a brilliant scholar and soon-to-be consultant doctor.

. . .

The famous gypsy meeting place is called SAINTES-MARIES-DE-LA-MER, not SAINTES-MARIES-SUR-MER. She doesn't point this out to him. She goes so far as to avoid saying the name so as not to correct Viktor until he happens to notice himself.

. . .

She calls him Vik.

. . .

She doesn't want to be the dominant one; no man can cope with that, let alone Viktor; he's a surgeon and is therefore used to people trusting him, and Marlis trusted him back then too.

. . .

One of Marlis's stock phrases is: 'Are you sure?' She'd like to know if C., a mutual friend of theirs in Basel, is actually homosexual; no sooner has he given his opinion than Marlis says, 'Are you sure?'

. . .

Waiting for her under the plane trees in Avignon, he suddenly feels like he used to when he still had a sense of humour. It's like a visitation. Sun on the plane trees and wind, probably the Mistral. Maybe things will be better today. He's not going to make his suggestion to cut their trip short. It's ridiculous really. He sits at a little round table under the plane trees and studies the *Guide Michelin* to work out the best route to Montpellier for later.

. . .

He is 42.

. . .

Once, when he was a student, Viktor spent a week in Provence. He thinks he saw the arena in Arles as they head for Arles and Marlis reads out details from the *Guide Michelin* about the diameter of the arena, the number of seats, the height of its sides, the year it was built, etc. She reads it out in French. It is written in French, and Marlis cannot help it if the moment he hears French, he feels as if he's in an exam; he does understand it though. When she reads the *Guide Michelin*, she doesn't look at the verge. Back then, as a student, he was with a woman from Hamburg; what has stuck in his mind is a memory of them sitting high up on the ring wall, a very precise memory of this arena in Arles. He describes it in advance. A nice evening in Arles—Viktor tells more stories than usual and is in good spirits. She likes it when he tells stories. They have a drink (which he doesn't do when he's on duty). The next morning they visit the arena—he realizes that it was the arena in Nîmes he remembered; Marlis doesn't notice, but he does.

. . .

She's slim. She has a wide mouth and full lips that always leave her teeth showing, even when she isn't smiling. Anyone who tells her she's beautiful has failed the test; yet she makes an effort to be beautiful to a man she thinks is clever.

. . .

An hour on from Arles he admits that he got the arena in Arles mixed up with the one in Nîmes.

. . .

She knows Viktor is waiting. She thinks they have time. Why does he always walk ahead so he then has to wait? She can't do things any quicker. He's always the same. Sitting there at the little round table under the plane trees, he tells himself that it's his fault, because he always walks ahead. She's right: he can enjoy Avignon. That's what he's doing. Sunshine on the plane trees. When he spots Marlis standing outside another shop window, even though she knows Viktor's waiting for her, he decides: patience. She says there are no shoes for her in Avignon either. What's more: she's far too lightly dressed. Will it be warmer in Spain? He guesses it will but says nothing so that if this trip really does go on to Spain, he won't have said anything wrong. Instead he says, 'Would you like a brioche?' offering her a croissant. He just about realizes but doesn't correct himself because she didn't hear his question. He now notices every single mistake he makes. At least he thinks he does. Then again, he doesn't notice, for example, that she's waiting for him to light her cigarette. 'Sorry!' he says, lighting it for her. 'Sorry.' The repetition is over the top.

. . .

In Basel she doesn't live with her husband but nor does she live at Vik's; as everyone knows, that would complicate her divorce proceedings.

. . .

The way he suddenly looks at her after lighting her cigarette—not nastily, just impersonally, the way you look at an object. She asks if he doesn't like her necklace. Then he calls, 'Garçon!' with sudden determination. It's unclear what he intends by his gesture of stroking her cheek. Unfortunately, though, the garçon doesn't come, even though he's wiping another table only five paces away. His hand gesture has confused her. He is determined to stay cheerful and relaxed. He says, 'What magnificent weather!' She asks, 'Have you still not paid?' A question isn't a reprimand; he taps a coin on the metal until Marlis calls, '*Garçon*?' He comes over now. He doesn't need to be irritated by the fact that she asks the garçon how to get to Montpellier while he pays; Marlis has no idea that he was studying the map closely just now. When the garçon finally leaves, she says, 'Did you get all that?'

. . .

What's he scared of?

. . .

One time (not on this trip) she said half-jokingly, 'You're not my surgeon any more, Vik, and you'll have to get used to that.'

. . .

Alone at the garage with the man who washed the car, he says BENZIN (nasally) instead of ESSENCE; it doesn't matter when Marlis isn't around. He gets what he wants.

. . .

Everything's different in Basel.

. . .

Only one time on their trip does she say, 'Idiot!' because he goes against her advice and turns into a one-way street. Why does Viktor take it so much to heart? Afterwards, he waits for the next reproach.

. . .

She's looking forward to Spain.

. . .

She is a Romance-languages scholar after all; Viktor should be grateful if she corrects his French from time to time.

. . .

He waits, smoking, in the car in Avignon with the top down while she buys something else. They have time. Holidays. He smokes; he's doing his best. When she eventually arrives, he welcomes her like a real gentleman, gets out of the car, opens her door and says, 'I found your sunglasses! They were under the seat.' Marlis says, 'You see?' as if he had lost her sunglasses, the second pair on this trip. Marlis didn't find what she was looking for, another nail file; instead, beach shoes, which he finds amusing. Why is she cross? She always has the feeling that Viktor is impatient. As in Marseilles. Half her suitcase full of shoes, and he doesn't understand why she has been wearing the pair that are too tight all the time since Marseilles. His suggestion that they drive via Marseilles again is not supposed to be ironic, but she doesn't believe it isn't. Now they're both cross.

. . .

Pity about their nights in bed.

. . .

Everyone knows that LA MANCHA isn't north of Madrid, as Marlis claims; after all, he had another look at the map before she came down to breakfast. Not to bring it up again. Just to be on the safe side.

. . .

They drive with the top down after he has promised he definitely won't speed. It's very different sitting behind the wheel or in the passenger seat. It is actually ridiculous that he doesn't overtake at all (as between Cannes and Saint-Raphaël) and stays behind every lorry; afterwards, he can't quite believe it himself.

. . .

He hates his name, VIKTOR, but he doesn't like it either when she says: VIK, especially when the people at the next table overhear her.

. . .

In his opinion, Europe must and will adopt a common currency; Marlis is unconvinced, but listens to his reasoning without comment. Why does this rub him up the wrong way? It isn't his arguments that doesn't convince her.

. . .

She has fully recovered.

. . .

When she stays silent, he does the censoring himself. Why is he talking about asparagus in Alsace now (food again!) instead of looking out for the Montpellier exit? She puts on her sunglasses and says, 'This is the way to Lyons' and as he doesn't say anything, 'I thought you wanted to go to Montpellier.' He dangles his left arm out of the car to look relaxed. Shortly afterwards, a sign: TOUTES DIRECTIONS. Back on their first romantic trip to Alsace she just trusted him. Another sign: TOUTES DIRECTIONS. Still no mistake.

. . .

When he thinks he is displaying a sense of humour, she generally doesn't think so; but then occasionally she'll laugh out loud at a comment he makes, and he doesn't know why.

. . .

She does up the headscarf, a new one she bought instead of the nail file; Viktor only notices when she asks, 'How do you like it?' He suddenly says, 'You're right!' as if she said something after his comment that he once drove from Baghdad to Damascus through the desert without her and managed to find his way; now he says, 'We're screwed!' which astonished Marlis because he doesn't usually say such things. He laughs as if they were standing on the famous Pont d'Avignon, which stops in the middle of the river; in fact, they are in an industrial zone with a sign marked PASSAGE INTERDIT. He puts the car into reverse, and she says, 'Don't get panicky.' When, following a series of mistakes (amplified by the engine), he has found the road that any idiot could find, Viktor still hasn't said whether he likes her new headscarf.

. . .

She is naturally clever.

. . .

If he could put on his white doctor's coat, everything would be different; the idea of driving through Provence and Spain in his white coat—

. . .

Why doesn't he talk?

. . .

It isn't true that he's never had an accident. It's just that Marlis doesn't know about it—it was a long time ago. A very fortunate accident. He'd more or less forgotten about it. When it pops into his mind, he looks at Marlis askance, as if her silence reminded him of it just after overtaking a 2CV.

. . .

What does 'plexus' mean? He's a surgeon and it would be strange if he didn't know. But he still waits for her to say, 'Are you sure?' She doesn't say anything, though. It's only when Viktor suggests that the route via Aigues-Mortes is shorter does she say, 'Are you sure?'

. . .

Marlis is sitting in the car in her bare feet because her shoes are too tight, but she doesn't say so. He commiserates—instead of simply talking.

. . .

Why does he put his hand on her thigh?

. . .

He shouted at her in Antibes, but now he can't remember what prompted it. He thinks he apologized later by saying, 'All right then!'—livid, not accepting that he was in the wrong—'I apologize!'

. . .

It doesn't really matter whether the flat landscape Marlis finds so gorgeous is officially Provence or the Camargue. Why does he insist it's the Camargue? Maybe he's right.

. . .

Not a word until AIGUES-MORTES.

. . .

Contrary to her warnings, which he doesn't even acknowledge, he manages to manoeuvre them into a tight parking space. No scratches, and first time too. Silently. A 100 yards farther on there are lots of empty spaces, and in the shade too. But Marlis couldn't have known that either. Nor does she say anything.

. . .

Aperitif under plane trees on his own while she looks around the town. He suddenly feels as if he's on holiday. The light under the plane trees, the light, etc.

. . .

He never thought she owed her life to him. It was the kind of operation that is usually successful. Maybe she sensed that—

. . .

They could stay here. It's 11 o'clock, too early for lunch, but they could stay here anyway. The old fortifications keep the mistral at bay. He'll look like a different man when Marlis comes back: jovial, relaxed—it depends on him, entirely on him.

. . .

Sometimes he fancies having a baby with her.

. . .

She doesn't know why Viktor makes scenes like he did in Antibes. First he shouts at her, then he suggests a restaurant, LA BONNE AUBERGE, three stars. She doesn't believe in these stars. He insists. He's in a bad mood again because his suggestion hasn't delighted her, and leaves her to stroll around Antibes on her own for an hour. What's he doing? When they meet up again, it's the same old palaver about where to eat; her objection that there are restaurants close by, why the three stars, etc. The area he drives to doesn't look promising for restaurants; when she finally asks, 'Are you sure?' he carries on driving in silence, turns off, turns off again, and there it is: LA BONNE AUBERGE. The head waiter shows them to their table on the terrace, which he booked specially an hour ago. Unfortunately it is too cool outside on the nice terrace now, and inside the walls are painted, the waiters are in traditional dress, the food is mediocre but expensive, but it doesn't matter. Marlis is kind to him, even though he was shouting at her an hour ago; she feels sorry for him.

. . .

There's also a poet called Mistral—Viktor knew that. However, the wind which is also called the mistral doesn't blow in off the sea, as Marlis claims. Incidentally. She is of course right that *Lettres de mon moulin*, which he read at school, is by Alphonse Daudet—not Mistral. It doesn't matter. What she actually said was: Mistral was a poet, as you know.

. . .

He drives a Porsche.

. . .

Under the plane trees at AIGUES-MORTES: he reaches into his jacket to check he hasn't lost his passport. Viktor has never ever lost his passport. His horror when he finds his passport isn't in his jacket pocket; but that same instant he remembers that his passport is in the car. He's sure, remembers precisely putting the passport in the glove compartment; but he'll have a look. He isn't sure.

. . .

If he had followed through on his decision in the bathroom to cut short this trip, they would now be in Lyons, in Basel this evening—whereas it's so beautiful here: the light under the plane trees, the light, etc. He'll make a suggestion when she arrives: a stroll by the sea.

. . .

Hopefully she'll find the right shoes.

. . .

Under the plane trees in Aigues-Mortes: an hour before the accident he feels like another black coffee. Is he too tired to drive? He praises the light under the plane trees, this light, etc. Pigeons are cooing around the memorial to SAINT LOUIS. Marlis would like to carry on, she really isn't hungry, she doesn't even want an aperitif. Now Viktor feels as if they have time. An old man with three baguettes under his arm.

. . .

Spain was her idea.

. . .

He doesn't regard himself as selfish. He's only happy when he thinks he can make someone happy. If it doesn't work out that way, he's appalled; he thinks everything is about him.

. . .

Anyone looking on would find nothing odd about the fact that she's reading *Le Provençal* newspaper while he drinks coffee with his long legs stretched out onto the pavement, waiting for a miracle—it would have to come from outside, from the cooing pigeons . . . He would be willing to get married. It just takes a sense of humour. 'Do you plan to sit here long?' she says. 'Sorry!' he says. 'You're reading the paper, not me.' He doesn't mean it the way it comes out, and she's accustomed to him carrying her handbag as he then does, a needy gentleman. No miracle then.

. . .

For the first time it is Viktor who wants to visit a cloister. Romanesque. She doesn't feel like it.

. . .

They walk along arm in arm.

. . .

For the first time it is Viktor who stops everywhere. A market with fruit and vegetables. It's touching when Viktor says, 'There are some shoes here!', showing that he still doesn't know what she's looking for.

. . .

Why do they have to go to Spain?

. . .

He waits in a lane. Marlis has forgotten her headscarf, but he isn't really waiting for Marlis. What would he do if he was alone? When he spots her approaching then stopping outside yet another shop window, he buys a *Herald Tribune* to find out what's going on in the world. When he looks up from his paper after a while, Marlis has vanished—

. . .

Tourists having lunch.

. . .

Later she says, 'Sorry!' She's bought a fun cap. 'No,' she says with a laugh, 'it's for you!' Marlis is in the best of moods. When he unlocks the car, she asks, 'Or shall I drive now?' He drives. Why is it always him? He beseeches her to let him drive. He has no real explanation. 'Don't you like it?' She means the brightly coloured cap. For the first time he's scared of the road.

. . .

She's a child.

. . .

His passport *is* in the glove compartment.

. . .

'You look funny!' She's put the colourful cap on his head so he doesn't look so serious, she says. He's surprised when

Marlis puts on her seatbelt without his asking. He leaves the cap on his head as he changes gear and glances back to make sure he doesn't bump into the car behind. No mistakes now—

. . .

So that was Aigues-Mortes.

. . .

She has a son of school age; she studied in Paris; she's getting divorced; she is a woman, not a child.

. . .

Camargue horses. Sometimes she says something, something he does. Luckily there's not much traffic. Then he tries to think about his work again: When is a person dead? That's the question with heart transplants. He catches himself saying, 'I have to change the oil tomorrow!' instead of saying what he's thinking. He's too easy on himself.

. . .

As a child she used to go horse riding.

. . .

He drives along behind a Belgian caravan without overtaking it; when he eventually overtakes, they just make it but it was hairy. She doesn't say anything.

. . .

Patients appreciate him: his composure, his certainty, his confidence, etc.

. . .

Now she's wearing the fun cap. 'Everything suits you!' he says, but he's got his eyes on the road. Is he listening at all? She's reading the *Guide Michelin* aloud so that he can look forward to the cave paintings in Altamira, so he doesn't only think about his oil change, so he knows why they're going to Altamira. She means well.

. . .

He's always been lucky compared with other people, with his health and his work and in general, not only as a mountaineer (Piz Buin)—

. . .

She says, 'Are you thinking about food again?!' He wasn't actually thinking about anything at all, just watching the road; he was going to say something about Montpellier because he sees a sign: MONTPELLIER 12 KM. He'd have been better off saying nothing.

. . .

Viktor comes out of it with only slight injuries, gashes on his temple, but he has no recollection of a lorry with a trailer. She dies on the way to Montpellier hospital. He can't even remember the avenue where it happened, where the overturned trailer is now lying between the plane trees; when he inspects it, it seems to him that this is the first time he's been on this avenue with the junction where he is questioned (in French) and discovers that it was his right of way and therefore not his fault.

. . .

He later becomes a consultant doctor.

. . .

For a decade he never mentions the accident near Montpellier; he doesn't know how it happened.

. . .

A few acquaintances know vaguely about it.

. . .

He becomes head of a clinic, a father of two children and travels a lot, but never to Spain.

. . .

A doctor shouldn't tell stories from his past on the eve of an operation, he knows; and yet he suddenly mentions his accident near Montpellier in France: 'As I said, it was my right of way, so not at all my fault . . . ' Afterwards he says, 'How did we start talking about that accident?' The patient doesn't know either. Why doesn't he just say goodnight, the usual things: 'You'll sleep. If not, ring for the night nurse.' But he's already said that. Then he picks up one of the books on the bedside table but reads no more than the title. He puts it back on the bedside table. What he really wanted to say was: No need to worry, he'll be there tomorrow, he won't be doing the operation but he'll be there, no need to worry, etc.

. . .

He never had another accident.

. . .

The patient is obviously disappointed but doesn't dare ask why the head surgeon isn't doing the operation himself.

. . .

Her question: Are you sure?

. . .

He never tells anyone anything more about the accident.

. . .

Marlis saw the lorry, she warned him; he saw the lorry but he didn't brake; it was his right of way. It's possible that he even accelerated to show he was sure. She screamed. The Montpellier police agreed with him.

VULPERA-TARASP, June

The things you do when you're convalescing!—I've been reading the (

,

190th year) every day for a week . . . Can it be said that this newspaper lies?

An old-style hotel. Nothing swanky. The lift is too small to accommodate a lift attendant as well; a wooden lattice door; when you push the button, it doesn't start up straight away and when it does get going, it shakes; it can be safely assumed that this technological factotum has already lifted a royal or two. The bathroom and toilet are modern, though. Not like Hilton hotels for high-earners with no sense of tradition; this style of hotel knows how aristocrats live when they're at home—just like here: with simple and reliable and unobtrusive service, as I said nothing swanky, even if we have been accustomed since we were small that someone opens the car door for us and lays our pyjamas on the bed, sleeves folded, as if praying.

What is not clear from the first day is what line of business they're in. What is immediately clear, even when they talk about the weather, diet, a son-in-law in Lisbon, dogs, the deceased, etc. is that they are property owners. Characteristic of this tone is that they can naturally choose, they make requests without hesitation—nothing improper, just services that they pay for at the appropriate price, and friendliness makes them friendly; they are certain that they will only be asked what they would like. Their air of entitlement—

Young people have daubed the high court in Zurich with red paint after disrupting the traffic again. (11 June.) The press strikes a serious note, rebuking the authorities. Only robust intervention from the police will do, or else popular rage (against young people) will be unstoppable—'militias'. Not a word about the cause, though: the fact that young demonstrators from the summer of 1968 are in court, whereas the police perpetrators from the summer of 1968 cannot be brought to trial; they haven't been identified. At least there is no longer any dispute about the abuse of people in custody, but the opines that we really have heard enough of that.

Hikes in the National Park.

[1969]

Their paper cannot be said to lie; all it does, three times a day, is prevent elucidation. Its trick is to present the property-owning class as dutiful—not just in business and industry, but in the army too. The property-owning class is dependent on labour, but not on workers' opinions; however, the majority dependent on the opinions of the owner class, which is what produces the owners' sense of duty. It is there in every NZZ article, often between the lines. They make the layout as boring as possible to make it look serious. This then rubs off on the readership because they think they are serious just by holding the newspaper in their hands. Their facial expressions while reading are even more serious. And afterwards they know just how frivolous any alternative report would be—so they don't even need to bother reading it. From time to time a sneaky piece of character assassination, either humorous or tastefully condescending; it is only those who are familiar with the particular case that can detect the spite. The better columnists stick closely to the facts as long as they confirm the paper's stance, i.e. they let the facts speak for themselves. Particularly in foreign news. Swiss neutrality may not constrain citizens in their thinking, but it does constrain the state in its pronouncements; and thus to a degree this newspaper, as the voice of Switzerland. Its stylistic neutrality (someone like Ulbricht is presented no differently from a colonel in the junta in Athens; someone like Brezhnev is never personally defamed; Kiesinger or Strauss are quoted without comment; the problems of the

Italian Communist Party reported with some sympathy, Nixon not criticized for a minor troop withdrawal from Vietnam, etc.) does occasionally shine a light on the nature of politics: the battle between power interests abroad, whereas with regard to domestic politics the tone is more moralistic. ('Nip it in the bud.') Given that local events, with which readers might be familiar, do not automatically suit a style of reporting that allows the facts to speak for themselves, its judgement must be indicated adjectivally now and then: 'irresponsible', 'foreign methods', left-wing intellectuals', 'masterminds', 'rioters and their backers', 'allegedly progressive', 'who is secretly pulling the strings in the background', 'monkey business', 'hooligans and layabouts', 'agitators', 'at the taxpayer's expense', 'the well-known lefty socialist's attempts to play it down', 'destructive', 'un-Swiss', etc. A portrayal that runs contrary to the paper's own bias is presented as 'biased'. Occasionally it makes for an amusing read: 'It has ultimately been proved that tolerance and patience are, contrary to initial expectations, sadly not sufficient to achieve the desired outcome.' This not only defines the essence of tolerance but also shows what exactly is desirable. The art of this subtle lie consists in presenting the opinion that approves of the power of the property-owning class three times a day as definitely not a class opinion but as an ethos in its own right and therefore in the interests of the majority.

The National Park: even though people stick to the marked paths, the marmots whistle and disappear, red deer keep to the far side of the valley and the chamois to binocular range.

Daimler-Benz has recorded gigantic profits. Things that are legal: free shares for shareholders; one major shareholder earns 140 million. To maintain peaceful industrial relations, employees also get a share of the profit: a one-off payment of 320 marks per worker.

Literature: when it is possible for your social opponents to present themselves openly as your admirers.

How the Greeks must have imagined Hades: an elderly couple from Zollikon playing Nine Men's Morris, elsewhere a family with chaste daughters, at the bay window a fat Finn (reading Malraux), always alone, others are drawn together by boredom and, after some discreet bowing, they pull up their armchairs. What are they talking about? From the next table I hear about the best places to shop. They're drinking coffee, like in real life. Later in the bar: the best places to eat in Hong Kong. But then the lady tells a rabbi joke: laughter, like in real life. The wives are better preserved, their sexuality too has faded but they chat more and more animatedly and sit up straighter. A man without a walking stick shuffles slowly along, one shoe in front of the other; there is constant anxiety: what if he comes to a doorsill? A wife looking after her husband after his stroke, draped in pounds and pounds of jewellery like the spoils of war, from time to time tells him all the things he used to know. The couple from Zollikon have danced a slow waltz and gone to bed. Connoisseurs at the next table: they collect Persian rugs—valuables of lasting value. It's 10 o'clock. Tomorrow is another day. Nothing will change.

The way they listen to the news before dinner, the gentlemen in dark suits, the ladies with fur stoles, not listening: Brezhnev curses China, Husák continues his purges, but the Czech writers are still resolute, even the Czech workers seem to be in favour of freedom, Pompidou is naming his government, Israel continues its retaliation, fish are dying in their masses in the Rhine, the Swiss government is going to inspect it, finally the general weather forecast—not all of it is pleasant, but all in all it confirms the course of events. In general, it is not too bad for the owners.

'The city council is not prepared to tolerate any further riots . . . People's right to freedom of expression and to organize demonstrations remains unaffected . . . The police have been clearly instructed as to the necessary course of action according to guidelines set out by the city council.' An additional news agency report: 'The motorized water cannons are apparently not filled just with ordinary water but also contain a chemical substance designed to make the water even wetter. At a higher level of alert, police officers will wear standard army flamethrowers on their backs, filled with water and liquid tear gas. Police sources stated that this chemical adjuvant to the water was previously tested in Germany.'

The Ofen Pass; in 1945 I had to heat a hut there for German deserters, faces down in capitulation. Schuls station: train wagons full of survivors from Terezín. Memories everywhere, even if I don't bring them up.

How does a majority come about (not just a majority in elections but a majority of public opinion on issues that are never put to a vote)? The postman—a civil servant—is not the only one who has a family; the professor, a civil servant, has a family too and, beyond that, a social role to play: research, which relies on grants. Is he meant to jeopardize these grants by signing something or making a speech? No one can demand that he does. Moral cowards? Individuals adapt to the social climate around them; any rate, contradicting public opinion is risky. The climate is generally unfavourable; the likelihood that a personal intervention has a greater impact than repression against someone. The more pussyfooters there are in a country, however, the more spoilt and sensitive the ears of those in power become; a constitutional referendum by students is already being called 'coercion' (   ). Anything that runs contrary to the prevailing opinion is deemed scandalous. As a consequence, I have become cautious. Am I supposed to make life harder for myself? I am therefore giving in to social pressure; but it is easy for the individual to succumb to an illusion: I see conviction in everyone else where in myself there is only caution and cowardice, or at best a lack of opinion. All the yes-people who keep their heads down ultimately enable those in power to perform a charade of representing public opinion; they have the wherewithal: schools, the press, television, universities, the church. Because public opinion is in essence not the expression of a consciousness of its own but a product of social pressure, it reacts angrily to any other consciousness; the majority always see consciousness as subversive anyway: NIP IT IN THE BUD. If the pussyfooters realize they are in the majority, they no longer need to pussyfoot around and become collectively aggressive: MILITIAS. They are understandably anxious to protect their reward for a life of caution. Public opinion, as the consensus of everyone who has been corrupted by social pressure, always presents itself as morally right; it has to compensate. This is true in every system. Fear of reprisals mutates into conviction. This majority does not take power because they are prevented from doing so by their belief and acquiescence with those in power; all they do is to take over the execution of reprisals from those in power. LAW AND ORDER, that is what the regulars at the pub support; those in power no longer really need to make sure that a teacher who has different ideas is kicked out of a school because it is taken care of democratically by the majority those in power have forged through reprisals. It is common to call the people of Switzerland SOVEREIGN: because, after all, the majority decides. But how sovereign is the majority?

Hike in the National Park.

There's a lot to laugh about, as always when Friedrich Dürrenmatt decides the subject menu . . . Recently it was Genghis Khan, whom he'd read up on, liberally garnished with Chinese dynasties, history larded with tall stories, and barbecued on searing wit. Today it was   , prepared to the same delicious standard: humans on the skewer of zoology, roasted on facts (blood pressure during sex: 200) and seasoned with speculation from his own garden. It's always a pity to request your own subject; the chef's own selection is always the tastiest. Not so long ago, in Berne hospital, it was Proust, marinaded in the vinegar of sleepless nights, served fresh from memory and flambéed with jokes at the bedside. Four-star cuisine! No hope of ordering the same thing again so your wife can enjoy it too; no Proust today, not even served cold. Today it's sauerkraut and sausage: , boiled to a pulp with jokes about doctors, innards from Konolfingen, made appetizing with drama along with calf's head from the applicable literary criticism, peppered with quotations. Washed down with Veltliner wine. Afterwards he gives me the paperback from which he gleaned his knowledge. I'm wary of reading the paperback. First, he always improves on it, and second, he is no longer intrigued by what the other person knows. Recently our conversation turned to a Godard film he hadn't seen; he changed the subject to another film he had seen and when it turned out that we too had seen that film, he broke off the conversation: this time he described a Japanese film that no one apart from him had seen. He needs an advantage, then it is wonderfully convivial. For many years it used to be astronomy; I was fascinated every time by his descriptions. He once gave me a fat book and I took it along on a three-week camping trip to Corsica as my only reading material, and the next time I visited him I had mastered the basics and thought that I was now better equipped for a conversation about astronomy; he said, 'You know what's interesting? Biochemistry.' He needs my ignorance, of which there is plenty. I've retained an interest in astronomy, and naturally so has he: it's just that we barely ever talk about it. By the time I get to supernovas, he has long since moved on to pulsars. Once, in Neuchâtel, Teo Otto, the set designer, turned out to be extremely interested in architecture; Friedrich Dürrenmatt listened for a long time, but it made him gloomy; he suggested we play boules. He thrashed us. The next day he suggested we play boules again, but this time his luck was out and we didn't finish the game; he felt like an aperitif now and had much to say about drama. He does all the giving. Recently in Berne, too, there was a very old LATOUR claret; the nurse opened it for the visitor, who kept a straight hospital face, as she did, but Friedrich Dürrenmatt burst out laughing. A mistake by a doctor, for example; without complaining, he tells the story as pure comedy. It's more than just humour. We've known each other for over 20 years. It isn't true that he can't listen. When the landlord sits down at our table to tell a story (for example, how the people in the Grisons are fleecing the Aga Khan or someone) and then lingers for a chat, Friedrich Dürrenmatt is a Herculean listener; it just depends who he's with.

Reasons to be Thankful

No organization asks for an annual or half-yearly list of thanks (as the tax office does) . . . Yesterday in the street I caught sight of a man in the distance to whom I owe a great deal, a very great deal in fact. It is a long time ago, but he seems to know that I can never shake off my sense of gratitude; actually, it isn't a sense any more, it's a consciousness. For life. I got the feeling, however, that he had recognized me but had kept walking and acted as if he hadn't seen me. What can he do about this consciousness of my gratitude? I could just about have caught up with him, but I didn't and was shocked that I didn't. It wasn't just my architectural studies that he made possible; to this man I owe Schopenhauer, Mozart and Beethoven, Nietzsche, Bruckner, Khmer art and so much more, including the Engadine. However, whenever he passed on his suits and coats to his friend, all of them still in good condition, they were always slightly too big; the sleeves in particular were too long . . . If an organization existed that required me to submit a list of thanks within the week, I would also add to the list:

a.
my mother

b.
the fact that I met a Jewish person at a very early age, a very German Jewish person

c.
my father's early death

d.
a practical experience of poverty

e.
not having been posted to Stalingrad or appointed to the Reich Literature Chamber

f.
a clean bill of health

g.
meeting the publisher Peter Suhrkamp

h.
meeting Brecht

i.
having children

k.
giving up my German literature studies

l.
all women—yes truly, all of them

m.
the Schauspielhaus Zürich back in the day (under Kurt Hirschfeld)

n.
my enjoyment of food

o.
practising architecture for a while; its valuable aspects: my experiences with clients, with contractors, with workers

p.
the tension between dialect and written German

q.
a Rockefeller grant

r.
late success

s.
friendships with colleagues

t.
financial independence in later life, i.e. with an awareness that it is unusual

u.
my neighbours in the village

v.
periods of poor recollection of my own mistakes and omissions

w.
the partner who lives with me

x.
waning ambition

y.
all dreams, even nasty ones

z.
all kinds of good fortune with cars

21 July
Moon landing (Armstrong and Aldrin)

News of a dog who walked from Calabria, where it was lost, to Turin, where it was joyfully reunited with its owners, in nine weeks.
Someone from the city's child protection services tells the story of a 15-year-old girl, an orphan, who set out from Cognac (France) in a panic because she had been raped

by her boss and walks the whole way to Basel where she has an aunt; there, the aunt's husband rapes her. A woman, a stranger who won't leave me in peace, asks for advice: her brother is soon to be sentenced for robbing a jeweller's shop and maybe also for drug smuggling, and I am known for being against injustice; her brother, who is essentially an artist, will not survive five years in prison, she says. Our cat Nina gave birth to another kitten—and ate it.

SKETCH OF AN ACCIDENT (II)

Gusts of wind during the night. No downpours, though it sounds like it. A broken shutter beats the alarm. The rustling of the dry trees. He is awake. There's no need to get out of bed. The windowpanes are sturdy enough. The two garden chairs don't matter; they're broken already. No sheet lightning, just gusts of wind, the sky is probably clear and starry over the sea. What's the worst that can happen? The car is in the garage. No lamps swinging around; no earthquake. Later, the electric light goes out. The idea that the island might be flooded tomorrow morning, the house left standing alone on the hill with the olives. Later on, he sits barefoot in the living room and falls asleep again, alone in the house that withstands the storm. The morning is blue and ordinary. A parasol has fallen over and broken; the island isn't flooded. He can't remember all the things he thought about during the night. The odd branch on the dry ground. He has breakfast in his pyjamas and wonders who might be able to repair the blind. Later, he picks up the branches from the dry ground, barefoot, before getting dressed. The phone line is down too, but he only discovers that now. Later, the post arrives, demonstrating that life goes on. Ground under his feet. He feels that there are more important matters. Thinks of selling the house. He doesn't know what prompted these thoughts. Everything is disconnected: his wife waiting for his phone call, the parasol, the letters, the blue and ordinary day, his shoes which he should put on. Around noon he walks barefoot to the beach. Memories of the wind in the night and on the avenue in Montpellier, the chalk on the asphalt, the tourists, the village, no need to be scared. He goes swimming. No ground under his feet, the cloudless sky over the sea. He'd like to know some day. He swims out as far as his strength holds, and it holds until there is no more land in sight.

BERZONA

Our fifth summer here already. Only rarely now do I pick up the axe to thin out the trees or the handier (a question-mark-shaped piece of iron); our land is reverting to jungle. Today I fought the advancing stinging nettles with the scythe, which is also rusty. These are fits and starts; they end in the insight, fuelled by sweat, shower and beer, that a proper jungle does not care about our fits and starts—

DER SPIEGEL, 28 July 1969

'About 2,380 West German business people and equity owners had an average monthly income of 190,000 marks in 1965. That same year, one third of those on wages and salaries earnt no more than 500 marks, meaning that in 12 months they earnt as much as the millionaires did in 23 hours.'

ADVERT BY THE SWISS VOLKSBANK

'Is it true that only the rich ever get richer? That was what one nineteenth-century theory claimed, but it has turned out to be wrong. It has long ceased to be true that society is divided into a small number of rich people (who become ever richer) and a large number of poor people (who become ever poorer). Nowadays, almost every working person can make a fortune—all it takes is willpower—and compared with earlier times and circumstances, practically all of us are rich.'

POSTER IN A DIFFERENT BANK

'Do you hate cash?'

QUESTIONNAIRE

1.
Do you hate cash?

2.
Why?

3.
Have you ever had to live without cash?

4.
If you meet someone in their swimming costume, knowing nothing about their circumstances, how can you tell after chatting for a while (not about money) that they are rich?

5.
How much money would you like to have?

6.
Suppose you are in need and have a rich friend who wishes to help you and he gives you a considerable sum of money (for

example, so you can study) and occasionally an old suit, still in good condition: which do you accept with less compunction?

7.
Have you ever stolen:

a. cash?
b. an object (a paperback from a kiosk, flowers from a stranger's garden, a first edition, chocolate at a campsite, biros left lying around, a keepsake, hotel towels, etc.)?
c. an idea?

8.
If you do not have a fortune and are on a low income, rich people are not inclined to talk about money in front of you, let alone about issues that cannot be solved with money, e.g. about art. Do you regard this as tactful?

9.
What do you think about inheritance:

a. if you have a chance of coming into one?
b. if you don't?
c. if you look at a baby and know that, however it turns out, he or she will own half a factory or a mansion, land immune to inflation, a holiday home in Sardinia or five rental buildings in the suburbs?

10.
Do you have savings? And if so:

11.
Can you explain why the central bank determines the value of the money you receive in wages and your savings, and who benefits from the sudden evaporation of your savings?

12.
Assuming you come from a modest background and you suddenly receive a sudden windfall so that money no longer really matters to you. Do you feel different? And if so, do your old friends think so too, or do they think that money does matter because it has warped your personality?

13.
How much does a pound of butter cost?

14.
If you were to be in a position to live off interest payments, would you consider yourself less of a parasite because you also worked, despite being able to live off the interest?

15.
Are you afraid of the poor?

16.
Why not?

17.
Suppose you are a great philanthropist, i.e. you distribute to people you appreciate a portion of the considerable interest payments you have derived from other people's labour. Do you understand the public esteem you enjoy as a philanthropist and your own peace of mind about this?

18.
What wouldn't you do for money?

19.
One day, Timon of Athens served bowls of water to test his friends' friendship; he found out what he already knew and was bitterly disappointed about humankind because, lo and

behold, they only ever came to see him for his wealth and were not his true friends. Do you think his vehement cursing of others was justified? Rich Timon of Athens had obviously believed he could buy friendship.

20.
Would you like to have a rich wife?

21.
How do you explain the fact that, as a rich person, you like people to notice if you deny yourself something you could easily afford (e.g. a yacht) and that you feel an almost child-like joy when you buy something particularly cheaply, dirt cheap, that anyone could afford? And why are you simultaneously so keen on priceless objects such as icons, swords, Ming porcelain, copperplate prints, Old Masters, antique coins, autographs, Tibetan prayer mats, etc.?

22.
What do you dislike about the nouveau riche:

a. that they get by without a coat of arms?
b. that they talk about money?
c. that they are not reliant on you?

23.
How do you justify your own wealth:

a. by thinking of it as God's will?
b. by telling yourself that it is entirely the result of your own labours, i.e. with the assumption that other abilities that cannot be converted into income are worth less?
c. through dignified behaviour?

d. by telling yourself that it is really only the nouveaux riche who can boost an economy so that everyone benefits, i.e. through their entrepreneurial spirit?
e. by giving to charity?
f. by your higher education, which you owe to inherited wealth or to a foundation?
g. by leading an ascetic lifestyle?
h. through scrupulous observance of all moral issues that don't affect the bourgeois system of profit and by internalizing the circumstances, sensitivity for cultural pursuits, taste, etc.?
i. by paying a substantial amount of tax?
k. with hospitality?
l. by telling yourself that since time immemorial there have been poor and rich people and there always will be, i.e. you don't even need to justify it?

24.
If you were to revert to being poor—not of your own volition (like St Francis) but due to circumstance—would you be as tolerant of the rich as before, as paralyzed by respect, having grown familiar with their way of thinking as their temporary equal?

25.
Have you ever used a lighter to burn a bank note with the portrait of a great poet or a great general on it, their grandeur passing from hand to hand, and then looked at the ash and wondered what became of its guaranteed value?

[1969]

BERZONA, August

A visit from two very young girls who have barely sat down at the granite table when they start asking questions: How is freedom possible? One of them, Barbara, has just discussed this with her father (a teacher); the other, Verena, cannot or doesn't want to discuss it with her father (a banker), 'or they'll stick me in a home'. What both of them want is 'complete independence, without having to live at others' expense'. The banker's daughter sees only one option: leave for Amsterdam or London, disappear without an address, without her father's money, and laze about. The teacher's daughter also wants to reject this false system, not become dependent on money and 'do something useful' instead; she wants to finish school, become a teacher and independent by not allowing herself to be conned into buying things she doesn't need. Verena: 'And it just isn't possible.' Barbara: 'You need a minimum amount of money.' Verena: 'Then you're part of it.' Barbara: 'Not if I don't want to be; I don't need a tape player.' Verena: 'I could do without my tape player right now.' Barbara: 'What are you going to live off as a layabout?' Verena: 'I don't hate my father, but I'm dying at home and he doesn't see.' Barbara: 'You heard my father saying he was against you just lazing about too.' Verena: 'Mine doesn't even get where I'm coming from. He thinks I'm crazy.' etc. Raspberry juice with our discussion. What do I think is the right path? Though different in background and temperament, the two of them are united by their disgust for the prosperity of a world that forces people into prosperity. Barbara: 'Lazing about isn't an objective either.' Verena: 'You've heard what my father thinks my life should be like.' Barbara: 'But you don't have to do that. When you finish school you can do whatever you think's right, but at least you'll have learnt something. You'll rot away if you just laze about.' Verena: 'I'll do any old job if I need money, I just want to need very little money.' Barbara: 'So do I.' Barbara: 'I asked her father for reasons not to laze about and now I'm asking you, Herr Frisch'; after my answer she says: 'And if I drive around in a sportscar and study art history and get married, that's parasitic too and I'll rot away. Ultimately, it's my life. You said so too. I think you at least find out about yourself in one of those communes.'

29 September

Like landowners who still haven't realized that the divine right of rulers has long since been abolished, even in Germany, they flaunt an entitled arrogance that only they and their kind are capable of governing, then dismayed by the news that the stableboys really do intend to enter the palace and subsequently aggrieved that their attempted bribery didn't work (Kiesinger is offering the FDP six ministerial posts rather than the maximum of three to which they would be entitled and eschews the first-past-the-post system, already promising the turncoats they will be selected for the necessary constituencies for the next Bundestag elections), to have the smile ultimately wiped off his face: 'the social democrats have diddled their way into power', 'power hungry', 'a government with no plan', etc.

Notes for a Handbook for Members

If he has always been conservative in his political opinions, the marked man is visibly satisfied by actually being undaunted by world events; the daily news confirms his political opinions; he never invested much hope in progress. If he does opine on world events, then he is by no means cheerless; his age lends him an aura of wisdom. He never had any illusions, which is why he has no need to think any differently from 40 or 50 years ago, back when he was young: in that respect, conservatives feel younger for longer than revolutionaries.

Why does an old man who has not lost his revolutionary ardour make at best a loveable impression but not a convincing one: the younger generation do not reckon with the fact that history will one day reveal their rhetoric to be pathos. It is better not to let any of these apostolic figures into a meeting to discuss revolution: their appearance has a cheering effect—paralysing in its demonstration of how rhetoric becomes threadbare.

The pre-marked man faces a certain temptation to become liberal by virtue of the fact that he, unlike the young, is forced to live with an awareness of his errors—he doesn't have to succumb to this temptation, though; the less he is able to bear this awareness, the more some men are driven to seek political power that would grant them infallibility. The authors of the great purges are generally pre-marked men.

In many cases a man's political opinions have come about due to a natural revolt against paternal authority; it only becomes clear when the father is dead and buried to what extent these political convictions actually correspond to the man's own constitution, i.e. to what extent they were ever political convictions. Age acts as a sieve.

If he describes himself as a left-winger, the marked man catches himself thinking that most texts (pamphlets, brochures, manifestos, school newspapers, etc.) bore him in spite of his political allegiance; anything that teaches him only the doctrine he already knows by heart strikes him as irredeemable.

The difference between a young person talking about the political future and a pre-marked man talking about the political future is an impression that the latter is actually interested in the future.

In general, there is less political temperament than democracy requires. Most people thought that using political vocabulary to be sociable was a sign of political convictions; as marked men, they might be disappointed in their lives but not politically, only privately.

Even if people who have been exploited have nothing more to fear, other than the old people's home, they tend not to become more progressive in their political convictions as they age; the opposite, in fact: however much someone may curse the exploitation he has suffered throughout his lifetime, it is possible to sense a hint of envy in him when he learns that these circumstances are about to change.

Something that is not yet true of the pre-marked man but is of the marked man: as his capacity for pleasure wanes, politics is occasionally the last area in which he can feel superior, especially as a marked man. He is seldom seduced by a spontaneous thought or action nowadays; his calcified brain registers very little irritation; political decisions come easily to him, not due to impetuousness but due to calcification; it happens automatically; he is neither hooked on risk nor does it scare him; he has survived many a wrong decision; his dwindling imagination allows him to weigh things up objectively without fearing the consequences; he cannot regard people's lives as so important, not crucial, given that he himself has almost no life left to lose and is increasingly suited to being head of state. (*Gerontocracy.*)

Elderly heads of state are covered by the taboo on talking about age; although their subjects have experienced themselves the effects of ageing, they never apply this sure knowledge to heads of state.

Unlike workers, whose sole asset—their labour—declines for physiological reasons; unlike intellectuals, who notice their regression earlier in proportion to their intelligence; unlike artists, who are forced to acknowledge that all creative powers are clearly linked to hormones, politicians have the least to fear from ageing; it is presumably intrinsic to political power that they can have the greatest impact without being at all creative.

[1969]

JAPAN, NOVEMBER

What am I doing on a Tokyo boulevard at five in the morning? The short workers with yellow helmets, illuminated by the flames of their blowtorches. No fruit. The temptation to think that people are naive just because they're smaller.

They giggle when I speak to them, puppets with flesh under their white makeup, almond eyes: I never know which way they're looking. They can also bend their hands back as if they were boneless.

The express train travels at a smooth 140 miles per hour; rice fields after harvest; they give you a terry towel: steaming hot to refresh your face and hands—thus refreshed, I realize that most of what usually occupies my thoughts back home is irrelevant.

A discussion with Japanese students at the university: 'Annihilation of the Existent', 'Ask about the goal and you won't bring about revolution', including self-destruction. 64% of the students at this university are working class. An agitator explains himself in metaphors: like a kaki fruit on the kaki tree in winter, etc. They don't think in concepts but in images: antirational.

When you can't read any writing it's as if you hadn't lived. It always looks like poetry, but it's actually advertising.

Shoes are always removed beforehand: the street stays outside (we are barbarians), squatting down for meals. Immediately a different relationship to space; you occupy it and have pretensions to be graceful. Two geishas prepare the low table. Everything has to be beautiful. You eat little by little, paying tribute to the different dishes; the two geishas on their knees are so noiseless in the midst of all this that no one makes any noise. As if you were picking up the German and English words with chopsticks too. A ginger-haired British man, a poet, can no longer contemplate going back to the West; he's 40. They don't offer, they simply attend to our every wish: HAI, they nod as soon as one looks at them, HAI, HAI, they wipe every drop from the table and bow as they do so, HAI, with silent grace. Later, they prepare the beds on the floor; they disappear noiselessly behind a bow. I sleep ecstatically.

Reading from the handbook on ageing.

Police in the city: squads waiting with shields, truncheons at their belts, gas pistols, helmets with Plexiglas visors. A large helicopter circles over Ginza Avenue, spitting out noise and seeking out youths with its searchlight. Shops lower their shutters. Squads marching with their gleaming shields, smoke billowing from the subway, youths with shields and metal bars, a snake dance, but good natured so far; then sirens, squads marching back in the opposite direction. One officer trips over his shield. Truncheons also used on the crowd, who don't take sides. Molotov cocktails clear spaces. Torchlight, loudhailers. I end up in a department store, MERRY CHRISTMAS, kimono dolls to the sound of

German carols; shopping goes on. It is clearer on television (an hour later).

Evening with a Zen Buddhist; he laughs as he imitates the famous gesture of Rodin's The Thinker: It's impossible to think like that!

Morning at NOH rehearsals, conversation with the school director: he sits upright like Buddha, as handsome as Buddha; matchwood architecture with a view of overhead railways, chimneys, industries, etc.; he speaks quietly, someone nearby is practising on a drum; son of a NOH dynasty: 'I'm 40 and I'm beginning to understand what NOH is.' Japanese politeness, no contradicting, they nod at each question, HAI, they bow to keep their secrets safe.

Boxing bout with kicks to the liver and as far up as the head; the victim drops like a dead man and has to be dragged away while the victor skips and whoops.

Weekend in the Japanese house of my translator, KOJI NAKANO, fishing village; the children ask if I'm a general because I'm so fat. A wife's chattering constitutes legal grounds for divorce in Japan. Her giggly laughter: a sign of polite agreement, or ? If I say something trivial ('I'm not thirsty'), there are sudden giggles; with the Japanese woman, facing a mountain of hacked-up, bloody and stinking dead fish; she stares for a while, then giggles.

Rock gardens, moss gardens

The quiet gentleman with the very bald head in the imperial garden: JUAN MIRO. He sits for a long time, watching them gather the fallen leaves under the trees and place three especially beautiful autumn leaves back under the tree.

Mothers, each with a child on her back, the little black shock of hair poking out of the bundle, wobbling like a bird; the child is more Asian than its surroundings; impression in the bus: the future is increasingly Asian.

OSAKA, visit to the docks where they're building the world's largest tanker. The company replaces the clan. I stand there in helmet and work jacket, a larger size for visitors from the West; I ask and nod, understand this and that, but don't know what use this knowledge is to me.

Tourism as an existential holiday.

Mountains small, islands small, frizzy forest of low-growing pines, bamboo, thickets with the occasional cedar towering over them: the bizarre silhouette of the foreground, branches in front of a distant landscape that looks like empty silk. Knowing a country's paintings and finally seeing the country itself; nature as plagiary. Carp ponds, lotuses, swans, cranes, dwarf trees in pots. May art and nature all be one.

Industrial landscape with virtually no land: shantytowns, hut after hut, a slum.

Japanese massage: the girl walks barefoot along my spine, afterwards I feel wonderful—

1969

'People were once categorized by the colour of their skin, the width of the bridge of their nose, the shape of their skull, and their physique. Modern ethnology pays little attention in external aspects such as these; ethnologists have discovered that peoples can be more accurately distinguished on the basis of the ideas and values that are especially important to them. In our case it is the ideal of human freedom within a community of our own choosing that predominates.'
(p. 15)

'Social national defence consists of maintaining healthy social conditions so that life in a liberal state is worth living for everyone and there are no weak spots that opponents can attack to stir up our people and undermine our political system.'
(p. 31)

'Long before it comes to violent conflict, the enemy is striving indefatigably in the middle of peacetime to sow mistrust and discord, destroy our natural sense of identity and erode our inner resilience.'
(p. 145)

'In peacetime we have taken all the precautions in our power. We can face up to danger. We are prepared. / Those who wish our ruin are deliberately sowing doubt and fear. We do not believe them. / We are not scared by so-called scientific theories predicting the demise of nations and cultures or even of the world itself. No one can foresee that. We are critical. / Our lives and fate are in God's hands. He alone knows what our future holds. Those who believe in him have no fear.'
(p. 146)

'Switzerland reacts in the same way that a strong and healthy organism reacts to infections.'
(p. 152)

'The enemy is striving with all the means at its disposal to shatter our inner strength . . . With everything we hear, see or read, we consider carefully whether the arguments hold water. We do not believe anything if we do not know where it came from or who spread it . . . We are not overawed by things that we have learnt only from certain newspapers and books, from foreign radio and television stations and films.'
(p. 175)

'Switzerland does not have the death penalty in peacetime. However, as the security of the nation, our people and our active soldiers are at stake, Switzerland cannot do without the death penalty in times of emergency . . . Drastic measures are needed to preserve the country from serious danger.'
(p. 186)

'Proving ourselves in war means doing our duty through commitment to the common cause, even when many things turn out differently than we had expected.'
(p. 191)

'The aggressor's government and parties adopt the following approach: For the sake of appearances, we form a political party. It does not need to be big. It relies on a small core of trustworthy and uncompromising members. It is not really about gaining power in democratic elections. At a specific moment, our goals can be pursued through terrorism and with a minor coup. The party must maintain a veneer of legality . . . It is not easy to win over the masses in countries with a high standard of living, which is why we must handpick some malcontents. Intellectuals make good decoys and figureheads . . . '
(p. 228)

'We respect scientists and artists regardless of their political views. We do know, however, that totalitarian systems make no distinction between politics and culture.'
(p. 231)

'The enemy ridicules all religion but is not afraid to quote liberally from the Bible in its propaganda.'
(p. 235)

'The enemy wants to attract partisans.'
(p. 230)

'He does not succeed.'
(p. 231)

'The enemy tries to lull us to sleep.'
(p. 238)

'We never sleep.'
(p. 239)

'The enemy tries to intimidate us.'
(p. 240)

'We leave him no opportunity.'
(p. 241)

'The enemy seeks to undermine our economy.'
(p. 244)

'We can see through him.'
(p. 245)

'He drives a wedge between the people and the authorities.'
(p. 256)

'The people and the authorities stand shoulder to shoulder.'
(p. 257)

'In this phase of the battle too, newspapers, radio and television are our main weapons. But watch out! If the opponent fails to intimidate them, he tries to infiltrate them.'
(p. 259)

'A small state is unassailable with the tools of revolutionary war as long as it remains internally united and strong. Switzerland reacts to subversion in its neighbouring country without anxiety yet swiftly and firmly.'
(p. 263)

'He encircles Switzerland.'
(p. 266)

'We hunker down.'
(p. 267)

'He tightens the noose.'
(p. 268)

'Switzerland will not take orders from abroad.'
(p. 269)

'We shall stick together and stay strong. We place our trust in our federal councillors for their whole term of office. The kind of governmental crises they have in other countries, which shake people's trust and rob the country of an effective government, do not happen here. There are far fewer opportunities for subversion. We are a politically judicious and watchful nation. Every man has a gun and ammunition at home . . . A sudden revolution is impossible. We shall fight in all circumstances.'
(p. 271)

'After the majority of our country has been occupied, leading Swiss figures will assemble somewhere abroad and establish the Swiss resistance movement. They will include surviving members of the government and of the Confederation, senior army officers who

have escaped captivity, parliamentarians, party and union leaders, and representatives of women's organizations. They will form a government in exile based on an emergency constitution. For the first time people will listen to RADIO FREE SWITZERLAND.'
(p. 280)

'Shortly afterwards, millions of pamphlets will be found around Switzerland. They will be dropped from missiles by night. They will read: "Citizens of Switzerland! We are not yet strong enough, nor does the international situation yet allow us to organize an active campaign of resistance. This could be the case for some time. The slogan for the time being is therefore 'Keep quiet and grit your teeth'." '
(p. 282)

'Don't do anything stupid. / Drunken soldiers broke into a church in Buchgraben and desecrated it. They yelled and bellowed, smashed paintings and cultural artefacts and shot at the cross. A man who lived nearby was seized with rage. He fetched out the gun he had hidden under the hayrick and fired it at the miscreants, wounding one of the occupying soldiers. The next day, the commander of the occupying forces sent some military police from the party militia into Buchgraben. All the men were herded together in front of the church and massacred by machine-gun fire. The women and children were taken away and the village was set ablaze.'
(p. 286)

'A resistance struggle is not the time for an outpouring of sentimental feeling. It requires smart and sober planning.'
(p. 287)

'Last but not least, this [occupying power] also takes on the Church. Religion is not explicitly forbidden, but its devotees face discrimination everywhere. Religious education is banned in

schools. The training of vicars and priests is prohibited, and as a result numerous parishes find themselves without pastors.'
(p. 289)

'Uphold intellectual freedom. / Two young authors and a female journalist are in the dock in a grand show trial in one of the occupying power's courts. They were members of the avant-garde before the occupation and famous throughout Europe. They had often commented cynically on conditions in Switzerland and were therefore suspected of sympathizing with the current occupiers. After the invasion, the cultural commissar of the occupying power tried to enlist the two authors and the famous journalist for his own propaganda purposes by offering them well-paid jobs in the cultural commissioner's office . . . They stuck steadfastly to their task of telling the truth, even in the new system, just as they had done in the old one. They were convicted of posing a danger to state security and sentenced to long prison sentences.'
(p. 290)

'Their example is a spur to us all. Now everyone knows what to do. No one should take the occupying power's cultural bait. Each of us must stand up for the truth in our own way—mothers, teachers, vicars, writers . . . No one is to toe their line.'
(p. 291)

'Many Swiss men and women are shot or deported to concentration camps. Villages are destroyed. However, these sacrifices are meaningful because each blow brings us a step closer to freedom. Those who fall in this battle have given their lives for their country and for freedom, like soldiers on the frontline. The resistance government is committed to looking after its own—indirectly for as long as the country is occupied, but openly after its liberation.'
(p. 295)

'On the day the advance from the Alps begins, it is possible that the supreme commander of the Swiss resistance army will issue an order to the Swiss population similar to this: "Citizens of Switzerland! The hour of freedom is upon us. The resistance forces are advancing from other countries and from the Alps. We shall be with you in a matter of days . . . Do not commit any hateful acts against Swiss people you consider to have been enemy collaborators. Many of them were undercover agents of ours . . . " '
(p. 299)

'We have presented this scenario of war to enable us to familiarize our minds with what it would really be like. This is the only way we will be able to steel ourselves so that we do not crumple in the face of danger.'
(p. 300)

EMERGENCY LUGGAGE
(p. 304)

In rucksacks, kept to hand at home:

Robust, warm, waterproof clothing, underwear, spare socks and stockings, hat, scarf and towel (sun protection), handkerchiefs, boots, slippers, a woollen blanket or sleeping bag, toiletries, toilet paper, gas mask, protective eyewear, a spare pair of glasses for those who wear them, a torch with spare batteries, sewing kit, first aid kit, string, shoelaces, safety pins, candles and matches, pots and pans, mess tin or camping stove, canteen, penknife and cutlery, battery-powered radio with spare batteries, plastic sheets.

Two days of emergency rations in dust- and gas-proof packaging:

Lightweight, concentrated food such as crispbreads, biscuits, tinned soup, processed cheese, cured meat, tinned meat and fish, chocolate, sugar, tea, instant coffee, dried fruit, milk powder or condensed milk.

A file containing:

ID papers, social security card, ration cards, insurance policies, health insurance booklet, professional credentials, money and securities, civil defence book, Red Cross identity tags for children.

BUNKER SUPPLIES

(p. 305)

In case of war and radioactive contamination:

. . .

Food must be stored in the bunker in a dry place and in its original packaging, plastic sachets or cans to keep it safe from radiation. It should be regularly moved and replaced each year or according to the instructions on the packaging. There are ongoing studies regarding special parcels of provisions. You will be instructed at the appropriate time via the press, the radio and television.

PATRIOTIC SONGS:

(p. 314)

'Call'st thou, my Fatherland?
See us with heart and hand
Vowed to thee, all!
Helvetia! hail to thee!
True still thy sons shall be,
Like them Saint James did see,
Leap at war's call.
There where no Alpen-bound
Circling thy land around—
God's hand hath thrown—
Steadfast we stand alike,
Blenching not, mountain-like
Still, even though death should strike,
Scorning to groan.

(Excerpts from *ZIVILVERTEIDIGUNG* [Civil Defence], published by the Federal Department of Justice and Police on behalf of the Federal Council with a foreword by federal councillor L. von Moos. Every household in Switzerland receives a durable linen-bound copy of this handy book in all national languages.)

Japan

It's no secret, but how exactly do I explain it? Take-off from Copenhagen in daylight; Greenland beneath the clouds, as we are told over the tannoy; it just refuses to get dark; once, for an hour, the Arctic; twilight could be morning or evening, and I have no idea which way is north now, whether it's today or yesterday; Alaskan mountains, but the sun is never where I expect it to be; the clocks in Anchorage simply say noon; then we fly on, but back in time again; again, only clouds for hours and hours; I write you a letter until suddenly there it is: FUJI, its white peak in the blue sky, as on posters; Japan under cloud too; we are told to buckle up once again . . . A month later, as the plane flies over Vietnam (they don't tell us over the PA system), it is night, and night in Bombay, a warm night, still night in Athens, and when it lands in Zurich, the sun is just rising: punctually, in the east, where I've come from. 'Tell me!' I do; suddenly the trip has meaning.

I read the papers, afterwards the feeling that nothing is really happening. Down to work in good heart; more attempts to write a play . . . The TV evening news confirm that nothing has happened: more shots fired at the Suez Canal, deaths; the Vietnam conference in Geneva. It's all familiar. At last the weather forecast, high pressure moving away as usual, the prospects for Thursday and Friday, and again that feeling that nothing is happening or at least nothing I don't have the slightest idea about—

Reading:

Tenth anniversary of the Cuban revolution. Dates. It begins on 25 November 1956, embarkation in the Mexican port of Tuxpan, a yacht with 82 revolutionaries on board crosses the Gulf completely undetected. Landing on the beach at Las Coloradas beach in Cuba's Oriente province on 2 December 1956. They are spotted and scattered; on 5 December 1956, a group of only 12 partisans remain who are planning to liberate Cuba. I probably read in the newspaper later about bandits and a legitimate government in control of the situation; three years later, presumably on the front page: Batista flees. At some point then the first photo of the bearded bandit. (I wonder, as I read, what might have been on my mind in 1959.) From time to time, more news from Cuba: executions. And so the name gradually brands itself on our memories: Castro. A savage dictator, apparently, though this time a Communist one; which explains the US boycott of Cuba, all of this explained in commentaries: Castro nationalizes, but most of the cultivated land (tobacco, sugar) belongs to American citizens; Castro talks about compensation in the long run but gives no guarantee that Cuba will remain a profit-generating colony; American investments in jeopardy, violent expropriation, a threat to the free world. Occasionally, more news that offers no surprises, just confirmation: the disastrous economic situation as a result of Communism, terror. We're familiar with this now. Nothing new. Only once do we hold our breath: Kennedy orders the US Navy to fire if the Soviet missile transports continue on their course to Cuba; Khrushchev diverts them. We breathe out. But Cuba is still a threat to the world . . . I wonder when I actually found out what happened in Cuba. Not today. But no one could know back in 1956, when it all began with 12 men in Oriente; or during three years of guerrilla warfare either. I wonder which things I have no clue about on a day like today. Was today a date?

Kabusch

Kabusch is not an immigrant or a foreigner, so that can't be the reason. What do they have against him? On the odd occasions he wears a tie, it cannot be ruled out that Kabusch will shout out something at a party, collect art and tell stories about lion hunting in Africa; he'll suddenly start shouting like a cowherd. He is a painter. If his name comes up in conversation, it's hard to find someone who will stand up for him. Nor is there any point in describing him as my friend. This doesn't win people over. Someone who makes casual fun of Kabusch can do so with the near certainty that they will not be contradicted; Kabusch is well known. For what? One time he played guitar on a washboard and sang nonsense; you have to admit that everyone burst out laughing. Why admit? Many people think Kabusch is arrogant. Should someone meet him for the first time and actually be charmed by the man, for instance about his spirit, his unselfish interest in everyone and everything, his spontaneity, etc., he will discover, too late, on the way home that his enthusiasm isn't shared and nor does his enthusiasm rub off on anyone. There are no allegations against Kabusch. It just cannot be helped that he leaves people sceptical, as a person. Why does he paint? He had a lot of success in his previous career, though. Why is Kabusch always getting involved in public matters? His name is sufficient to ensure his interventions are a flop. Doesn't he know that? Sometimes he has had enough and sneaks away to Paris; you cannot rely on him, they say. Whenever you could do with someone like Kabusch, he's in Paris. When he comes back, they think he's showing off. Kabusch is an enthusiast; if he advocates a cause, he can look like Savonarola one moment and like a gardener the next, sometimes like an eagle owl with a human laugh. He enjoys life. He eats moderately and doesn't drink—an ascetic with an inclination to overconfidence. He sometimes says, 'We are kings! We are kings!' Kabusch is naive, even though he is a 50-year-old man who has no sense of irony to protect himself. What he does always take seriously are art and scientists' latest discoveries. He was excited by the May protests in Paris. In his studio, a large hut, he wears navvy boots and a craftsman's blue apron; he receives visits from collectors from Chicago. Kabusch sells his works, but it can't be that either; others sell their work too. It isn't envy that has led to his being sidelined in recent times; his worldwide success doesn't cover him in glory but in suspicion instead. Sometimes he sits there and shrugs his shoulders, but then his good humour picks him up again, yet he still knows that Kabusch has done something wrong—

. . .

His father was a worker, a sturdy man who was always a bit too big for the humility a Jehovah's Witness ought to show when he walks up to someone's front door and hands out pamphlets. When he came into some money later, he bequeathed a small temple to his fellow believers and was removed from his holy duties for lacking humility.

. . .

Kabusch has let a luckless young writer use his house; for example, he wasn't able to control the heating and some pipes froze up as well as the loo. These things happen. The unlucky devil moved out so as not to sit there shivering in Kabusch's house—without telling Kabusch, and leaving behind a big pile of phone bills. What does Kabusch do when he gets back? He shivers for a week until the repairs are done and tells no one. The anecdote the wrecker tells, on the other hand, goes down very well with folks; it's funny. It's typical Kabusch. Another guy Kabusch helped get to Paris because he was having a tough time of it cannot stand up for him either, unfortunately; he had a really tough time in Paris too. Anyone who stands up for Kabusch meets with scepticism. I tried again. To a group in need of more comrades I put forward, among other names, that of Kabusch, and they reject the proposal out of hand, the young wrecker getting particularly worked up; all he says is, Kabusch?! That's all it takes; even people who don't know Kabusch personally think he is impossible and immediately raise their hands against the proposal. Kabusch naturally knows nothing of this incident, when the young writer, another kind friend, turns up at his place soon afterwards and asks if the house might be available again for a month—

Etc.

Where is Kabusch going wrong?

ZURICH, DECEMBER

A reception in honour of Varlin is being held in a large house belonging to an art collector (a lawyer, on the boards of about 80 companies, honorary consul of the Republic of South Africa, also a member of the executive board of the NEUES SCHAUSPIEL AG ZÜRICH). High society. A Herr von Kastelberg is genuinely surprised when he reads the place card of the young woman sitting next to him and says quite openly: he doesn't believe it, no she doesn't seem unhappy despite being married to a psychopath. He is deeply concerned. Does she live with this psychopath? After a few drinks, he gazes deep into his own soul and finds that her husband cannot be a psychopath if he has a wife like her, seriously, and now he's happy. As a token of his happiness Herr von Kastelberg asks her to pass on a cigar to her husband, whom he has unfortunately never met. She does so the next day. I smoke the cigar, HOYO DE MONTERREY, my habitual brand.

[1969]

Where have left-wingers gone wrong in recent years? What they have managed to do is to misplace their intelligence—conscious of their powerlessness as long as they are concerned with workers only as a category.

1970

Kabusch II

He is not a painter, no Savonarola, no eagle owl with a human laugh, etc. That can't be why. He doesn't shout out at society occasions or anywhere else. He wears frameless spectacles. He can refrain from playing guitar on a washboard. So where is Kabusch still going wrong? A well-read man, admittedly, and not too forward; he has to be invited to speak. What Kabusch knows about this or that subject remains debatable unless someone else happens to agree, which isn't always the case; there isn't always someone sufficiently knowledgeable there. The topic is then dropped. He's a librarian. He has recently started lecturing at the university, somewhat to the surprise of his acquaintances, but people do not begrudge him it; Kabusch clearly needs this kind of recognition.

. . .

What Kabusch (whoever he may be) cannot afford is pride. It simply looks insulted and is therefore an embarrassment.

. . .

In certain circumstances he forgets he is Kabusch; for instance, he once had to give a eulogy because he knew the dead man better than anyone else. A younger colleague told him afterwards that his speech wasn't at all embarrassing, I swear; not embarrassing in the slightest. He is shocked by this acclaim beside an open grave.

. . .

Kabusch was his nickname in his schooldays. His class refused to dismiss a rumour that his mother had been in the circus. That caused his fits of rage. Did he think he was special because his mother had been in the circus? For ages he didn't realize what Kabusch meant. For example, he got hold of a football, a leather one, and he also obtained permission to use the field for the year's biggest event. Did he intend to guarantee good weather too? When the class of which he is a proud member picked the team, Kabusch seemed to be the only one surprised that he wasn't chosen as goalie or an attacker; all the other positions had also been filled while Kabusch—who is, incidentally, the only one with proper football boots—paced out the penalty area and carefully marked the lines with sawdust. Maybe they would need a substitute? That remained to be seen. Who actually decided? No one in fact; this was just the way things were. Kabusch shouldn't get too big for his boots just because he had supplied the ball; he could have it back after the game. That was it.

. . .

Everyone occasionally cracks a joke in company about someone who isn't there, but only Kabusch can't afford to do this. People laugh, but he immediately realizes his joke is unfair and is shocked; Kabusch relies on fairness.

. . .

Another person from roughly the same background who moves in the same circles would hit back by becoming a big businessman, a big advertising tycoon, a big board director, etc. He wouldn't think of letting someone wreck his house or telling him his speech wasn't embarrassing, or settle the bill for everyone just because he is sensitive, or fall silent because no one nods, or generally get things wrong; he doesn't think of any of those things and yet he too has worked his way up from caretaker's son to Rotary Club member, an affable and charming character.

. . .

Does Kabusch feel sorry for himself?

. . .

When he was an apprentice, he protested against doing overtime that had nothing to do with his job description. Protesting doesn't come easily to Kabusch; he can stutter sometimes. On the other hand, he wins a prize in a citywide competition for apprentices; this speaks volumes for his master.

. . .

It has nothing to do with his background. His father wasn't working class, his mother not even rumoured to have been in the circus. That can't be the reason. His family played a role in national affairs until the late nineteenth century. He drives a Volkswagen—why not a Bentley? People believe none of this coming from Kabusch, incidentally. In the studio an impatient actor shouts out, 'Who's the cameraman here?' even though Kabusch has been standing by the camera for an hour. He doesn't fit the part (as an actor might say); for instance, when he needs something, he has to ask the workers in the studio three times; if he yells, this just creates the impression that he isn't sure what he wants so he'd rather take care of it himself. Later, during a test screening of the footage, he apologizes: it's only a rough cut, the copy is unfortunately underexposed, etc. Everyone's indulgent: No problem! Afterwards an actor says, 'Man, that was great!' One day he turns up with a new girlfriend who creates a stir—a black beauty. People flirt with her as if she and Kabusch weren't together: they simply can't believe it; our cameraman shouldn't get ahead of himself. When it becomes apparent that Kabusch and the woman are indeed a couple, she is gradually subjected to the same treatment as him. He can't stop it. It has nothing to do with racism, believe it or not.

. . .

You can find a Kabusch in every walk of life. I once observed a waiter. Although the other waiters are serving the same food from the same kitchen, customers never complained to them; Kabusch was the only suitable victim. Kabusch was called to tables he wasn't even serving because of a draught, no mustard, etc. He doesn't misconstrue this; he knows they like Kabusch. Nothing really changes when he becomes head waiter; unfortunately, a bottle uncorked by Kabusch always smells corked.

. . .

It can be a woman too. For example, no one believes that her career (psychiatry) is anything other than a substitute. What she says is admittedly intelligent. Why 'admittedly'? She is also an excellent cook, even though she has recently started speaking at conferences. She is praised for her willingness to help, which people take advantage of, and she is surrounded by a mixture of goodwill and pity which makes her insecure and sometimes tense. What is she doing wrong? She has children. When conversation turns to children, there is an immediate change; people let her speak, and Lisbeth can open up and it all sounds impressive until she puts forward scientific arguments. Nothing against the arguments, but coming from her people don't buy the same jargon they use themselves—jargon as a means of expression that impresses the person speaking. As already mentioned, she is an outstanding cook. Of course, she knows more about her field than the guests do; this they admit. They listen to her too. Only her husband looks on edge, but he is careful not to change the subject. Does Lisbeth not notice? The longer she speaks, the less present she is, and there's nothing to be done about it; her expertise, backed up by two degrees, just doesn't suit her. She dresses very elegantly, and the inevitable question comes: Where did you get that wonderful coat? accompanied by the assurance: 'It really suits you!' and a glance at her husband, 'Don't you think so?' as if each time it was an astonishing stroke of luck; as if the psychiatrist couldn't have her own taste. Later that evening, in the hallway, if not before, her husband cannot resist dropping into the conversation, clearly against her wishes, her many achievements as a psychiatrist, for example at the institute, not to mention the conferences and congresses, and she's writing a book too, etc. Why does this embarrass her? Her brow furrows above her beautiful nose; no, it isn't a book—more of a brochure. It's embarrassing; the guests are standing there in their coats, waiting to say thank you and leave.

. . .

Kabusch's error: he thinks his achievements should and will lend him legitimacy, which only devalues his achievements in advance. It's not that he doesn't enjoy the odd success; it's just that it doesn't make him shine.

. . .

It's better if he doesn't drink like everyone else; if he does, he forgets he is Kabusch and wakes up in horror the next day.

. . .

Kabusch is a TV newsreader. The news he enhances with his precise diction is usually so important that people accept it. He can feel this without seeing his audience, people in living rooms and bars. What people don't take so well are his colourful tie, the tailored suit, the signet ring (he hasn't worn this signet ring lately; someone has clearly had a word with him) and his hairstyle—his entire personality, in fact, even though he goes to great lengths not to display one. The news is about state visits, disasters, coups, summit meetings, crimes, the pope's travels, etc. He avoids showing any reaction to these announcements—Kabusch can't afford to—apart perhaps from an involuntary expression of relief when he comes to the weather forecast. For a few seconds he is covered by the weather map superimposed with the country's familiar outline. When, at the end, he is back on camera and looking straight ahead, wishes people goodnight as usual, someone in the bar says, 'And to you too!' and everyone laughs.

. . .

It is not easy for his children to have Kabusch as a father. At least, that's what he thinks; his magnanimity comes across as a kind of self-publicity, even a form of compensation.

. . .

He occasionally describes himself as an idiot.

. . .

Occasionally he publicly rises to the challenge: he stares out from election posters and is elected mayor. Voters have seen through Kabusch: this man will make an effort; this man won't surprise them; this man has no margin for error.

. . .

What he gives himself credit for: he is not a conman. But Kabusch doesn't have a hope in this regard; if Kabusch refuses to put up with something, there's a whiff of megalomania about it.

. . .

The hotel receptionist recognizes Kabusch with a friendly, almost familiar nod. After handing everyone else their keys, he even asks, 'How are you, Herr Doktor, how are you?' and after chatting briefly to the doorman, gives Kabusch his key.

. . .

It makes no difference when Kabusch wins a cinematography award at Cannes; everyone knows how these things work, and it is kinder not to mention them. He doesn't mention it either, which is a good thing.

. . .

How ambitious is Kabusch?

. . .

If I make what seems to be a winning argument and then Kabusch arrives and makes the same point (in his own words), that is one less argument I can make in future. It's contagious.

. . .

It sometimes occurs to Kabusch that all it would take is for him to disappear around the next corner, for instance, wait a moment and then come back—without Kabusch. As someone else. No memories, no inhibitions. That would do it. No apologies for making them wait for a while, a quarter of an hour or a quarter of a year. That would probably be the decisive thing—no apologies for Kabusch.

. . .

Another person might think that it was down to his father being a well-known national figure. Even though he's 50 now, people still ask him, 'So what do you do?' He tells them. Why does Kabusch shrug as he speaks? But for a while people are especially nice to him.

. . .

Someone happens to be telling a story about a man who gave up everything one day—his teaching job, his salary, his marriage. Which of us would dare to do the same? Kabusch sits there in silence; there is no need to bring up what he has done, not even with a twitch of his face. It's never the same when Kabusch does the same thing.

. . .

No one would believe Kabusch's suicide; that is to say, they would accept the fact, but in his case people would find it quite embarrassing.

. . .

Another man tries emigrating. Kabusch in Canada. Even though he thought he had no illusions, he makes the big time. For example, as an architect. His summer house in the woods, with its own bay, cattle, etc. is magnificent and comes as a greater surprise to him than to his guests, who are used to such things. One day someone says, 'You'd never have dreamt this was possible, would you?' He realizes how deluded he was to think that no one would recognize Kabusch in Canada.

. . .

Does *he* think he's hopeless?

. . .

What I observe not from his behaviour but from others': they've felt freer in his presence recently, less constrained; he has stopped being Kabusch. He has the same tics, the same abilities; he dresses no differently either, and yet he could fool them. They don't know what has happened; almost no one pats him on the shoulder any more, or if they do, merely out of habit; it's clear that he isn't cut out for this—he laughs . . . We must find another Kabusch.

BERZONA

Is our phone being tapped? And if so, is it worth it? Best to discuss the matter over the phone.

LUNCH AT THE WHITE HOUSE, 2 May

The officer sitting watchfully in the antechamber is as friendly as a hotel porter happy with our passports; we are announced. The Black taxi driver on the other hand was a little sullen when we told him our destination. We have to wait. The officer seems bored, his cap on the table, revolver at his belt. I notice I'm incapable of sitting down; I'm nervous, though now we're here I'm less curious than I reckoned I would be. A secretary goes to the toilet; an old Negro empties the ash-trays in the corridor. No signs of alarm. Now and then young men in shirt sleeves walk down the corridor to fetch a Coca Cola from the machine, swapping small talk. The mood in the building is not at all on edge. Administration. Everyday life at the helm of a superpower—

The US invaded Cambodia two days ago, the usual pictures on TV today: tanks from behind, swarms of helicopters, soldiers with skewed helmets and heavy packs, gear, weapons, ammunition, more gear; they're working or standing around looking somewhat lost, waiting for orders, somewhere in the jungle. According to the reporter they don't yet know that they've crossed a border; you can't tell from the vegetation. When the reporter lets them know, their faces betray no emotion. Only when they are asked what they think does one say to the mike, 'This is a mistake, I'm sure.' Another says: 'We're going to make history, that's all I know.'

We wait in the corridor which is narrow and nothing like a corridor at IBM. No chrome or leather. We sit surrounded by petty-bourgeois furnishings. Not a hint of the Reich chancellery. It could be a dentist's waiting room, except for the photos: Nixon in Hawaii with a garland of flowers around his neck, laughing; Nixon with the men from APOLLO 13 after the accident has been brought under control, laughing and waving; Nixon and his wife on some stairs, laughing and waving; Nixon getting off a plane, waving; Nixon as *pater familias* in a garden, not waving but laughing; then Nixon in public again, shaking children's hands; Nixon at a gala dinner with Negroes to his left and right, lots of Uncle Toms, all in black tie; the same gala dinner again—

No one can say how big the BLACK PANTHER PARTY is. 'The BLACK PANTHER PARTY regards itself as a socialist organization and believes that the means of production should be in the hands of the people. They declare that men only live creatively when free from the oppression of capitalism.' As a White person, you are advised not to go into Harlem any more; we go to Harlem anyway and walk around on foot; the only White people in the Apollo Theater. No trouble at all; nor are there any hostile looks in the street as long as, as a White person, you don't gawp. Roughly the same consumer goods and the same language; but a different continent. No slogans on the walls. It's hard to say what has changed in the past 20 years; but a lot has. At the cinema: laughter at the White hero.

Our host sends apologies that he will be busy for another few minutes, which we can easily understand: there's a new theatre of war since the day before yesterday. I'm still somewhat surprised by this corridor; with the exception of the Nixon photos in cheap and tasteless frames there is nothing here to suggest that we are in an organization that is ploughing billions into war. It is only while looking for the toilet that I find a photo of Nixon in Vietnam: soldiers receiving his fatherly gravity—

I have come to the country as a tourist, primarily to see American art in its own environment—studios on the Lower East Side. On the way there we run into demonstrations: Vietcong flags waving outside the public library, loudspeakers, a big fat helicopter circling over the park where they sit on the ground or on balustrades, others lie under the trees, young people with guerrilla beards and Jesus hair, lots of young people, both men and women, groups with guitars, police officers standing around the park as the young people shout, 'PEACE NOW, PEACE NOW'; the police are quiet, not looking at anyone, their truncheons dangling from their hands by a loop: 'PEACE NOW, PEACE NOW, PEACE NOW.' No one is being threatened, the police look surplus to requirements, the skyscrapers don't need protecting. A few people shout, 'REVOLUTION NOW' but they're referring to the constitution. Nothing happens; it is just that the war-mongering doctrine of salvation no longer has the desired effect. A few voices cry, 'ALL POWER TO THE PEOPLE', accompanied by the two-fingered sign, then all of a sudden 15,000 people yell, 'PEACE, PEACE NOW, PEACE, PEACE, PEACE.'

Our host, Henry A. Kissinger, greets us warmly and shows us into his antechamber. We know him from Harvard; as professor of government at the time, he was an occasional adviser to President Kennedy. Now he is a full-time member of the White House staff as an adviser on military policy. He is in his mid-forties, short, inconspicuous but cosmopolitan; he's an academic in the German tradition, though he often has his hands in his pockets. Another phone call that keeps him busy for a few minutes is from Nelson Rockefeller, and so we sit there with not just understanding but also some embarrassment in the knowledge of how precious his time is. Two secretaries are sitting in his antechamber, eating hotdogs. Here too there is a photo of Nixon: the president is seated, surrounded by flags, listening to his adviser Henry A. Kissinger, who is standing; it's like a scene from a Kipphardt play—Henry A. Kissinger, now free, introduces us to a lady who isn't part of the White House, an actress; he cracks a joke about Siegfried Unseld, 'my friend and left-wing publisher'. Here too there is a photo of Nixon, a portrait with a dedication to Henry A. Kissinger: 'Grateful for ever.' I don't manage to read the date because Henry A. Kissinger asks what I'm working on at the moment: a novel or a play? No one's actually very hungry, but there are other reasons for lunch; ordering our food is a welcome postponement of the inevitable questions—questions about the American invasion of Cambodia. We agree on mineral water. When the White House waiter has left us, Henry A. Kissinger starts off with an account of his personal situation: letters with death threats, every day. No sign of the secret service man who shadows him as a result, though. Is he the waiter, or are we totally trustworthy? We move on to the conflict between the generations: it's our fault that fathers and teachers are failing, giving in to the slightest empty threat, surrendering, capitulating, etc. instead of standing up for what they see as right and setting an example. Henry A. Kissinger tells us of how, while taking part in debate at one university with students, he was called a 'war criminal'; roughly half the students showed their support for this statement by getting up from their seats and remaining standing. Henry A. Kissinger was willing to continue the debate, but someone cried 'war criminal' again and so he left the lecture theatre. Quite a few of the youngsters, he says, wrote letters to thank him for his attitude and apologize for the incident.

WAR CRIMES AND INDIVIDUAL RESPONSIBILITY, a memo by Richard A. Falk deals with the Son My massacre on 16 March 1968. which saw the slaughter of over 500 civilians: 'The US prosecutor at Nuremberg, Robert Jackson, emphasized that war crimes are war crimes no matter which country is guilty of them.' The Nuremberg Charter not only defined massacres, deportation, torture, etc. as crimes, but also contained an Article VI: 'Crimes against peace: planning, preparation, initiation or waging of a war of aggression in violation of international treaties, agreements or assurances.'

As far as the invasion of Cambodia is concerned, not only are we laymen but aware of it too. Henry A. Kissinger has been doing theoretical work for decades in a field laypeople can talk about only as war, which is why he is so relaxed two days after the invasion of Cambodia. The food is decent enough, but no distraction. What am I going to say—just to avoid asking Henry A. Kissinger the question millions of American citizens are asking? He's friendly, perhaps even glad to have lunch with laymen, and he asks my publisher about his publishing house; but Siegfried Unseld, who is happy in any other situation to talk immediately and in detail about his company's plans, keeps his answer brief so he can ask a question that Henry A. Kissinger (they have been on first name terms since a Harvard seminar) answers easily: the Cambodia operation will last for a fortnight until the rainy season starts. Our host's attempt to steer our conversation towards marriage also fails. There's another silence. Someone who advises President Nixon has it harder than a publisher or a writer; he cannot avoid talking about his job by switching to a more general and more important topic—war, for instance. War is his job, and neither personal modesty nor tact on our behalf can alter that fact. Henry A. Kissinger says they didn't take the Cambodia decision lightly. They had to choose the lesser of two evils (lesser for whom?) and—obviously I didn't hear properly the first time—the lesser evil will last six weeks at the most. Henry A. Kissinger, who is on a diet, speaks without zeal and not too much; he is under no pressure. The President is at his country residence today. In need of something to say, I could tell him what the Americans I've met think about it; but Henry A. Kissinger gets there before I say it: those are students, professors, artists, writers, intellectuals. He says: 'Cynics have never built a cathedral.' The nationwide protests can't knock the decision makers off course; they alone know the facts, which are secret. Henry A. Kissinger is an intellectual who has shouldered the burden of responsibility, although he claims that 'we' didn't start this war in Vietnam—meaning, not the Nixon administration. An unwelcome inheritance. On the subject of the invasion of Cambodia again: the US has no interest in Cambodia; it is merely about forging a position for negotiations. He asks what we would like for dessert. An opinion poll shows 63 percent in favour of the invasion of Cambodia today, 25 percent against it. (*The New York Times* is against.) So I order fruit salad and am glad when a man in shirt sleeves comes to announce quietly: 'The President is on the line.' Left alone for quarter of an hour, we eat our dessert in silence; everything our host can tell us, Nixon has already said on TV—

No violation of Cambodian neutrality as the Viet Cong had already violated it. No aggression against Cambodia because there are no people living in the designated district, only Viet Cong, whose bases are being destroyed. The rainy season will prevent the Viet Cong from rebuilding bases for the next six months. No escalation of the war; just the opposite because this was preparation for the withdrawal of American troops; after the rainy season, the South Vietnamese army will be capable on its own, etc.

The White House restaurant is as cosy and dignified as a gentlemen's club, dark wood-panelled comfort; it could be on Lake Constance . . . There is no photo of Nixon here, instead four paintings of old ships, three of them in distress . . . 'The President is on the line' . . . I'm eating fruit salad in a place where millions of Americans can't make themselves heard. Why is that funny? A host who receives daily death threats; he shows no fear about it and no indignation either. An occupational hazard. Perhaps he even feels flattered; its suggestion of Caesar. What could they be discussing on the phone right now? I imagine Henry A. Kissinger, standing with his hand in his right trouser pocket as we eat our fruit salad. I consider why I don't like to contradict a man who lives with death threats—as if I were protecting him by staying silent, no matter what he says. 'Intellectuals are cynical, and cynics have never built a cathedral.' That's what men in our administration think too; it goes with the brownish clubhouse ambiance.

Professors from Harvard visit Henry A. Kissinger a few days later to terminate their previous joint cooperation; they call the invasion of Cambodia irresponsible and the way the decision was taken antidemocratic.

Of course we would like a tour of the White House, but we could make do with a different guide whose time is less precious. Our host clearly doesn't fancy any more talk of Cambodia at the table when we've finished our coffee, and we are honoured that Henry A. Kissinger himself is going to show us around the residence. (There are specific times when anyone can visit.) The palace guards are no more numerous than museum attendants and they don't salute; our host, his left or right hand in his trouser pocket, gives a curt, familiar greeting and the uniformed staff sit down again in the act of standing up. Some of this aura of familiarity rubs off on us too. I still don't dare to light my filled pipe, though, clutching it in my hand or between my teeth without smoking it. The walls are white, the carpet red. I'm not sure what to make of it all . . . This, then, is the seat of power. It comes across as an entity that loves quietness and cleanliness, starting with the ashtrays; an entity with tradition; one that loves the peaceful grounds, the green lawn and seasonal flowers; it probably doesn't love street battles, even if the victims only have themselves to blame, and it must regard massacres like Son My as an abomination. It doesn't even like normal traffic noise. There is not the slightest sound to disturb its meditation; it appreciates the view of a distant obelisk, the sound of a fountain. All those who are part of the seat of power, whether as military advisers or guards, walk around without haste, clearly without any cares, and so you have to smile when thinking of the cries, 'REVOLUTION NOW!' Lincoln and others have been shot, Kennedy most recently; what upheaval did it cause? Their oil portraits create an atmosphere that makes visitors immediately lower their voices; even the portrait of L. B. Johnson, not yet gazing down on us from the hereafter, makes us feel that modesty is required. Only Henry A. Kissinger, explaining less than the normal tour guides, simply doesn't remove his hands from his pockets, wordlessly demonstrating that life in the seat of power is completely natural, civilized, humane—in sum: casual. He even cracks a joke about Jacqueline; that's all right. Most of all, though, power always seems to be nicely brought up, a creature of taste; taste, for example, in china and period furniture. It lends an aristocratic touch to everything that happens here. Every president has his own set of porcelain and later, when he has left office, it goes on display in cases; that way, each respects his predecessors' personal porcelain, and they are all united in their taste for porcelain. Without asking many questions, we walk along if not solemnly, then at least decorously; for instance, when we walk up the marble staircase, I do not place my hand on the banister. The paintings that deck the halls of power stick to the last century; no Rothko or Roy Lichtenstein or Stella or Jim Dine, no Calder, etc. There's a need for tradition, but that tradition begins with Lincoln and Washington; hence no suits of armour. There are no tapestries depicting military victories or I didn't see them; there is no military braggadocio here, no braggadocio whatsoever. Power makes a show of being an understated creature that does not wish to scare anyone; the reality is colossal but not the villa where the creature lives and receives its guests. Another view of the grounds; even a jumbo jet we can hear doesn't actually fit in with the surroundings. History walks on fitted carpets here. There is nothing here to remind you of oil, of the Pentagon's computers, of the CIA, of the United Fruit Company, etc. Here is a large desk, and I take my pipe out of my mouth: So here—I believe—is where the president works, currently Richard Nixon. Behind the empty chair is the Stars and Stripes, on either side the flags of all the branches of the armed services. The desk is empty and tidy, but authentic. The only object that lends credibility to the idea that historic decrees are issued from this seat as well as the only one that isn't an antique: a telephone, white. And so we stand there as you would at the Escorial, forced to tell ourselves: So this is it!

Nixon to the press (8 May 1979) about the US invasion of Cambodia: 'Decisions, of course, are not made by a vote in the Security Council or in the Cabinet. They are made by the President with the advice of others. I, as Commander in Chief, I alone am responsible . . . I made the decision. I take responsibility for it. I believe it was the right decision. I believe it works out. If it doesn't then I am to blame.'

So as not to enquire what use it is to the victims, in the event of a disaster, civil war or a world war, that Richard Nixon takes personal responsibility as commander in chief and potentially kills himself like Hitler, I ask his adviser what kind of a mind the president has. An intelligent one, I hear, sharper than Kennedy or Johnson. But what kind? I hear that he has an analytical mind; the tour continues . . .

Two days later, on 4 May 1970, four students are shot at an antiwar demonstration at Kent State University, Ohio, by the National Guard who were supposedly acting in self-defence against snipers, although this is disputed by all eyewitnesses; the photos (*Life*) show the National Guard shooting into the crowd from 30 metres away, where they didn't even have to fear being hit by stones. Without warning. They supposedly lost their nerve because their supplies of tear gas ran out. Nixon says: 'The needless death should remind us all once more that when dissent turns to violence it invites tragedy.' *The New York Times* notes: 'which of course is true, but turns the tragedy upside down by placing the blame on the victims instead of the killers.' Nixon writes personalized condolence letters to the parents.

Next, we visit a small room, not larger than an actor's dressing room, where the president can rest; a narrow couch, a chair and a wardrobe, a wash basin. What's missing: a dressing table. I see: so it's here that Nixon takes a break between performances . . . I gradually shed my inhibitions; what we are seeing has nothing to do with reality. Why are we even looking at it? The White House isn't very big, and yet I still have the feeling that our walk is going on for ever. The walls are white, the carpet red, which gives the corridors a cheerful feel; it is almost a pity when our host breaks in: This, for example, is where a reception was recently held for Willy Brandt. But I'm still thinking about the words he let slip at lunch: What happens in Cambodia when we leave Vietnam is not our problem! I nod: so this is where Willy Brandt had to eat. The same jocular tone with a colleague to whom he introduces us: 'my friend and left-wing publisher'. I now know that there is a spirit of open mindedness in this building. Like the young men we saw in the waiting room, this colleague too is shirt sleeved, trim and casual; the early news from Cambodia is good, as was to be expected. (Back at Harvard, in 1963, Henry A. Kissinger could be more open as an intellectual without the heavy burden of responsibility; he was more worried when he spoke then.) I actually have a question but don't get round to asking it; we visit a drawing room where Henry A. Kissinger and the ambassador of the USSR normally meet. I nod, as if this required my assent. The drawing room reminds me of the spa hotel at Tarasp; lots of small clusters of armchairs, all of them uncomfortable but tasteful; they're probably genuine antiques. Now Henry A. Kissinger has both hands in his pockets as if to show that he isn't responsible for the decor. Nor is Nixon. The apartment that each president furnishes to his own taste is on the floor above; we only see the state rooms which, as I have said, any American citizen can visit at specific times. Democracy keeps no secrets from the voters . . . This (I now nod before I even know what I'm acquiescing to) is where the cabinet meets. An impressive room. Leather chairs are arrayed around a long and wide and heavy table; not too pompous, just right: chairs that force you to sit upright. Here you could negotiate over whether to invade Cambodia or not. What I hear is that cabinet meetings are not often held here and if they are, they're just boring. Henry A. Kissinger smiles; he just wanted to show us the room. This is not where the decisions are made, he says—

Walter J. Hickel, Secretary of the Interior, complains in a leaked letter that the President only consulted him three times in a year; he writes: 'Permit me to suggest that you consider meeting, on an individual and conversational basis, with members of your Cabinet. Perhaps through such conversations we can gain greater insight into the problems confronting us all—'

My question would have been what Nixon actually wants from power. There are goals you can achieve by coming to power. (Abolishing poverty in the world's richest country, integrating Negroes, peace without exploiting other nations, etc.) What is Richard Nixon's goal?—but I can save my question; his goal was to become President of the United States, and he achieved his goal by having no others, power as the goal of power, and I can believe without question that Nixon will definitely want peace when there is no other way of staying in power—

Everything is getting out of hand: the garbage, the young people, hair, drugs, the Negroes, the riots, the students, the street protests, fear of America. The new skyscrapers, even the guitar is getting out of hand. In the autumn, when they again converged on Washington, there are said to have been a quarter of a million of them gathered around the White House: PEACE NOW, STOP THE WAR, PEACE NOW; no one died; President Nixon had the window closed and watched baseball on TV (by his own account). Half a year later, on 9 May 1970, they are once more camped outside the grounds, OUT OF CAMBODIA, this time only 100,000 people, many no longer believing that they'll be heard, but Nixon spends a sleepless night, according to the press: early in the morning the president goes to the Capitol where he talks to a few students and tells them they have to understand him because he has responsibility for ensuring that the United States remain the leading superpower. The students say he talked about sport. According to the press: the president had bacon and eggs for breakfast. War works well in a crisis, but what works when youths are getting out of hand? 400 universities go on strike because of the shooting of students at Kent State.

Out in the grounds which, as we saw through the windows, are very beautiful but don't answer any questions, Henry A. Kissinger says that he's not going to stay in office for very long; he barely has a private life any more. Now the White House from the outside: as we've seen it in pictures. Out here I light my pipe at last as we walk along, hearing only our footsteps on the gravel. What should we talk about? A summery day. Someone who makes decisions affecting millions of people cannot afford to entertain any retrospective doubts about whether the decision was correct; the decision has been taken, for the rest you have to wait and see. Now would be a good time to tell a joke, but I can't think of one.

At Jimmy's Coffee Shop this morning: a chat with a cheery waiter who, taking me for a German, says that he isn't for Hitler and not against Hitler either 'but perhaps we have to see that Hitler was a great philosopher'. Noting my hesitation, he changes the subject to McCarthy 'who was considered to be a fool' but now it is clear: if people had listened to McCarthy at the time, 'we would not have all the trouble with Vietnam.' He, the waiter, is Greek himself, a patriot there too; he thinks Pattakos is quite all right, 'only some Communists can't stand him'. We're not alone, incidentally; the man selling tobacco nearby is for Hitler. Why? Because Hitler had a grand belief. Which was? 'He believed that the Germans are a superior race.' He, the tobacco guy, is a curly haired Puerto Rican who is of the opinion, incidentally, that the United States should have occupied Europe after the war. This reminds me of a conversation at a motel in California in 1952 when the landlord assured me that 'depression is worse than war', by which he actually meant a war in old Europe. Why in Europe? 'Because they're used to having wars over there.'

There is nothing to see in the grounds, which makes the silence all the more noticeable; I'm relieved when Siegfried Unseld starts talking about his publishing house. Every business has its problems. Henry A. Kissinger, modest like most people of exceptional intelligence, almost vain in his modesty, a specialist who has thought through every eventuality with weapons of mass destruction and wants the best, i.e. the least possible destruction in the world; he knows what very few people in the world know (historians will know it one day) and would rather listen to someone else, even if somewhat absently. I have met no other man whose potential error could have a correspondingly great impact; a surgeon who botches an operation, a locomotive driver, even a federal councillor, a pilot with 160 passengers on board, or a Herbert Marcuse, a publisher, etc. Those are all responsibilities that a person can take on. But White House adviser? I understand better and better why Henry A. Kissinger puts his hands in his pockets whenever he can; his responsibility has grown out of all proportion to a man who wears the same kind of suit as we do. The more lethal the potential error, the less one can do about it. Without my letting anything slip, Henry A. Kissinger says that he prefers to put up with responsibility rather than powerlessness. I didn't properly catch an afterthought he added, facing the other way. We are walking very slowly. Henry A. Kissinger doesn't yet know what he's going to do when he steps down from the White House. Go back into academia? He thinks that would be very difficult. Our walk across the gravel will soon be over, and it seems that there are no more questions. Why did Henry A. Kissinger, an avowed opponent of Richard Nixon before his election, become his adviser? More becoming is my wife's question: how has his academic theory been backed up or changed by practice? He's often been asked that question, Henry A. Kissinger says; he doesn't have time to think about it. Those are terrible words, but we are just passing through some swing doors, and all I hear is: Once you're on the tightrope, there's no going back—after the swing doors—no policy is without the risk of tragedy. A tragedy for whom?

Another dream about the denouement of a play. My joy woke me up (an egg of Columbus, which God gives to his own in their sleep!) I could simply write the words down—the denouement of a nonexistent play which I haven't even started to write and can't plot backwards from the denouement sleep gave me.

The first thing that occurs to a contemporary who discovers that I am not a German writer but a Swiss one are THE GNOMES OF ZURICH. These gnomes seem to be generally reviled, but there is nothing I can say about them. Close behind our bankers, who represent our country in our contemporaries' minds, comes FONDUE, then lots of nothing, and I don't wait to hear the rest. I would be sorry for any venerated compatriot whose name is proffered to save our honour. I just wait for the conversation to move on naturally.

Paintings and sculptures where they were created: I am suddenly convinced by paintings 19 metres long and sculptures of such volume that no gallery could exhibit them. Not an internalization of the world but a counterattack. And Paris is no longer the place where coronations take place——

A public question-and-answer session at Columbia University. What do they want to hear? No political questions; when one of my answers does allude to politics, they are tolerantly and irritatedly silent. Older people ask things tinged by C. G. Jung and Freud, the younger with a tinge of Levi-Strauss.

What I hear from a teacher from Queens: a pupil of his refuses to understand Anna Karenina's distress because she doesn't want to grow as old as Anna Karenina anyway, as 12 years or so from now there won't be any oxygen left in her neighbourhood anyway——

On Writing in the First Person

Norman Mailer's method in *The Armies of the Night* is striking; he describes himself as a demonstrator outside the Pentagon, where he was arrested, in the THIRD person. Norman Mailer writes: Norman Mailer laughed, just then he hesitated, then Norman Mailer let himself be pushed along by the crowd too, etc. After being arrested he registers his astonishment that the police officer doesn't know his name, so he spells it out: M-A-I-L-E-R. One of the things this method does is to give the writer the liberty of looking at even his own self-satisfaction objectively. That is not impossible in the direct FIRST person which would contain a hint of machismo if it did the same thing.

. . .

Maybe the FIRST person is especially advisable in situations where there is personal bias; it offers greater control. For the sake of control it would be possible to write in the FIRST person, then transpose it into the THIRD person to be sure that the latter isn't merely camouflage—but that leads to sentences that gain objectivity only in the FIRST person whereas they seem cowardly when translated word for word into the innocent THIRD person; writers don't escape their own shadows in the THIRD person—they simply chicken out.

. . .

Do I really think that my state of mind (the mood I woke up in today, etc.) is of general interest? Yet still I note it down occasionally and even publish it. A diary as an exercise in assessing my state of mind while fully aware of its irrelevance—

. . .

Something that is commonly characterized as indiscretion: information from the writer's private world that is none of the reader's business. And yet the real indiscretion is: someone telling everyone what is the reader's business, which the reader knows but never admits—

. . .

Even the THIRD person doesn't prevent the reader from suspecting autobiography precisely where personal involvement shades into invention.

. . .

The difference between the narrative FIRST PERSON and the direct FIRST PERSON of a diary: the latter is less comprehensible precisely because it conceals too much about its conditions and that creates an imposition:—not a character, because part of a character is what they hide, what doesn't interest them at a particular moment, things they aren't aware of, etc.

. . .

In confessional literature (maximum honesty towards yourself) the THIRD person has greater potential.

. . .

The THIRD person is easier at the beginning than later when the conscious or unconscious deposits of the FIRST person have become apparent in the more versatile THIRD person. It is not because the writer takes himself more seriously, but because the writer has no disguises left, he can later be forced to adopt the bare FIRST person.

. . .

Explicitly FIRST PERSON writers like Henry Miller, Witold Gombrowicz and others don't write confessional literature and are bearable because the FIRST PERSON becomes a role. These writers seem quite innocent; they write first-hand and live out their writing every step of the way and barely ever give the impression that they are exhibiting their personal and private affairs. They are their own literary subject, the character their writings describe, so there is no vanity to conceal—it is part of the character, along with everything else.

. . .

Why does resignation always seem indiscreet, unlike arrogance, which can indulge in all sorts of nakedness? The late Gide, for example: he writes no more indiscreetly than the earlier Gide, but his resignation makes him seem more indiscreet.

. . .

What remains questionable in the keeping of a public diary: leaving out names and personal details for reasons of tact. The Goncourt brothers didn't hold back: through their diary everyone who dined with them became public knowledge. Why do I hold back? This gives the impression that the diarist sees only himself as an individual and treats his contemporaries as an anonymous mass. There is no point in holding back if someone is already a public figure; yet this creates the impression that the diarist lives surrounded only by famous contemporaries or sees no one else as worth recording. So why not include the names and personal details of all the people in whom the diarist shows an interest? Of course there is no place for nasty gossip, but even the opposite would be indiscreet. What entitles me to spill the beans about others? The price of this discretion is overinflated self-absorption—or, to escape this, of politics?

ZURICH SCHAUSPIELHAUS

Last winter it almost became a major playhouse again, a political one. Though long since faded, it derived its fame from Hitler's time; it is still remembered as an antifascist theatre. Later the bourgeoisie began to take pride in it too and now they say 'our Schauspielhaus'. Not without good reason as it turns out. The board of trustees noticed the new left-wing tendency and when the right-wing press ensured takings began to fall below expectations, the director and his dramaturge (Peter Löffler, Klaus Völker) were fired three months into their first season. The board of directors—who include a couple of bankers and some city council representatives but not a single theatre person—were unlucky because the new director was unable to rebut suspicions that he didn't exactly cover himself in glory during the Nazi era. No one was aware of this. We also recognize that a man can change his beliefs. That has no bearing, however, on the fact the man's successor was sacked for his left-wing tendencies, as the trustees see even Edward Bond as a Marxist (incidentally, the social democrats also approved this). Our public efforts to first topple the board, which receives public funding according to the bankers' need for art, have failed. Today's papers say that Friedrich Dürrenmatt is to become artistic adviser and a member of the board of trustees.

Postscript to My Travels

When you tell people this isn't your first time in the United States, they almost always ask the question: Do you think it has changed? The last response they expect to hear is that it has changed for the better. But that's what I think . . . Back then, the first question on any long-distance bus was: HOW DO YOU LIKE AMERICA? A cheerful, upbeat question that naturally anticipated applause; their only real surprise was what impressed us the most. I was most impressed by the desert back then. It was the McCarthy era. There has been no lessening of anti-Communist sentiment without any knowledge of what Communism is trying to do, combined with repressive patriotic fervour (quite similar to our own); what is on the decline, however, is the arrogance of power, even if they do say: We are the richest country in the world. Which is true. They're spooked. Air pollution is merely a metaphor for all the other facts that spook them. In any event, they are no longer so sure that everything getting bigger and bigger is such a good thing. Hardly an evening passes without some expression of concern, frequently the frank question: Are we heading towards fascism? There are various reasons to dispute this, e.g. the legacy of puritanism. The debates they are having among themselves about America are growing longer and come to no optimistic conclusion—not even, in most cases, with an endorsement of history. The annihilation of the Native Americans no longer appears to be the glorious accomplishment of a God-given mission but genocide. The hunting mentality of their ancestors can be explained but its outcome is now called genocide. The President is right: never in its 190-year existence has the United States lost a war. But nor has there been victory. The things everyone has heard about

Vietnam will cause lasting shock, even if the troops are one day withdrawn. People are no longer confident that America is the moral superpower it was at Nuremberg. Things have happened and continue to happen on a daily basis that they believed only others were capable of. WHAT ARE WE DOING IN INDOCHINA? say people who have never had anything to do with war crimes, not even indirectly; they are the ones who have changed most, it seems to me, even in their daily lives. They are amazed that we have come to this country of our own volition. A terrible country, is how more than one person describes it, even if they immediately add as an afterthought: And yet we're the richest country in the world. Construction workers beat up marching flower children; that's not going to bring back the American Dream. What wasn't there 20 years ago was this scepticism about America's being on the right path. The old tone of confident self-righteousness is still present in commercials and official speeches, which are of course just another form of advertising, but not in private conversation. America is scared. Those in power insinuate that this is fear of Russia, fear of China—because this fear legitimizes their strategy and the costs of this strategy. In small bars or studios or among scientists or in public parks or wherever, at their prompting, we engage in conversation, we notice a different tone: America is scared of America . . . I mean it when I say it has changed for the better, even compared with 1956 when I travelled around this huge country for the second time; I may not have heard any criticism of the system, even from opponents of the President and his administration; but their fear of themselves makes them individually more humane.

Travelling

It's easier to speak in dialect. Does it make me feel more at ease? After a conversation in High German I have a more precise memory of how I have phrased things; as a rule, we speak dialect more unconsciously, and we feel more sure of ourselves and uninhibited. But are we? Swiss German (as we repeatedly have to explain to foreigners) is not slang or gibberish but an authentic if unwritten language—our mother tongue, regardless of social class. Its syntax is simple, precisely because it's a spoken language; there are barely ever any complex sentences. It's especially well suited to storytelling. How much do we have to tell one another? On the whole, we are all pretty fed up of one another when we're together; our dialect breeds automatic familiarity. Dialect almost always creates a pub-like atmosphere, a sense of matiness; whether we argue or agree, we communicate with a down-to-earth informality, although that doesn't make us completely identical—we've grown accustomed to it, like a role . . . Even my fellow citizens who depend on High German in their jobs and derive their knowledge from the written word are embarrassed when called upon to use High German in the presence of a fellow citizen and immediately slip back into our dialect, despite the fact that courtesy to strangers would normally forbid this; it's just that we know one another in dialect. Something is not quite right when we hear each other speaking High German; everyone acts as if they were themselves in dialect and only in dialect, even though their thoughts can be more precisely expressed in High German. Dialect, on the other hand, affirms authenticity. Why is that necessary? I sit down in a French buffet car; the gentleman opposite me keeps a low profile until he recognizes me as a compatriot and therefore speaks in dialect and becomes authentic: different from before, down to earth, and our tone immediately strikes both of us as slightly off . . .

BERZONA

Meet up with an East German friend I haven't seen since 1945. Why, despite the warmth on both sides, is it like walking on eggshells? They are trained to know what they mustn't say and yet they pretend to be very open minded. The child plays with a model railway but can already tell from the buildings that there are fascists living inside. We talk about other subjects. The parents are proud of their antiauthoritarian educational methods. Suddenly, touchingly, the child calls its father by his first name and says it's had enough. It's tired and wants to go home. The father agrees: in five minutes. He wants to finish his story and says tenderly: in two minutes. The child wants to leave now, not in two minutes, right now; it says, 'Or I'll have you arrested!' Laughter. Out of the mouths of babes . . .

Notes for a Handbook for Members

Those who entertain a superstitious belief that old age might even be an asset ('intellectually') tend to make reference to artists, writers, philosophers, etc., but only famous ones. The existence or even strong influence of their work in the public mind misleads us into confusing the individual with their fame, which ages more slowly.

The artist fears ageing because he thinks that it will take away his creativity; and he generally hasn't learnt a profession or lifestyle in which this doesn't matter.

An exhibition of a lifetime's work in three rooms . . . The older the painter, the faster we move on from one picture to the next; his skill gets the upper hand, our curiosity wanes, even if we don't admit it, and we are simply quicker to praise. This is in the second room. Here he tries to surprise us and almost succeeds; the only thing is that we get the impression he no longer surprises himself. As we walk through the final room, the painter is standing there in person; we are actually surprised—to discover that he is still alive. Not an old man. He chats away cheerfully. Even a pre-marked man can catch himself feeling deflated by his own success; at an increasingly early stage in his work he is conscious of what is not going to work and he spends less time pursuing blind alleys. In this sense, he is more effective in his work (the productive stage). But he used to feel freer at the start; his failures offered him greater hope.

Some older works are more than just an extension of perfection (Matisse). They are rare, however.

I have only heard second-hand accounts, from other people who were there, of how his nearest and dearest treated Stravinsky: it sounds unbelievable and yet it's so easy to believe. It is only from a distance that fame protects someone.

There are famous old men who declare all their past accomplishments to be meaningless (Ezra Pound); there are others who revere themselves as if they were Old Masters; this latter attitude can also be found in pre-marked men.

The pre-marked man likes to attribute his artistic crises to the fact that ageing and success have made him more self-critical. This is not necessarily true; his creative drive has become weaker than his critical faculties, which have stayed the same and will only decline when he becomes a marked man.

The need to teach, have pupils, manage an institute, be on a prize jury, etc. should not necessarily be interpreted as a sign of senility.

A marked man who shows us his studio doesn't notice that all his excited plans are things he did decades ago; he mistakes his urgent desire to copy for an impulse to create; he doesn't feel remotely old; on the contrary, he keeps up a constant show of his temperament, his vitality, his great appetite, etc.

The marked man recognizes himself as such by his addiction to fame, which is unlike his earlier ambition: it is more sensitive than ambition, which still depends on our expectations.

Dilettantes age less noticeably.

The marked man discovers, for example, that even if he hangs around in a pub for a long time, he no longer wishes to do anything with beermats—he doesn't try to build a pagoda out of them which then collapses; he's not even tempted to fling the beermats out into the lake. Beermats, lake: nothing about them attracts him, and so he tears up some bread and feeds the swans because he assumes this will attract the swans. If you traced his progress through the city with a piece of chalk, the chalk trail would follow a different course than in the past: fewer zigzags due to temptations. He can even walk past an accident (broken glass on the cobbles, police, people jostling to catch a glimpse) the same way he does shop windows. The marked man doesn't need to be tired and he doesn't look old either, it's just that he sees less and less reason to lend a hand where it isn't necessary. He can, for example, see one of Calder's mobiles without blowing at it or setting it in motion with his finger. He enjoys it when someone else does, though. He's seen it before. But even if he hasn't seen something before, for instance if he spots an unusual object in someone else's home, a material he's never seen before, he still behaves as if he's in a museum: Ne touchez pas les objets. *Someone has to place it in his hands for him to feel it. Do they feel it? The marked man is surprised: he's holding a length of wire, copper wire that can be bent without pliers, and he can hold it without playing with it, without bending it this way or that—he knows what this means, and it comes as a shock to him.*

There is no doubt that older works (Theodor Fontane) *can be significant; this is principally a source of comfort to people who have no creativity to waste, and we should leave them be.*

A marked man whose paintings are on display in every major museum—one day he decides that he needs a new coat but he doesn't dare to go out any more and so he requests that a selection of new coats be brought to his home. He tries on a dozen but cannot pick one, so he keeps a smaller selection of three coats and realizes he doesn't need any of them. He works for another week, then (aged 66) *slits his wrists at the height of his fame.*

Apart from poverty, ageing is easier for the unappreciated artist; his unconsummated claim to be a rising talent keeps him young.

Painters or sculptors whose works have been destroyed for ever by a disaster (force majeure) *always seem as a result to be a little younger than their peers . . .*

It may be true—prodigies excepted—that artists tend to get old later than other people; on the other hand, they notice the onset of ageing earlier—long before those around them notice it—and what we would call mastery can scare some artists.

It is possible that the marked man finds his art comes more easily due to the fact that our sense of touch declines, our hearing declines, our sight declines, our brains take in less and operate more slowly, our emotions decline, our curiosity declines or at least narrows, our reflexes repeat themselves or stop entirely, our associations falter, our imagination dries up, any kind of desire declines, etc.; he only thinks of things he already knows how to do (*late style*).

Senility can produce its own artistic flowerings. That is presumably why marked men often curse their art as well as art in general; everything else is art.

The look in the ageing Rembrandt's eye—

```
The national play of Switzerland (in the
Second World War) was not               but
                          . However, we wouldn't
like the fact that the wicked cousin, who
actually makes the good deeds possible, might
also be Swiss. So it will have to remain
            .
```

Questionnaire

1.
Do you think you are a good friend?

2.
When do you regard it as betrayal:

a. if the other person does it?
b. if you do?

3.
How many friends do you have at the moment?

4.
Do you see the length of a friendship (if it lasts) as a measure of its value?

5.
What could you not forgive a friend for:

a. duplicity?
b. stealing a woman from you?
c. being sure of your friendship?
d. being sarcastic towards you and others?
e. being unable to cope with criticism?
f. liking people with whom you have fallen out and enjoying their company?
g. not having any influence over him?

6.
Would you like to be able to do without friends?

7.
Do you keep a dog to be your friend?

8.
Have you ever been completely friendless, or do you simply lower your expectations?

9.
Have you had female friends:

a. before sex?

b. after sex?

c. without sex?

10.
What do you fear more: the verdict of a friend or the verdict of your enemies?

11.
Why?

12.
Do you have enemies you would secretly like to become friends with so you have less trouble admiring them?

13.
If someone is in a position to help you out with some money, or if you are in a position to help someone out with money: do you see this as a threat to your existing friendship?

14.
Do you consider nature your friend?

15.
If you find out indirectly that a friend has told a nasty joke about you, do you end your friendship? And if so:

16.
How much honesty can you bear from a friend in public, in writing or in private?

17.
Suppose you have a friend who is greatly superior to you intellectually: does your friendship console you for this or do you have your secret doubts about a friendship that is entirely reliant on your admiration, loyalty, helpfulness, etc.?

18.
Which of these have you fallen for most frequently out of a natural need for friendship:

a. flattery?
b. the company of a compatriot abroad?
c. the realization that you cannot afford to make an enemy in this particular case, e.g. because it would endanger your career?
d. your own charm?
e. feeling flattered to be able to publicly claim that you are friends (on first name terms) with someone whose reputation is currently riding high?
f. ideological agreement?

19.
How do you talk about lost friends?

20.
If it comes to a situation where friendship obliges you to do something that clashes with your conscience and yet you do it for the sake of the friendship: did that friendship survive?

21.
Can friendship exist between people who do not share a sense of humour?

22.
What else is essential for a relationship between two people to feel like friendship and not just as set of shared interests:

a. pleasure on the other person's face?
b. that you can let it all out in private, i.e. trust the other person not to reveal everything?
c. a good measure of political agreement?
d. that one of you can give the other hope purely by dint of being there, calling or writing?
e. indulgence?
f. the courage to contradict openly but with the feelers to pick up how much honesty the other person can bear at this time, and patience?
g. an absence of problems about status?
h. that you allow the other person to have secrets and are therefore not hurt when something comes out that they have never mentioned to you?
i. a similar sense of shame?
k. when you bump into one another: automatic delight, even though you don't actually have any time?
l. that you can entertain hopes for the other person?
m. the guarantee that you will both at least ask for evidence before siding with slanderous rumours about the other?
n. a meeting of minds regarding your pleasures?
o. shared memories that you would both cherish less if they weren't shared?
p. gratitude?
q. an ability to see the other's flaws without becoming judgemental?
r. the absence of any stinginess?
s. that you don't shackle the other to opinions that once united you, i.e. that neither of you has to suppress a new opinion out of consideration for the other?

23.
How big can the age difference between friends be?

24.
If a longstanding friendship fades, e.g. because it cannot include a friend's new partner: do you regret that you were ever friends?

25.
Are you a friend to yourself?

Theatre with puppets? No facial expressions: they are slightly taller than a human. Their brusque gestures are produced by a stage performer (silent, work clothes) during the scene. Occasionally, a gesture lingers on and no longer fits the text. For example, the raging plaintiff with the outstretched arm, finger pointing at the accused when their innocence has already been proven. Or the reverse: a gesture of indignant innocence when the text of the play has long since condemned them. It does no harm if a puppet falls over and lies there for a moment until the text needs it again: their gestures of great rejoicing. Because the puppets do not move themselves and have to be operated, there is repeatedly a slight lag in their gestures. As the news comes that there are unfortunately no grounds for rejoicing or, on the contrary, that the beloved will never return, the puppet is still standing there with its gestures of great rejoicing. The performer follows a score they hold in their hand, without emotion and in no rush but very precisely, whether they be preparing the puppet's gestures before the text makes them intelligible, or only managing to produce the missing gesture afterwards. The performer is as invisible as possible; we forget them just as we forget a waiter when everything is going smoothly. The text comes through loudspeakers: it has to be written in such a way that we can effortlessly understand to which puppet the respective lines are imputed. While a text is being read, the relevant puppet stays still; the performer waits until the end of a lament before lowering its head, for example, or raising both hands to its face. There are also breaks in the text; everything is silent and the gestures of various kinds of silence are shown, e.g. an abashed silence, a challenging silence, bored, obstinate or expectant silence. Perhaps the text that silenced everyone will be repeated. A puppet that according to the text has suddenly taken on a leadership role is calmly moved forwards or put in an armchair, with it hand clenched into a fist and its arm raised. It holds this position, even if the other puppet's text doesn't require this. This can make the puppet, if we pay any attention to it, look extremely comical; it doesn't seem to understand what is going on. On the other hand, a puppet's gestures will sometimes remain nonsensical for a long period before suddenly falling into line with the text again. Its lamenting gesture is now fitting, its rejoicing gesture right, and now it alone is alert. The text contains nuances, whereas the puppets are restricted to a series of basic reflexes, reducing the action to the few twists and turns that are not verbal but factual . . .

ALBUM

Here, he is on the album cover, looking just as everyone who has been following the German press and international newspapers over the past decade knows him.

. . .

Here is a list of his works.

. . .

Here, he is still young, in 1955, he seems to have a moustache. He isn't wearing his flat cap at the table of course but a raspberry-coloured shirt, the collar open. An evening in a villa on the Zürichberg. Here, he is a nephew, not intimidated by the bourgeois china and silver and keeping out of the conversation; he is not interested. A sculptor. It's been pretty clear since the soup course what he thinks of today's literature; he won't even go and see Friedrich Dürrenmatt's new play, *The Visit*. He writes plays too. Dinner meanders on. I know this friendly household from earlier visits and am wearing a tie, which turns out to be a drawback when I realize why I've been invited this evening; I can only try to fend off the master of the house politely when he announces that his nephew is going to read something after dinner. We're still on the cheese and fruit. The young man has kept a low profile so far but he seems amused by the older man's embarrassment. (I was then about the same age as he is now.) He leaves us to make conversation; he doesn't ask any questions. When we get up from the table and go up some stairs for coffee, he takes out his manuscript and waits on the graceful sofa in silence until we all have a glass of brandy. I repeat my request to be allowed to read the play at home. He agrees to read only the first act. Some people can form a literary judgement on the spot, but unfortunately I am not one of them, as I've already mentioned. His acts are admittedly very short and so he reads them all. He's an excellent reader; he feels good afterwards, although I have understood very little.

. . .

This is a year later. He is sitting here in my country place in Männedorf where I'm not wearing a tie either. I also like the new play he sent me to read. He doesn't need to know more. He has come from Paris where he is writing a novel. I had a military inspection this morning; the helmet and pack and rifle are still lying in the narrow corridor. Back in Paris, he tells the amusing story of the Swiss man who keeps his helmet and his rifle ready in the corridor, all year round.

. . .

Here, he is rolling a cigarette, then slowly licking the brownish paper. This was in Berlin. He no longer depends on a single admirer. He wears his fame as if it was entirely predictable.

. . .

Here, he is laughing. That doesn't signal agreement or familiarity. He generally doesn't laugh with you but at you.

. . .

This is in Berlin again. In a pub. Beer and chaser, then the same again. All with an awareness of the divided city; Danzig in the background, Mecklenburg too; collegiality between two elective Berliners; literature is on the comeback. Here, he is wearing the flat cap. Anyone who doesn't move to Berlin has no one to blame but themselves.

. . .

This is in 1961. LA BONNE AUBERGE, the two of us for an afternoon; here, he is speaking for the first time about politics, not in literary terms, in an almost Swiss manner: politics not as utopia but in pragmatic terms. But I have to go to a performance of one of my plays at the Schiller Theater.

. . .

Here, he is during the interval, silent in the foyer.

. . .

This is the same evening, LA BONNE AUBERGE, the lead actor asks straight out: 'You were watching?' Actors are natural: they expect applause from everyone who was there, or at least some criticism as a courtesy. He is rolling a cigarette, licking the brownish paper, etc. Not a word about the performance (Lietzau) or the play. He doesn't like to lie.

. . .

Here, with colleagues, Gruppe 47.

. . .

Here, I don't understand his narrow-eyed look. A chance meeting in Sperlonga, Italy. We seem to have had some dispute, and it doesn't help to invite him home, look out over the sea at night. Here, he speaks as a judge in marital matters not his own, but only briefly because then I kick him out. He sits there and says, 'Let's at least finish this grappa.'

. . .

Here, the next day, we are playing boules on the beach.

. . .

This is at the Schiller Theater in Berlin again, a dress rehearsal; no one there apart from the director (Lietzau) and him, lots of camera people, but none of his German colleagues.

. . .

Here, you can only see his lower lip under his moustache and his mouth when he laughs; he laughs less offensively than he used to.

. . .

Here, he's dancing.

. . .

Here, he is sitting, a famed chef as well as writer, at our table, guessing every spice, expressing his admiration for the cooking by eating and talking about his own recipes. He raves about offal including testicles, which I've never tried.

. . .

Here, he is standing in Frankfurt. Young left-wingers have been jeering at him; he is rolling himself another cigarette, slowly licking the brownish paper, etc. Not beaten; he isn't scared of enemies; indeed he goes looking for them; that's what they're there for.

. . .

Here, one New Year's Eve in Ticino; he is less outgoing than the others. It is not his style suddenly to let his hair down.

. . .

Here, he is standing at his stove, adding some seasoning. It is clear from behind that he feels good in his own skin.

. . .

This is in Zurich; he is talking to Czechoslovak writers, friends from Prague, after the Russian invasion; here, he is listening, hands in his pockets, head bowed, a person with authority thinking about practical assistance.

. . .

Here, by the fire: not cosy, but relaxed. Even then, he doesn't indulge in flattery and doesn't hold back. When we've had a drink, he returns to his topic (development aid). I cannot imagine that Jeremias Gotthelf could have been any less dogged.

. . .

Here, he's addressing the nation on TV. A writer who feels personally responsible. He's speaking to the nation's presumed political consciousness.

. . .

Here, he is talking about literature: Alfred Döblin.

. . .

Here, he is swimming in the cold river Maggia. When he gets out of the water, he will talk about Willy Brandt; he knows what you need to know—facts that prove every opponent wrong. I'm not an opponent, though.

. . .

Here, with Gershom Scholem. If someone doesn't engage with his topic, he demonstrates his great erudition which encompasses a range of subjects.

. . .

Should a writer, etc.? His answer is his example. Can someone choose his camp for an election campaign and yet remain open minded as a writer? This is at his home; he's reading aloud.

. . .

Here, in a car; he doesn't drive.

. . .

Here, he is publicly arguing against some adversaries in a large venue, accustomed to their booing, steadfast but handicapped by his innate lack of cynicism. He debates knowledgeably and defiantly, but always means what he says.

. . .

Here, he isn't in the picture but we're talking about him and in that sense he is present—present enough for the mention of his name to divide opinion.

. . .

Here, it is just the two of us and he isn't saying anything, inscrutable, not cold but unwilling to leave the sphere of public affairs; he doesn't ask personal questions in private, remaining closed until I enter the sphere of public affairs.

. . .

Here, he's asking what I'm working on.

. . .

Here, he is maintaining his silence, a man considered invulnerable; we know of a slur against him, but he spares us any personal complaints. He will defend himself publicly.

. . .

Here, he's pleased. What about? He looks different when he's scored a political success; he's satisfied then, very serious in his awareness of how much is still to be done. Here, he's obviously pleased by a token of affection.

. . .

Here, he is fairly quiet; at ease in a domestic setting. In fact, we are his guests in the large dining room; we're eating mushrooms from the Grunewald forest. Tomorrow he has to leave for Bonn.

. . .

Here, he is being interviewed by the international press: GERMANY'S GÜNTER GRASS. He answers not as a government spokesman or a private author but as a normal citizen with a special reputation. He doesn't smile as diplomats do; he doesn't find the questioners a drag, quite the opposite, and he doesn't dodge their questions; his responses are not evasive. His persistent allergy to German extravagance builds trust in Germany.

. . .

Here, he is listening.

. . .

Here, he is keeping silent but not rolling a cigarette. I realize afterwards that I have also kept my silence to this day about his play that puts Bertolt Brecht on stage.

. . .

His face has thinned down, it seems to me, but is no less forceful than in that villa on Zürichberg; back then, he seemed both softer and more aggressive from the front. Here, it's snowing; otherwise he rarely wears the flat cap now. On the other hand, his face has sharpened in profile, it seems to me.

. . .

Here, I have just mentioned the name of someone he refuses to respect; he no longer says anything about the sad case. A break in the conversation. There are other matters to discuss. A meeting with Herbert Wehner. He'll make arrangements in Germany and I'll take care of Switzerland. We are on first name terms: 60 million versus 6 million. The difference is not only numerical. He's a public figure. What he can't quite understand is the situation of a private author.

. . .

Here, outdoors in summer, he's turning the roast suckling pig on its spit, sweating and giving orders on where to put more embers while we sit on the dark lawn or stand around the fire, looking forward to the food; every now and then he sprinkles some spices on the pig.

. . .

Here, I think, he is unaware that he is being watched; not knowing doesn't change him.

. . .

Here's a picture where I almost don't recognize him, one of many; sufficient for a wanted poster: forehead, nose, moustache, chin, etc. All too distinct, especially his gaze.

. . .

Here's his handwriting: an elegant flourish.

. . .

This could be anywhere. I don't know if it's at an airport or in a cave and it doesn't matter: he's aware that he's a public figure unlike any other contemporary German author; he neither sets any store by being recognized nor does it bother him, it seems.

. . .

Here, he is talking about Dürer's *Melencolia I*.

. . .

He has stubble, which means that he's currently in Ticino, working on a book; he shows us a bunch of snails he has collected on granite—a logo for the Social Democrats—and also a scorpion in grappa which he caught and rendered harmless while he was looking after the house. (August 1970).

SEPTEMBER

Three passenger planes (SWISSAIR, BOAC, TWA) have been hijacked by Palestinian irregulars and redirected to Amman and Cairo. A fourth surprise attack on an EL-AL aircraft failed; the hijacker ('Leila') was overpowered on the plane by armed security guards and another was shot, and there was also an element of luck—a primed hand grenade rolled around the cabin but didn't explode. The passengers on the other flights, 650 people in total, and their crews are being held as hostages in the desert with the threat that the planes and their passengers will be blown up if all the Palestinians who have been legally convicted abroad of earlier attacks are not immediately released. Ultimatum: 72 hours.

INTERROGATION III

A. Our interrogation began back when you were re-reading Leo Tolstoy's political writings and his unconditional condemnation of all forms of violence. You couldn't find it in you to back that condemnation at the time. Peasants in tsarist Russia, you said back then, had no other means of exercising their right to life—

B. I still think that.

A. How did you react to the hijackings by the Palestinian irregulars who also think that they have no other means of defending their right to life?

B. I have heard some of my compatriots say that the only proper response to this violation of international law is a Swiss parachute operation in Zerka. Others, however—the majority—would be happy for Israel to assume military responsibility. I believe there is general outrage. The Swiss cannot tolerate injustice against Swiss citizens. In Thalwil near Zurich a good, honest housewife reportedly used an umbrella to beat to the ground in public another housewife she took for an Arab due to her skin colour.

A. I'm asking for your reaction.

B. When I heard the news, I was surprised by how easy it seemed to be to carry out a successful hijacking. All it takes, apparently, is a gun and two people unconcerned for their lives, and everything follows a different path. Some evil deeds are secretly fascinating—not that that rules out anger . . . When I heard the news I was glad I wasn't sitting on that plane—that is, I felt sympathy with the passengers. Also, I remembered the Arabian desert near Amman. We drove through it in an Opel; one of our party burnt himself accidentally touching the body of the car . . . that's how hot it can get there.

A. The federal council has accepted the ultimatum, meaning that it has said it is willing to release the three Arab terrorists held in Zurich.

B. Swiss lives are at stake.

A. What would you have done in the federal council's shoes?

B. That depends how sacred you consider the law to be—the law *per se*. If it were as sacred as it is usually cast, then the sacrifice of 143 passengers would have been inevitable. I was both disappointed and relieved.

A. Why disappointed?

B. I think it is possible that the fedayeen would not have shrunk from committing a massacre. The federal council had to reckon with the possibility of that plane being blown up with the passengers and the crew—I was disappointed because I was brought up to believe that a constitutional state, or the Swiss state at least, does not cave in.

A. And why were you relieved?

B. It seems that it can be resolved without human victims. The aircraft is insured for its nominal value. The three Palestinian terrorists in Zurich, who were sentenced to twelve years in prison according to our laws, will be released as soon as the hostages are set free and will then be able to resume their terror campaign against air travel at any moment . . . We condemn violence, and yet the legal verdict will not be enforced; the constitutional state is capitulating to violence as soon as its own violence proves insufficient. What else could the federal council have done? Incidentally, it wasn't only the Swiss constitutional state that caved in; so did the British state and the German state. They didn't have a choice. Constitutional states depend on international law. If you want to make international law work, you must not violate it yourself; you shouldn't even derive any benefit from others' violations. For example, a country that supplies weapons, even if only for business reasons, is an actor in that particular theatre of war. That is a shock. The federal council does not envisage banning the arms trade and is therefore in a tricky situation when it makes references to international law. Who could have acted any differently in that position? You cannot do business with war without subjecting yourself to its rules, law or no law. This was a matter of the hostages in the desert near Zerka, a matter of saving lives—at the expense of the rule of law.

A. In February this year a bomb went off on board a SWISSAIR flight to Israel. It has not been proven but it is likely that it was a Palestinian attack. All 47 passengers were killed, along with the crew.

B. The federal council had no decision to make that time. Deep mourning was enough. That's the difference; this time there was a decision to make. Should 143 passengers and the crew die for the rule of law? The answer from Berne seemed clear to me: established law is not more sacred than human life. Revolutionaries think that too.

A. In the meantime, the planes have been blown up—

B. But the hostages are alive.

A. What have you learnt from this?

B. Established law is obviously not absolute or else the authorities, both federal and cantonal, would not have decided not to enforce a legal verdict. That would require sacrificing human lives, it would not be possible without tragedy, sacrifices . . . I've learnt that our established laws are humane laws. We owe this knowledge to violence, even as we condemn it.

A. How can you be relieved?

B. I understand the outrage. There is always outrage when it's not enough to be right. Presumably the Palestinian refugees think they too are in the right and are outraged that it isn't enough to be right.

A. Suppose you were on board that DC–8, flight number SR 100 to New York. What can *you* do about the living conditions of Palestinian refugees?

B. Hostages are generally innocent.

A. Do you think that endangering peaceful aviation with terrorist attacks can improve the living conditions of the Palestinian people?

B. That has been disproven.

A. And what do you think?

B. I must admit that I've barely given any thought to the Palestinian cause before.

A. So does it take a crime to force you to think about a cause? Or do you not consider Dr Habash, who masterminded this terror campaign against air traffic, a criminal?

B. It depends who else we brand criminals. I've read all the opinion pieces. In the language of our press, terrorism is always unequivocal: blackmail by violence—by the oppressed.

A. And what do you think terrorism is?

B. Blackmail by violence.

A. You support the rule of law.

B. I support the rule of law.

A. And yet you still shrink from condemning violence. It scares you and at the same time you're relieved that our administration caved in to violence, as you put it.

B. In order to erase the impression that the constitutional state may bow to violence in certain circumstances, there has been some thinking already as to whether and how the condemned terrorists in Zurich could simply be pardoned; that is meant to reinstate the belief that violence achieves nothing—whereas in actual fact, as we have seen, all it takes is a pistol in a cockpit.

A. It is of course not right to override the rule of law to free the hostages in the desert. The federal council's willingness to swap criminals for hostages neither rescinds nor revises the criminal law according to which the Zurich terrorists were found guilty. The federal council was acting in an emergency; in an emergency, human lives come before the law.

B. I agree.

A. Do you condone violence, yes or no?

B. There is violence to uphold the law without which the rule of law cannot survive, and there is violence that creates law; the latter is a response to the former, but the former has always emerged from the latter.

A. Do you condone the pistol in the cockpit?

B. It is not for me to condemn the pistol in the cockpit because I can make do without one. I have all I need to live without violence, which means: I have it through the violence that upholds the law. Other people are in a different situation; my belief in the law doesn't feed them or dress them or house them or give them the luxury of getting by without violence.

A. So would you say that the use of violence is justified if it isn't possible without violence?

B. That depends on *what* isn't possible without violence . . . I don't find myself in a position that justifies the use of violence.

A. But this is not about you.

B. Precisely.

A. You have admitted that you are horrified by acts of violence. And yet you're still not willing to condemn the use of violence on principle—

B. It is not for me to say.

[1970]

BERZONA

An evening ambush. Who are you? But I can see: young people. Five of them in windbreakers, sweaters, jackets, etc. Lots of hair. Better not ask: What do you want? By lamplight, though, they are not guerrillas but schoolchildren from Basel who state their case fairly unselfconsciously, without cliches; they've brought some Chianti, there's still some cheese on the table as well, but they've already eaten. Their names? They're from good homes whose parents presumably don't have much understanding but do have houses, one in Basel, another in Ticino. They are not bound by this state of affairs. The eldest one has as much hair as all the others put together, not straight or curly hair but the black frizzy hair of an Abyssinian, and glasses, and is learning the double bass at music school. He doesn't intend to disappear into a symphony orchestra for the rest of his life. Music is provocative. I uncork the bottle and understand. I'm able to say that we saw and heard THE MOTHERS OF INVENTION recently. Marketing provocation, HAIR, etc. is not in his plans either. But what can you do if the record industry goes crazy about your music? the younger brother asks him, the 14-year-old. This is proving easier than I thought; I'm in my own home, but I'm dispensed of expressing an opinion. The Abyssinian will always be a progressive. One of the others is thinking of becoming a teacher, but he isn't sure yet and it's still three years until he finishes school. Since nothing apart from provocation makes any sense, why have a career? Their discussion becomes more and more lively, and I am obviously not in the way; only the 14-year-old says nothing and scrapes his black pipe, which he then sticks back in his mouth like an old man, but it still isn't drawing properly. I have matches. When my wife says something, they switch back into High German, although it isn't necessary. It reminds them of school. He finds it totally impossible to read Kafka, the middle brother says. He's 17 and the wittiest at the table. The Abyssinian, who has got hung up on the double bass, quickly begins to bore them; maybe that's why he's got that hairstyle, which I don't mind but it just doesn't suit him. He mentions his hair once: the kinds of things he hears about it from his teachers and in the street. I have no idea what they were expecting when they rang the doorbell; no one asks. They sit there and they are the present. What they are thinking is their own business. Politics? What is definitely not on their minds is Marxism, i.e. that everyone should earn the same amount. This kind of nonsense occasionally creeps into their words, but I'm allowed to correct them. What is in is Zappa and others I know less about, their music and especially the person behind these records, their lifestyle as a model: excess and an early death. The 14-your-old has to step outside because he is feeling sick, from the pipe I imagine, but he insists it's the wine (two glasses) that has got to him. When he has puked, I bed him down outside in the night air; the face of an elderly scholar, but with a child's complexion. The longer the evening around the narrow wooden table goes on, the less I get in the way; my contribution is cheese and a ready ear, apart from one question about what their attitude is to hashish. They converse entirely among themselves. Hashish is the one area where no grandfather can butt in with his experiences, so all of a sudden experience does count after all. They have no desire to preach at me; why would they? Their coltish intelligence; their recently discovered thoughts that believe thought (without acts) capable of anything. Among themselves they are up for any argument; it is all about arguments, not about secret justifications for past mistakes. Their zeal is constantly upbeat. The mistakes, easy to identify, are the mistakes of their forefathers. Their suspicion is that when an old man thinks, he's basically always defending something, i.e. he isn't open to arguments. Irony disconcerts them. That's the other kind of encumbered thinking, a canny agreement between hoary souls, and it is often completely incomprehensible; the only thing young people sense is that there's the rub and it has nothing to do with them. So he reacts with gravity. The 14-year-old (who has done the washing up in the kitchen) turns out to be something of an expert on drugs and has read just about everything there is to read about them, can reel off statistics at will. And why do you use hash? One of them objects that this is escaping into a parasitic existence. The witty one is now completely serious and advocates that it's better to live fast and furious, everyone has the right to wreck their life. For example, he doesn't want to grow old —Sorry, sir!—no older than 25; and if everyone's shooting up, then your society's kaput, so what? The 14-year-old scholar, who has now given up on his pipe and is smoking cigarettes, differentiates between hashish and hard drugs, and lectures us on medicine, law and sociology. What I still want to know approaching midnight is: their experiences 10 years, 30 years from now—nothing could interest them less—

Questionnaire

1.
Are you proud to be a father?

2.
Do you like children in general?

3.
Are you sure you do not expect any gratitude from your grown-up children? And if you don't: gratitude for what? (Give a short list)

4.
Did you want to become a father at the time?

5.
If you think your children have it better than you did, does this please you, or do you mean it as a criticism?

6.
What is your attitude to babies?

7.
Were you conscious of your paternal responsibility before procreation or during procreation or, if not, when did it hit you?

8.
What makes you sad about children:

a. similarities with their mother?

b. similarities with you?

9.
To what extent does an unborn child seal your lifelong attachment to the respective woman?

10.
If other people (guests, neighbours, teachers, etc.) let on that they find your child nothing special, whom do you resent—the child or the other people? Or the child's mother?

11.
Do you feel a sense of kinship?

12.
Until the child is how old?

13.
Have you ever beaten a child? And if not, is that because you've achieved what you intended by other means or is it a matter of principle?

14.
When you see your children among other youngsters, e.g. at a sit-in, do you have the impression that you're closer to your own children than to their peers, and what are your grounds for this conclusion?

15.
What gives you the greatest pleasure as a father?

16.
Do you trust in your educational skills? For example, if you have a new car and your children see it as their own property, would you stop them using the car for educational purposes?

17.
When do you feel more comfortable as a father:

a. alone with your child?

b. when his or her mother is there?

18.
Do you still feel like a father when you go to bed with another woman?

19.
Does your sense of fatherhood decline:

a. when your child starts earning an income?
b. when your child gets married?
c. when it turns out that the child knows more than you or is more adept, better at coping with life, etc. than you are?

20.
What shocks you more: if your children suffer from your being their father or if you secretly prefer other people's children?

21.
Are you aware that you always behave somewhat differently around your grown-up children, and what are you hiding from them?

22.
Why?

23.
Suppose you no longer feel attached to the mother as a husband, are you sure that you're the father of her child?

24.
Can you imagine being childless?

25.
Have you ever managed to get to know your own children, i.e. not to see them as sons or daughters?

Catalogue

Conkers bursting out of their green hedgehogs, gleaming / snowflakes through a magnifying glass / Japanese rock gardens / printing / caravans of camels on the yellow horizon / rain on a train window at night / a Jugendstil vase at the antiques shop / mirages in a salt desert when you think you see puddles of blue water; the desert in general / turbines / morning light through green Venetian blinds / handwriting / coal piles in the rain / a child's hair and skin / building sites / gulls on the black mudflats at low tide / the blue sparkling light of welders / Goya / things you see through a telescope / woodchips under a carpenter's bench / lava in the dark / photos from early this century / horses in the fog in the Jura mountains / maps, old and new / a mixed race woman's legs under her coat / bird footmarks in the snow / suburban pubs / granite / a dead person's face the day after his or her death / thistles among marble in Greece / eyes, mouths / the insides of shells / a skyscraper reflected in another skyscraper / pearl fishers / kaleidoscopes you can shake / wilted, faded ferns | the hands of the old people I love / pebbles in a mountain stream / a Mayan relief in situ / mushrooms / a moving crane / walls covered with outdated posters / snakes swimming through water with outstretched necks / a play seen from the fly loft for once / fish at the market / fishing nets drying on cobbles, any sort of fish / sheet lightning / the flight of Alpine choughs when you're standing on a ridge; their flight over the chasms / a couple in a quiet museum / the hide of ordinary cattle from close up / whorls of sunlight in a full glass of red wine (Merlot) / a prairie fire / the amber light inside a circus tent on a sunny afternoon / X-ray pictures you don't understand; your own skeleton as if in cotton wool or fog / surf, a freighter on the horizon / blast furnaces / a red curtain seen from a dark street, with a stranger's shadow on it / glass, glasses, glass of all kinds / cobwebs against the sun in the woods / copperplate prints with yellow spots on the paper / lots of people with umbrellas, the glint of headlights on asphalt / my own mother as a girl, painted in oils by her father / the robes of the Church to which I don't belong / the olive-green leather on an English desk / Lake Sils / the expression of a distinguished man when he has taken off his glasses to clean them / the tangle of gleaming tracks outside a main railway station by night / cats / milky moonlight over the jungle when you're lying in your hammock, drinking beer out of a can and sweating, unable to sleep and thinking of nothing / libraries / a yellow bulldozer moving mountains / vines, for example in the Valais / films / a man's hat rolling down the Spanish Steps / the fresh paint when you run a wide brush over a wall / three branches outside a window, the winter sky over red-brick buildings in Manhattan, smoke billowing out of other people's chimneys / the back of a woman's neck when she's combing her hair / a Russian farmer looking at icons in the Kremlin / March on the shores of Lake Zurich, the black fields, the blue of a föhn wind over snow in the shade—

etc.

etc.

etc.

Joy (affirmation) just from seeing.

[1970]

BERLIN

My first visit to Alexanderplatz in ages. Had to pass through the sluice gates of suspicion: the green uniforms remind me, unfairly, of the Hitler years. Self-consciousness on my part, but why? I'm from a state that doesn't recognize this state; I recognize it. A walk through the capital with its Prussian past, posters of Lenin against a backdrop of architecture. My self-consciousness subsides during the drive through the Brandenburg countryside, a forested plain, the sky wide and bright. Visit Peter Huchel in Potsdam (22 September), who was once recognized as a resistance fighter against fascism and still hasn't been granted an exit permit.

FRANKFURT

Book Fair. The difference between a horse and an author is that the horse can't understand what the horse traders are saying.

ZURICH

Homely feelings at COOPERATIVO, a restaurant in Militärstrasse; the building is due for demolition soon . . . Lenin was a regular here until he left for Russia. Mussolini later ate here with Italian workers too: as a socialist. A picture of Matteotti, whom Mussolini, by then a fascist, had assassinated, and on the brown wood panelling of the smoke-stained wall is a recent poster for the Swiss Social Democratic Party; the text reads as if it were a matter of course, but it still hasn't become a reality. A jukebox gives away the fact that `it is the second half of the twentieth century, and the young men are bearded once more. Above the jukebox in a shiny frame is the faded portrait photo of the bearded primogenitor: CARLO MARX. Workers eat at long tables covered with white tablecloths, served by waiters in white smocks. The food is Italian. This is where antifascist newspapers were once written and smuggled into Italy. We have a beer under the smoke-stained bust of Dante. A convivial place despite its high ceiling, the site of historic hopes—`

INTERROGATION IV

A. Suppose a group of people who know how to handle weapons occupy the factories in Oerlikon and threaten to blow up the Bührle company's facilities if trading in armaments isn't banned—what would you say?

B. Leo Tolstoy condemns any use of violence—and that includes war, which he described as a crime. I don't think Bührle could invoke Tolstoy.

A. Do you think Herr Bührle is a criminal?

B. I note that this issue has been raised neither in court nor in public; the right to deal in war, as long as it is done without falsifying any documents, is accepted.

A. You've read the sentences the prosecution is demanding?

B. The crimes, namely constant falsification of documents and arms smuggling for a total sum of 90 million francs, have been proven. The federal prosecutor is demanding prison sentences—suspended—and fines that are insignificant to these gentlemen. It is the length and size of these requested sentences that has angered some people in the country.

A. Not you?

B. The law is the law. We are a constitutional state and even, I would venture, a model constitutional state: even a powerful man like Dr Dietrich Bührle, with a declared income of 3.4 million and declared assets worth 125 million, can be brought to court here.

A. Will he go to jail?

B. Dr Dietrich Bührle, the boss of the company, is a colonel and on the general staff of the Swiss army.

A. What do you mean by that?

B. As the federal prosecutor has stressed, the Bührle company enjoys the overwhelming confidence of our federal council, which is what makes this consistent forgery so embarrassing for the federal council, even though, as the defence has insisted, it is merely a peccadillo because the 90 million francs worth of business was done not out of greed but out of concern for national defence, the Swiss economy, etc. As Dr Bührle himself admitted, it is impossible for him to take care of everything at a company with a turnover of 1.7 billion. He did know about the falsification at the time though or he couldn't have said to a longstanding member of staff, as the defence has highlighted, 'that this kind of illegal dealings are not allowed in future'. The following words stuck in my mind: 'There is no reason to call Dr Dietrich Bührle's credibility into question.' All I meant was that if this were not so, the accused could not be a colonel on the general staff.

A. And his deputy director?

B. I don't know either of the men and rely entirely on reports in the right-wing press. Herr Dr Lebedinsky is not a colonel. As the defence has said, the long-standing member of staff was seriously conflicted, even though it represented only seven per cent of the turnover from arms sales. 'He committed or approved the acts for which he is accused in what he thought were the best interests of his employees.' That is why he is still drawing his annual salary despite having been sacked. We should understand Herr Dr Gelbert too: 'Like the company's other leading figures, he was faced with the dilemma of complying strictly with official directives or trying, in the interests of maintaining established business relations, to salvage what could be salvaged'—meaning, the Bührle company's profits.

A. We are a constitutional state—

B. We are.

A. There is a petition for a referendum to ban arms exports. I expect you have signed it too. If it leads to a referendum, you will have the chance to vote for a ban on the Swiss weapons industry. That is a constitutional process.

B. Certainly.

A. So what's wrong?

B. The man now sitting in the federal court in Lausanne with his long-time forgers is a major employer. The Bührle company doesn't just make arms and employs 14,000 people. As I said before, Bührle doesn't just manufacture twin flak guns and associated ammunition—we shouldn't exaggerate. He only sells guns and munitions to sustain our country's arms industry, which the federal council appreciates. We do not force other countries to make war; we just sell them the weapons because they would buy arms elsewhere if we didn't. They could also leave our guns and munitions to rust once they've been paid for. As a sign that Switzerland does not interfere with other countries' wars, we supply both Israel and Egypt at the same time. And always have done, by the way. In the Second World War, when it was touch and go for us, the Germans and the British fired the same Oerlikon cannons at each other in Tobruk. Leaving aside the fact that our arms trade is also mixed up with development aid, it doesn't mean we're meddling in Nigeria or South Africa; it is purely business, part of the free market. If the federal council hadn't introduced an arms embargo out of concern for the credibility of Swiss neutrality, pure business would not have required any falsified documents. That's what the defence lawyer said at the Federal Criminal Court . . . As far as the petition is concerned, we must consider that Dr Dietrich Bührle will only tolerate so much; he could move his company abroad at any moment and the state would miss out on his taxes, as well as his art collection. I understand that Dr Dietrich Bührle is being treated with the greatest of respect; unlike the swindler von Däniken, no photographs were to be taken of him in the courtroom. Fundamentally, we should be grateful to this man. Nationalizing the weapons industry would only make things worse.

A. How?

B. Because then the federal council would be responsible, and the parliament. Dr Dietrich Bührle relieves us of this responsibility; as an independent entrepreneur, he delivers arms according to his own conscience and our country shares his profits in the form of tax but not the moral blame. We organize collections for Biafra and send out nurses, who are hit by Bührle shells. Charity is charity, business is business—

A. The verdict has just been announced.

B. The verdict can only relate to falsification of documents. Nothing else is at stake here. It is not against the constitution to aid and abet genocide for commercial reasons, which means that our society does not consider the men from the Bührle company to be criminals.

A. Contrary to the application from the federal prosecutor, which requested only suspended sentences, it is prison for Dr Lebedinsky, Dr Gelbert, incidentally a Chevalier de la Légion d'Honneur, and Herr Meili, and the court has also opted for longer sentences. It cannot be said therefore that the sentence is lenient. The only one who doesn't have to go to prison is the boss: an eight-month suspended sentence and the fine has also been reduced to 20,000 francs because it cannot be proven that he was motivated by profit.

B. I understand why he's laughing so hard.

A. Aiding and abetting genocide for commercial reasons, as you call it as a layman, is not up for discussion here. So you cannot be surprised by the federal council's verdict.

B. No.

A. Nor are you surprised that the federal court, protected incidentally by special police measures, has condemned the act of consistent falsification of documents but has been incapable of elucidating a single case of how these falsifications came about, which middlemen facilitated them and which federal officials, who check these documents, noticed anything for years?

B. No.

A. You're not surprised?

B. Three or four guilty men are enough for our people, who believe in the rule of law; otherwise, it's about preserving the established relations between business and administration and the fatherland.

A. Do you think our people are stupid?

B. Looking at the company boss's booming laughter in the photos in the press, I think I'm stupid. He's right to do so. The fine imposed by the court that he has to pay to remain a free man can be written off as expenses and is, by the way, a trifling sum compared with the bribes the company has paid in the past—expenses towards the constitutional guarantees protecting him from any violence.

ZURICH

A small demonstration, gathering outside the Kunsthaus (Bührle once donated a million) and marching along Bahnhofstrasse to the stock exchange; here and there the odd onlooker gives a pitying smile, a shake of the head. A woman says, 'Bravo!' but doesn't join us; a man keeps repeating, 'I feel sorry for you! I feel sorry for you!' Most people, seeing the banners, keep walking; a young man says, 'You Communists can go to Moscow!' About a thousand marchers.

Word of Honour

Where would you like to live, sir? First of all, I'm not a sir and secondly, I say: Please take your hand off me! I don't know the man. Sir! he says and now he gives a longer speech, his hand still clutching my coat collar, mixing several languages and after a while, when he has confused me enough, suddenly in Swiss German. So, a compatriot. Where in the world would I most like to live? This, he says, is a question that can only be put to a sir. 97 out of every 100 earthlings have no choice of where to live and from that they derive reproductive urge. That's right: I think of Czech friends, Greek refugees, millions of Indians. When I tell him I like being where I am, he shakes me around in my raincoat and says in a gangster voice: Come on, man. Come on! This is on the Helmhaus bridge in Zurich. We're blocking the road. What business is it of his, I ask, without grabbing his hand again or else he'll give me another shake. We're no longer alone; a few people, one of them with a briefcase, others simple folk who initially stop as if they'd like to help, agree with him when he says: Why don't you live in Moscow then? Why not in Havana or somewhere? I was born here, I say, nodding, I was born around here. It comes across as gauche. To sound more plausible I say the name of my neighbourhood and start defending myself: Did I say I *didn't* like living here? At least he's removed his hand from my collar now, as if his question was enough: Why not in Havana, why not in Peking or somewhere? We're not standing at the side of the road so as not to block the traffic as I adjust the collar of my raincoat without looking around for help; they find the question entirely justified, and of course I know the answer the majority expects from me. There aren't actually so many of them, but they have the appearance of the majority. My words sound less and less credible with every sentence: Word of honour, I don't want to live anywhere else; word of honour, I was born here and grew up here and went to school here and also live here. Do I need to show my passport? Do I need to give my social insurance number or the approximate number of days of military service I've done without either medals or punishment? Few people have hung around given there's no prospect of a punch-up. Why do I say a third time: Word of honour! It takes me a little longer to admit that I have asked myself before where in the world I'd like to live. This is good enough, it seems, it's good enough. I can go.

1971

BERZONA

Snow, lots of it. The twigs are white and fluffy, like pipe cleaners. We dig ourselves out during the daytime, then it snows again during the night. Only the television, TELEVISIONE SVIZZERA ITALIANA, is here to confirm that the world continues to turn with official visits, space travel, the pope, Vietnam, music and sport. No reason to panic then. The mail comes too: page after page of sociology.

Luck

'I was lucky, Fyodor Ivanovich. I hardly dare think about it. Incredibly lucky. As you can see, I am travelling first class. I have a passport, I have a title, I am a free man. I still don't understand how I didn't end up in Siberia because it was close, God knows it was a very close,' he says, pushing tobacco not into his nose but into a Charatan pipe; there is no samovar humming away either, but it is winter, on a train, and when the pipe is finally drawing properly, the traveller says, looking out of the window, 'It's snowing.' However, it isn't Russia they see outside. 'I had no reason to be jealous,' he says, as if no one wanted to listen to his story. 'Not the slightest reason. Natasha was married, but I didn't know that from the start. Maybe I was even happy that Natasha was married. I bet you're thinking now that it was improper because Natasha was married. But things are different nowadays, Fyodor Ivanovich. Her husband was a quiet and gentle man, younger than me in fact, a just and gloomy man. It is possible that Natasha misjudged him. In any case, I had left my wife and children for her. I didn't see that as moral at the time, but it made me happy. I loved her, Fyodor Ivanovich, I loved Natasha.' There is no one in the compartment who might be called Fyodor Ivanovich or Vassily Vassilikov or such like, and yet he still has to tell this story once. 'You see, I don't often think about it, so not to shock myself,' he says. 'I was an adult at the time, a respected man so to speak, and I think you have guessed, Fyodor Ivanovich, that I could very well be a murderer!' Even the ticket collector, who walks past once and peers into the compartment is clearly not a Russian but a Swiss conductor, a young, rosy-skinned chap with a red bag dangling around his knees; not unfriendly, but he too has no time to listen to half a novel, as people in Russian trains used to, and once he has left the compartment, the traveller says, 'Are you genuinely interested?' He was in the dining car before; people sit there staring at their plates or past each other, and when they've settled the bill, maybe they nod, but by then it's too late to say, 'I'm a sick man . . . A bad man . . . I'm a repellent man. I think I have a liver complaint.' Who wants to know? 'God knows I'd already raised the little axe and Natasha was sitting there in front of me and I wanted to split her like a log. Of course I didn't want to, but the axe wanted to—the little axe in my hand, Fyodor Ivanovich.' It's not something you say in a dining car nor in a compartment after a man gets in and barely says hello and would like to read his paper. His name might be Hubascher or Vogelsanger, a man from here, and of course it wasn't in Russia that the terrible act occurred but in the Grisons. 'Do you know the area around Bivio?' That's the kind of thing you can say, even if the other person is surprised and says, 'Why?' As I've said, there's no samovar bubbling away; just his Charatan pipe sizzling. 'Nice pipe, don't you think?' he says. The man who is invisible behind his open paper is surely not a bad person; his coat is a nice one with an elegant lining. 'I'm a sick man, or maybe I'm not; I'm a ridiculous man,' he says out in the corridor. 'By the way, I lied before, Fyodor Ivanovich. You might have noticed. I didn't leave my wife and children for her sake. That's nonsense. I did it for my own!—and later I left Natasha—and Vassa . . . Now you think I'm a man with no conscience, Fyodor Ivanovich, but the opposite is true. She was too good for me—this time I mean my first wife. I never hit her, may God be my witness, but it was a blessing for her that I left. Everyone admits that now. They were always too good for me, and one day I had to acknowledge that they were suffering, you see, sooner or later. There was gossip each time, the same old gossip. Which is why I have travelled so much. I now know that the opposite is true. Why feel guilty? On the contrary, the women always felt happier after I'd left them, or at least no less happy than they were—there weren't actually so many of them, Fyodor Ivanovich, if that's what you're thinking . . . Now we're in Biel, I think,' he says before correcting himself. 'Bienne.' It's still snowing. The trains don't stop for long nowadays; travellers cannot get out to fetch some hot water and nor do they have tea in the dining car any more, only the menu.' 'I had no reason to be jealous,' he says, resuming his story, 'because it was her brothers . . . I don't know what came over me that evening. It was in a ski chalet. Anyway, she was making her brothers some mulled wine because it was cold; she spent the whole evening talking to her brothers and the brothers only spoke to her because I wasn't part of the family. I thought it was funny—I mean, I tried to find it funny and it was funny, Fyodor Ivanovich, but I am a vain man. I couldn't accept that Natasha was closer to her brothers than to me. Am I a covetous man? I wasn't drunk because she made the mulled wine for her brothers; I didn't want any. You can imagine how merry it all was. I didn't say a word because they were now talking French, you see—that too. It's ridiculous. All of a sudden I hated her; I watched from side on and hated her with utter clarity. Or at least that's what I thought; in fact I loved her, but I hated the clan part of her. The clan!—I always find clans nasty, ripe for killing . . . It came over me as we were getting into bed, all of us alongside one another, Natasha and her brothers and me. Or to be more accurate: Natasha between her brothers and me. It was cold. I'd been fetching in the firewood all evening long, but she made the mulled wine for her brothers. They were already snoring when rage took hold of me and I felt it suddenly tearing off my covers and taking hold of me from the outside, that rage, and sitting me up in the dark . . . Did I say that her older brother was an officer? He was the more stupid of the two, but Natasha never corrected him. The younger one was a dancer though, a choreographer or something, an artist. Natasha especially admired him—I realized for the first time who I was: her lover . . . It's possible that Natasha then asked, in the dark, if I felt unwell, in a whisper so the brothers could carry on snoring; I didn't hear her. I went to university, but I'm still a primitive person. Natasha didn't believe I had it in me. And her brothers didn't believe it either, without knowing anything other than that I loved Natasha . . . It was winter, as I've already said, and it was night time, and I didn't know where to go. Out into the deep snow. I wanted to freeze to death, you see, while they were snoring away in the chalet,' he says and pauses because there's another person walking along the narrow corridor. 'Fyodor Ivanovich, do you believe in God?' he asks, without expecting an answer. 'I would now have been in Siberia for 15 years for a stupid murder. I might have learnt. It doesn't take much—that's all I've learnt. I might have learnt to believe in mercy, Fyodor Ivanovich. Now I only believe in luck,' he says, scraping out the Charatan pipe while the gentleman whose name might be Vogelsanger or Bärlocher or something picks up his leather briefcase and vacates the compartment, though not without a nod. 'In short,' he says when he has taken his seat in the upholstered compartment again, 'I wanted to freeze to death. I hated myself, Fyodor Ivanovich, I was ashamed. It wasn't cold enough to freeze to death. Merely unbearable. A starry sky. To be a stiff corpse in the snow the next morning was not only a ridiculous and vile plan but also unfeasible because I was only shivering by the time day broke over the mountains in the east. Natasha was asleep. She knew nothing of my plan. No one under the starry sky knew how ridiculous I was. Only me! . . . Now we're in Brugg, I think,' he says, then glancing out of the window, 'Brugg or Baden.' These are not epic distances. 'Maybe I'm boring you, Fyodor Ivanovich, but you are the first person I've told my story . . . When I went back into the chalet, I believed I had my wits completely about me, sensible and cold in my resolve to get my skis silently, ski down into the valley at first light and write Natasha a letter. She was too good for me as well. An angel! . . . I've no idea, Fyodor Ivanovich, if you're familiar with it, but this consciousness of ridiculousness, this consciousness of baseness more vicious than a starry night out in the snow—at least that is how I felt when I heard the brothers snoring up above me. What had the officer and the artist done to me? Their sister had served them mulled wine, and I can understand a bit of French . . . So I picked up the little axe to cut some wood because I was freezing in my ridiculousness after two hours out in the snow. I was chilled to the bone. I had lit a fire for them and now I was going to light a fire for myself. Of course, a log makes a lot of noise when the axe gets stuck in it and you bang the log on the block with the axe. The clan's snoring grew fainter. Now I was happy that I was shivering because that gave me the right to bash the piece of wood and cut it up into firewood, the way we do here, not without putting ourselves in danger. It must have looked funny, but it wasn't funny at all, Fyodor Ivanovich. When Natasha came downstairs and asked what in God's name I was doing, I said, 'Mulled wine.' She was sleepy and not as beautiful as usual, as she had been the whole previous evening, and as she was sleepy, I made myself plainer: Mulled wine for me! But I was ashamed. Her reasonableness, Fyodor Ivanovich, her feminine reasonableness! You don't know Natasha. We'd been lovers for three years—I mean, she is irrationality personified, an authentic person, but her unreasonableness at five in the morning was suddenly irritating. Mulled wine, I shouted. Go away! Natasha thought she knew me or else she wouldn't have sat down on the block as if it was made for it; Natasha in a pair of blue overalls with her hair down and warm from sleep. Woken by my wood-chopping, the brothers were listening in; she said, '*Qu'est-ce que tu fais?*' I said again, 'Mulled wine! 'Like that, with that emphasis, you know; Natasha thought it was a joke, I don't know, or an obstinate lack of consideration for the others and not just for her two brothers. I forgot to tell you that there were other people in the chalet, daughters and sons and God knows what else, a whole clan when I said: Go away! and raised the little axe,' he says, 'to make firewood, kindling' and again he scrapes out the pipe to be silent, but then he doesn't manage after all: 'Now we're in Schlieren,' he says, glancing out of the window. 'Fyodor Ivanovich, have you ever thrown a chair out into the street? Then another and another? I never got any better, you see, that was with Vassa, that was later, I had reason to be jealous and I was drunk, a drunken pig; there were these iron chairs that my rage took hold off and hurled them off the terrace into the road, and I wasn't a murderer, Fyodor Ivanovich. How can you explain that?' He says nothing until the pipe is drawing properly again. 'You believe in God, Fyodor Ivanovich, or else you wouldn't smile at what I say. Be honest and say you feel sorry for me, Fyodor Ivanovich, me—a stupid and superficial person. I don't feel sorry for myself . . . I wasn't mad, I knew precisely in that instant that all my ridiculousness had nothing to do with Natasha, who was looking at me, nor with her brothers, but now I simply couldn't hold the little axe any longer, even though Natasha was sitting in front of me, looking at me. I think I couldn't even pronounce her name, her beloved name, as all I could hear was: *Qu'est-ce que tu fais*? Then the little axe was stuck in the block and she was standing next to it; I was still holding the log I'd been meaning to split—that was it, Fyodor Ivanovich: Luck! he says and looks out of the window again at the yellow lights of a station flashing past. 'That was Altstetten already,' he says indifferently, and it is almost time for the traveller to take down his coat and his other things, not much, a small parcel, perfume for his wife. There is never or only rarely a peg for his coat so he tends to toss it into the luggage net, and when he looks around to see where his coat is he seems surprised to find Fyodor Ivanovich sitting opposite, directly under his coat, with a faint smile on his face: 'Is that your whole story, uncle?' There is already a throng of people in the corridor. 'No,' says the traveller, without taking down his coat, then with a similar hint of scorn, 'Fyodor Ivanovich.' The latter is a short man, not very old but he clearly has prematurely grey hair and strikingly piercing eyes; he's sitting there in a threadbare Astrakhan coat with a fur collar that was obviously made by a good tailor, and wearing a fur cap on his head; when he unbuttons his coat, it reveals a *poddiovka* and a Russian shirt with brightly embroidered edges. 'My name is Posdnyshev,' he says as if it was important to know his name, and then, 'May I offer you some of my tea? It is strong, mind you.' The tea he brewed at the last station but one that does indeed taste like beer. 'Posdnyshev,' he repeats bitterly, and coughing slightly he says, 'Uncle, why don't you tell your whole story, your true story, when you can see someone's listening?' Now they can feel through the soles of their feet that the train is starting to brake. 'Fine,' the traveller says, 'I will tell it to you,' as if he hasn't heard the conductor announcing to every compartment, 'Zurich main station, all change!' He says nothing, rubs his face with his hands for a few seconds and begins: 'If I want to tell the story, then I have to start from the very beginning. I have to tell you where I was born and who brought me up, who my friends were, what I studied and everything leading up to my sorry story—'

[1971]

NEW YORK, February

We have rented the apartment of a child psychiatrist I've never met. Her diplomas on the wall. A psychiatrist's couch: neither sitting or lying I relax, with the result—the things I have repressed:

a) my father
   (He died in 1932.)
b) the 1918 general strike
   (Students with caps in fraternity colours driving trams, behind them soldiers in helmets and with mounted bayonets to protect the strike breakers.)
c) the first time I read a newspaper.
   (I wanted to find out if a motorbike rider who had crashed due to a prank we played with our handcart had died as a result.)
d) poverty
   (Stealing fallen fruit.)
e) war children from Vienna
   (I preferred playing with them because they knew different games, but I could only do so in secret and when I was caught, I was in disgrace; I was a traitor.)
f) fear of God
   (Wearing swimming trunks in the bath.)
g) fear of people
   (You had to walk through a sewage pipe to be accepted into the group of friends, barefoot through the sewage and the stench, with the small hole of daylight in the distance.)
h) Lenin
   (The thin little man who went in and out of the house next door; my father said he wanted to wreck the whole world.)

and a few more things.

Incident

No cause for panic. Really, nothing can go wrong. The lift is stuck between the 37th and 38th floors. It's happened before. The power will come back on any second, no doubt. Amusement at first, followed by more general complaints about the property managers. Someone flicks on their lighter, maybe to get a glimpse of who's standing in the dark lift car. A lady with a bag of food on each arm has trouble understanding that it's no use pressing the alarm button. People recommend, in vain, that she put down her bags of food on the floor of the car; there's more than enough room. No grounds for hysteria: we're not going to suffocate in the lift, and no one voices the possibility that the car might suddenly go hurtling down the shaft; it's technically impossible, you'd think. One man doesn't say a word. Maybe the entire neighbourhood's without power, which would be of some consolation; in which case, lots of people will be dealing with it and not just the caretaker down in the entrance hall, who may not have noticed anything yet. It's daytime outside, sunny in fact. After a quarter of an hour, it has become more than merely annoying—it's desperately boring. Two yards up or down, and we'd have access to a door, although with no electricity it wouldn't open; the design is crazy, really. Shouting doesn't help, either. Quite the opposite: it leaves you feeling more abandoned, that's all. Surely, somewhere every effort is being made to fix the problem; the caretaker, the property managers, the authorities and civilization are all obliged to. When someone jokes that at least with the lady's shopping we won't starve to death, it's too late—no one laughs. After half an hour, a young couple try to have a discreet conversation—as far as that's possible with a bunch of strangers listening in—about some everyday matter. After that, more silence; there's the occasional sigh, the kind of emphatic sigh expressing reproach and displeasure, no more. As has been said, the power will come back on any second. Everything there is to say about the incident has already been said several times. Power cuts have been known to last a couple of hours, someone says. Luckily, the boy with the dog got out earlier; a whining dog in this dark lift would have been the final straw. The one man who doesn't say a thing might be a foreigner who can't understand much English. The lady has now set her bags of food down on the floor. Her worry that frozen foods thaw elicits little sympathy. Someone else might need to go to the toilet. Later, after two hours, there's no more indignation and no conversation either, because the power has to come back on any second; everybody knows this isn't the end of the world. After 3 hours and 11 minutes (according to later press and TV reports) the power returns: light all over the neighbourhood, where it's evening now; light in the cabin, and all it takes is one press of the button and the lift rises as usual and, as usual, the doors slowly open. Thank God for that! People don't even leap out at the first stop; no, everyone selects his or her own floor, as usual—

EMERGENCY DIAL 911. OBSERVE THE FOLLOWING RULES OF SAFETY WHILE WALKING THE STREETS:

1. Try not to walk alone at night—have someone accompany you through the streets.
2. Have a friend or relative meet you at the subway or bus station.
3. When you arrive home, ring your bell to alert a relative or neighbor and have a key ready in your hand to open the door.

4. DO NOT enter an elevator with a stranger of any age.
5. Walk in an area that is well lighted. Don't take shortcuts.
6. Know the location of police call boxes and public phone booths in your area.
7. If there are doormen in your neighborhood, know when they are on duty; they may be helpful.
8. Remain ALERT while walking. LOOK AROUND YOU.
9. If you observe any person or group that appear suspicious, do any of the following:
   a. Use a police call box and call for assistance.
   b. Go to a public phone booth and dial 911.
   c. If no phone is available, enter any store or residence and call police. Your neighbors are willing to help.
10. DO NOT carry large sums of money, conspicuous jewelry, or other valuables; when you cannot avoid this, secrete the cash and other valuables on your person. NOT in your wallet or handbag.
11. DO not place your house key together with other keys. Keep them separate. If you lose identification papers together with your house keys, someone may have access to your home.
12. Carry a whistle or a cheap battery-operated alarm when possible.
13. Carry your purse close to your chest. Don't dangle it loosely at arm's length.
14. If you hear screams, day or night, try to pinpoint the location and help your neighbor by calling 911 immediately.
15. DO NOT answer the bell downstairs unless the caller is expected and known to you.

Ptl. Charles E. Delaney
Community Relations Office
26th Precinct

[1971]

NEW YORK, February

It seems to be true: a compatriot tells me he had three knives pulled on him at eight o'clock in the evening on 10th Street (where we live), two from behind, one from the front. They were Black: their only question: 'Where is it?' When they found only 10 dollars in his wallet, their knives moved closer. Luckily he didn't move until they found another 20 dollars in his pocket book, and then they threw his pocket book with his passport in it out into the street so that he had to fetch it while they ran away. A passer-by to whom the shocked man tried to explain his situation, shrugged his shoulders——

Seminar at Columbia University——PROBLEMS OF STYLE AND EXPRESSION——in German. Who are these students? Their course fees are 1,200 dollars per year; a student costs his or her parents 4,000 to 5,000 dollars per year. Who are their parents?

Demonstration in Times Square: it's against the same war with the same banners as last spring, but attendance is lower. They walk around in circles inside an enclosure established by the police, carefully separated from the normal pedestrians and traffic. Like in a cage: 'PEACE NOW'. There are lots of police officers, equipped with helmets and nightsticks and radios, but to the majority they say casually, 'KEEP MOVING, PLEASE KEEP MOVING'. The majority, the papers say, is now 70% against the war. Demonstrations have outlived their usefulness.

An old taxi driver explains why he's heading home after this trip and why he no longer drives at night: 'Too many characters, you know!' But he understands them, he says; they come back from Vietnam and don't know how to get by and so they shoot up, but heroin's expensive so then they mug him and take his whole day's earnings. That's why he'd rather go home around this time. There are good people too, he says: they say at the end of the ride that they don't have any money and so he gives them his address and sometimes they really do send him three or four dollars.

ALCOHOLICS ANONYMOUS. They meet three times a week. A young, attractive woman tells her story of alcoholism—one of the cured. Very unselfconscious, direct, completely unsanctimonious. The only condition for joining is to want not to drink any more. There are some 150 men and women of all ages, poor people and better-off people too, White and Black. Those taking part in the discussion introduce themselves: 'Joe. I am an alcoholic.' Then he asks what the speaker did when she suffered relapses, though. They understand each other. One man is very drunk, says something and then leaves after a bit, which nobody holds against him; everyone here knows how hard it is. I even see him borrow a dollar. Only a few of them are obviously drinkers. In the next room kids are playing a noisy ball game. There's free tea. Those who have tasted the blessing of being tee-total accompany someone else after work; without any condescension at their attempts to keep the craving at bay, because they know alcohol and they know the devil promising to keep it to one glass and the excuse that today there's something to celebrate. The old Negro I ask for brochures offers me his hand and says, 'Bobby.' I say, 'Max.'

WOMEN'S LIBERATION

—and every time he concludes by saying that he's for it, all for it, but we women have to do it on our own. Then he pulls the covers over his bare shoulder, this nineteenth-century man. I could kill him, just because he knows I can't. Why can't I? Someone who snores is not human. We've been at peace for months and months. He accepts that vaginal orgasms are a myth so that I leave him alone. If I mean to kill him, he says, I first need to learn how our car engine works and other nonsense. I didn't know what I'd married. A woman's body is different, he says, which is what I say too, just differently from him. Have I read Norman Mailer? Then he doesn't even put up a fight when you argue with him, just says again that he's all for it. Women are like Negroes, he accepts that, but what's he doing about it? This June who's flirting with him is really all I needed—this June with her sausage legs who doesn't even notice that this man can't take her seriously. Why do I take him seriously? That's what he asks before he falls asleep. I ask myself the same question. I don't read Norman Mailer. They never learn. *Lysistrata* was invented by a man too, that ancient male joke that a sex strike by women would always fail because there are women like that June, strike breakers of only faint consciousness. The most progressive thing he's capable of thinking is that women's emancipation so far has turned out to be a boomerang in that it hasn't liberated women but fitted them into categories of male thinking instead. That's exactly what we've been saying. If he can actually bring himself to be serious, he accepts that things cannot go on like this. He has in fact dropped certain habits; he used to say: *your* children. Then he makes a casual reference to Margaret Mead: human fatherhood is a social invention, (do I hear) an invention, not a biological necessity like menstruation, for example (do I hear?) a social construct and therefore repressive. No, I don't think long hair suits him particularly well; maybe because I know him. Joe is no lion. They act all progressive, these artists, and then he gives himself away: women aren't creative, he says. Helen told him better than I can; she doesn't get worked up when he argues with her. With me he doesn't argue any more, he's nice; not always, though, only when he feels the urge to or thinks I feel the urge to. He does admit, though, that he wouldn't want to be a woman. I am one though. Or if he were a woman, he says, then a lesbian. I'm not one, though. When he puts himself in my position, though, it turns out that: I'm lazy (by his standards) because he sees it as work when he fiddles around with his Plexiglas; I'm emotional because he thinks of himself as rational as soon as he doesn't agree. I'm motherly and identify with the children when he kicks them out of his workshop; I'm not stupid (again, by his standards) and so he thinks I'm even more stupid when I can't accept something that proves him right. I could kill him. There's only one woman he obeys: LA MAMMA in Bologna. The fact that young women he doesn't take seriously fall for him—not only June—doesn't make me jealous, it just prevents him making any progress. I'm possessive, he says, even though I'm really not asking him to put himself in my position; then he says that I have qualities (by his standards), for instance he thinks one of my qualities is that I'm feral, etc. and Irish. He says those kinds of things out loud. Women, he says in public, are naturally conservative. He actually still believes such things. FREE OUR SISTERS—he's back on board when they're jailed. I'm free, he says. And when I threaten to leave him? He suddenly brings up

Strindberg, whom I can't stand, apart from the letters. Helen says, We mustn't discuss, we must create facts. Now he's snoring, this 31-year-old patriarch who agrees with Norman Mailer whose books I'm not going to read. We've known how they think for 3,000 years. They've learnt nothing new. Not Joe anyway. He thinks Gertrude Stein is great, but he wouldn't be able to put up with her, I say; he can barely put up with me. Now he's snoring because as soon as he's asleep he's unable to keep his mouth shut—like a baby.

NEW YORK, February

Today (8 February) American television (Channel 2) and   are reporting that in Switzerland, 'the world's oldest democracy', women's right to vote was introduced yesterday.

NEW YORK, March

You wake up, go out into the street and survive. That makes me happy, even exuberant. Nothing special needs to happen; it's enough that you have survived from one normal day to the next. Someone is murdered somewhere and we are standing in a gallery, enthusiastic or not but there, and it isn't a lie when I reply, 'THANK YOU; I'M FINE.'

Woken at 3:30 a.m. by an explosion. A double bang with the echo. A few minutes later the police are in the next street; I'm too tired to stand by the window for long; you can't see anything either, just the revolving blue light reflected in the buildings. Half asleep I think: someone has shot someone. Voices. Then a noise that continues for nearly an hour:

glass shattering and shattered glass being shovelled up. Sleep won't come; when I open my eyes: the revolving police lights on the ceiling until I do fall asleep . . . It was at the NEW SCHOOL on 11th Street, a small bomb, the vestibule in ruins; students (adults) at the library loans counter in the foyer as every day. When I ask the doorman about potential reasons for the bombing, he shrugs his shoulders. Nothing new. It happens.

A year ago, at the FILLMORE EAST, a psychedelic lightshow was suddenly interrupted and a rocker came out to the front of the stage to ask us to check there wasn't a bomb anywhere under our seats. They'd got a call. The theatre can hold an audience of 2,884. Most people bent down briefly to look under their seats, like a woman whose handbag is missing; others remained sprawled in their seats, clearly in a trance. After three minutes the band started playing again. I asked the young man with the Jesus hair and kind eyes next to me why there would be a bomb here of all places. 'For no rational reason.' And when I still didn't get it: 'You know, these days——'

Seminar on narrative positions:

a) Homer

b) the Evangelists

c)

d)

e) contemporary literature

When political activism achieves nothing: all kinds of sects, Krishna children, etc. The eclecticism of doctrines of salvation. You can't butt walls down with your head; but you can adorn it with colourful headbands. They look picturesque. What used to be a revolutionary impulse has been reduced to an escape into our minds and a dereliction of will. If it weren't for rising crime due to drug addiction, those in power wouldn't need to worry: their revolutionary children are destroying themselves.

Yesterday a young man was murdered in our neighbourhood (9th Street). Today I was among sociologists again. There's not much that they do not immediately translate into their language. Humans have a choice of doctrines.

Went for a walk after work through the jungle of cities, 'of which all that will remain is what blew through them: the wind . . . ' It sweeps and swirls the garbage along the streets, which look like a battleground. Rust and decay, buildings reduced to filth. Elsewhere, not far from here, new skyscrapers shoot up from the ground. Despite the desolation of these streets, you don't feel afraid; now and then a limousine. Fear resides where the white-gloved doorman stands on a fitted carpet. There are no traffic lights here, you can have a proper hike. A blue evening; planes drawing their brown veil of jet poison over Manhattan. This isn't even a slum; ruins with such a marginal rate of return it isn't worth demolishing them; capital currently seeks its returns in other parts. Here, there is only land, land as property, which nature is gradually reconquering through weeds. One-time storage sheds have long since collapsed, some of them gutted by fire. Even the dogs here have abandoned all hope. An elevated highway: it shows we're in a metropolis, not at the end of time. I don't know what it is; all of this together makes me happy when I hike here. We come to the glittering water, but from close up it's a black cesspit, barges carry diggers to stop it silting up; names still recall the Dutch who landed here once; the jetty is rotten, sunset behind brown smoke.

When the doorbell rings, I simply open the door. I still haven't learnt. A man with a workbag—I ask him what he wants; and when I don't understand what he says, he steps inside. WINDOWCLEANER! He cleans for 10 minutes and asks for 9 dollars. Presumably the property managers sent him. Afterwards I hear that I was lucky; but he really did only clean the windows.

We know about the war crimes from witnesses who were interviewed on television (Channel 13) and gave their accounts of what they did under orders in Vietnam: take no prisoners. FREE FIRE ZONE: anything can be killed including children. The reward for three dead Vietnamese: a week's vacation by the sea. They brought in ears and genitals as proof of the killings. None of the witnesses, who give their names and present addresses, can remember anyone ever being punished or so much as warned for atrocities against prisoners. The public meeting is chaired by a professor of jurisprudence at Columbia. If prisoners weren't killed, then for one reason only: for interrogation purposes, which included every form of torture including sexual gratification involving both women and men before they were shot. The incidents, described by the young witnesses as normal occurrences, are dated: 1967, 1968, 1969, 1970. Even though they are now speaking in a different state of mind (very objective), they still use the same expression when talking about the Vietnamese: GOOKS. When asked by journalists whether they were aware of the criminal nature of this warfare, all of them admit that you soon got used to it. What happens if someone doesn't go along with it? The young man, now a sales rep, shrugs: transfer for disciplinary reasons, another six months in Vietnam. You turn into an animal. Nothing in their faces suggests this. Prisoners are generally shot from the front, but for a change they can be tied to a helicopter and dropped from a certain height. An elderly gentleman protests against the witnesses: his son, his only son, was killed in action in Vietnam; he wanted to be a conscientious objector but he, the father, told him that he was fighting for his country and for freedom, and that's what his only son did. Then he starts to weep. The chair asks for further questions—

WALL STREET

Lunch on the 60th floor . . . Even in the lift (doors chrome or brass?) there are lots of men dressed for work as if going to a concert—from dark grey to black, hardly any blue. Despite the packed lift (it is lunchtime), appearances of unshakeable rectitude. Their skin is smooth and pink and generally firm, their eyes alert, their voices not soft but respectably virile;

occasional laughter can stand out forcefully and youthful in contrast to their extremely relaxed gestures. Even with their hands in their pockets they are gentlemen.

Reception in the lobby:

I have made it as a writer and that has earnt me this invitation; the other gentlemen are diplomats; we look out together at the lower skyscrapers on Wall Street between the two rivers and immediately agree: a magnificent view. Although our host is used to this view, he gives us time to drink it in. It's a hazy day, unfortunately, or we would see Brooklyn, etc. You can't come to lunch here if you're scared of heights; when you look down, the people in the streets are moving around like maggots or lice. You really shouldn't look down. Fitted carpets, glass, potted plants. It is quiet here: Manhattan as a panorama beyond the glass. Only men meeting more men, an intact world, and incidentally no old men and no fat men apart from me; they clearly have little time but are also not in any rush. They're accustomed to an awareness that their time is very precious. I am more on edge; it is not done to have doubts here. The suggestion that we are somehow all in agreement is as silent as walking on a fitted carpet. Only my trousers—corduroy, no creases—are a little out of place; but that merely increases the honour of being allowed in. We go to lunch in groups. A private room with a round table, works of art on the walls, a view of Manhattan again. A hazy day, unfortunately, but we've already said that to one another; we can see the Statue of Liberty though. There is water with ice, no alcohol; the financial world here is puritanical but cheerful. Today's news (in passing): the family of the Russian tsar weren't killed; they're still alive, supposedly, somewhere in

America. If true, that means that there is a fortune in London, millions of old roubles. I can't remember the menu now. Four of the guests are German; the question is who will be chancellor, Barzel or Schröder? No nasty words against Chancellor Willy Brandt though; they think it is possible that the Social Democrat government might survive until the elections. In spite of his Ostpolitik. Unless it founders over the economy first, that is. Franz Josef Strauss is not mentioned, even though he was recently here and robbed by two prostitutes. Schröder is polling ahead of Barzel, I hear and am able to assure the American host that I really don't find the subject boring; these men know a lot that a normal newspaper reader doesn't. I've noticed the CHASE MANHATTAN BANK's art collection. I know Liechtenstein, Lindner, Dine, Fontana, Glarner, Bonnard, Dali, De Koning, Sam Francis, Hartung, Segal, Albers, Calder, Goya, Vasarely, Steinberg, Pomodoro, Beckmann, Nevelson, etc. from galleries. What surprises me more: there are no suggestions of US imperialism. Did I say something? Following the experiences in Indochina it is to be feared that the American people will be inclined to return to isolationism, i.e. American aid to Latin America might fall. What then? I have little to report on the theatre. If anyone's imperialist it's the USSR (I don't contest this), which is losing enormous sums in Arab countries, our host says, Luckily. Actually, this isn't our lunch topic. There isn't one. Not much to say either about the WORLD TRADE CENTER under construction, 1,350 feet high, even though it's just outside the window; it will draw in another 85,000 commuters to rob them of their vitality in the daily back and forth. Who can stop this? Then I have the same old question for the experts: Why is gold a backstop? What is the advantage of gold compared with oil or labour, etc.? There are a range of different answers: a Swiss banker once said that gold was a complete myth. Today's answer is: nothing in the world is secure apart from gold which has kept its value since time immemorial and will continue to do so. Why? A goldless financial system is only conceivable in a state-run economy and thus a dictatorship; a liberal economy, on the other hand, requires a refuge, stability, and gold is also (lest we forget) good for jewellery, etc. My lack of understanding doesn't exactly grease the wheels of our conversation. What am I writing at the moment? That there are also idealists among the hippies, I confirm without beating around the bush; and also that there are no riots in Switzerland. We eat with breaks. It would be awkward to mention Vietnam. They know more than me. None of the men around this table represents the authorities; they are simply at one with them, and thus smart. Asked about my experiences with 'my' students, I can assure them that they are well behaved, no protests. I have coffee. On the other side of our table they're talking about Japan: conquering markets with low prices, but wages will rise in Japan too. They have figures. China? They have figures. They are certain that there has been no other motive in world history other than profit. Sadly, there aren't any cigars, and the gentlemen have to get back to work. I thank them sincerely; it was more interesting for a writer than they think. Our host insists on accompanying us to the subway in person; marble until the reception desk and then we go through the turnstile—and out.

[1971]

AUSTIN, TEXAS, Late March

Saw a skunk in the wild for the first time as it ran around the park at night: Don't get too close to it though, says my friendly host, a German literature scholar on the edge of the prairie, the dean. The flight was long, like Zurich to Moscow, but then you land to find the same brand of beer. So Austin is the capital of Texas—not Dallas, as I thought until yesterday. The classical dome of the Capitol, illuminated by spotlights at night, is proof of this. When was it built? it's already summer here, oleander losing its flowers. It's not really a city but one big park; the waste land means it doesn't feel urban, more like an oasis of comfort.

Not so long ago, about a year, a young man climbed to the top of the dome, a madman with a machine gun and shot at the crowd on the big square down below at random, killing some fellow students—

Embarrassment at my great motel; they have everything a person could dream of needing. They are all so nice, the people and also the facilities. Life couldn't possibly be more comfortable than this. Outside (I imagine) is the prairie; but here there's everything and it's clean, grounds too, a summer's night with lines of gleaming cars and neon signs. It's all so familiar, not intimate but completely familiar; I don't know where I am. No sense of place. I have no wishes (they've asked me again), just a calm sense of panic.

[1971]

Lieutenant Calley has been found guilty of murdering at least 22 Vietnamese civilians at My Lai. Without superior orders. All that remains to be decided: death penalty or jail? The guilty verdict alone has sparked national protests. One man writes on his limousine: I KILLED IN VIETNAM, HANG ME TOO. The young lieutenant, soft looking in photos, hadn't reckoned with a guilty verdict and can only restate that he was serving his country. Today the court stands accused of dishonouring the troops, backed up by 60,000 telegrams even after a death penalty was dismissed. First Agnew and then Nixon issue a reprimand to the justice ministry.

Lecture on Bertolt Brecht.

Questionnaire

1.
When you are abroad and meet some of your compatriots, do you feel homesick or anything but?

2.
For you, is home associated with a flag?

3.
What could you more easily do without:

a. a home?

b. a fatherland?

c. other countries?

4.
What do you call home:

a. a village?

b. a city or a particular neighbourhood?
c. a linguistic region?
d. a continent?
e. a flat or house?

5.
Suppose you were hated in your homeland. Would that cause you to deny it is still your home?

6.
What do you particularly love about your homeland:

a. the landscapes?
b. the fact that people have similar habits to your own, i.e. that you have adapted to the locals and can therefore count on them to agree with you?
c. the customs?
d. that you can get by there without a foreign language?
e. childhood memories?

7.
Have you ever considered emigrating?

8.
Which dishes do you eat when you're homesick (e.g. German holidaymakers in the Canary Islands have daily packets of sauerkraut airmailed to them), and do they make you feel more secure?

9.
Suppose that, for you, homeland means forested mountains with waterfalls. Are you moved when you see similar forested mountains with waterfalls in a different part of the world, or are you disappointed?

10.
Why do no right-wingers feel they have no homeland?

11.
When you pass the customs barrier and know that you are back in your homeland, do you ever feel lonelier at the precise moment when your homesickness evaporates? Or do you feel that your sense of home is reinforced by the sight of familiar uniforms (railway workers, police, army, etc.)?

12.
How much homeland do you need?

13.
If you and your wife have different homelands, do you feel excluded from the other's homeland or does each of you feel freer as a result?

14.
If homeland is the natural and social area in which you grew up, then home cannot be swapped: are you grateful for this fact?

15.
Grateful to whom?

16.
Are there regions, cities, customs, etc. that make you secretly think you would have been better suited to a different homeland?

17.
What makes you feel you don't have a home:

a. unemployment?

b. banishment for political reasons?

c. a career abroad?

d. that your thinking is increasingly divergent from that of people who call the same place home and govern it?

e. wrongfully swearing allegiance?

18.
Do you have a second homeland? If so:

19.
Can you imagine having a third or a fourth homeland, or do you then revert to identifying with the first?

20.
Can ideology become a home?

21.
Are there places you are shocked to imagine could be your home—Harlem, for instance—and worry about what that might mean, or do you thank God?

22.
Do you ever think of the earth as your home?

23.
Soldiers are said to die for their homeland on foreign soil: who decides what you owe your country?

24.
Can you imagine yourself without any sort of home?

25.
How do you know that animals like gazelles, hippos, bears, penguins, tigers, chimpanzees, etc. don't feel that the zoo is their home?

The second time I've heard from an American intellectual that the only hope for their nation to get back on track is military defeat in Indochina—no diplomatic arrangement, a clear defeat.

A Chilean poet, a former diplomat who is no longer tolerated by Allende's left-wing government, is looking for a house in Ticino, Switzerland, or near Salzburg, until better times return—

A young American writer from a rich background, a navy lieutenant in Vietnam, would like some advice on whether Ireland or Provence or Sicily is best; he has to get out. When he came back from Vietnam, he made a fortune on the stock market. A piece of cake, he says, if you have some starting capital. He doesn't say what he saw in Vietnam; only this: the officers would no longer speak to him, nor would his crew when he—educated at an elite humanist college—couldn't comprehend what went on there. So that's what he wants to write about; not about the well-documented wartime incidents, but about his shock. Back here, he says, you even lose your sense of shock; he would like to be among foreigners who don't believe it (as he didn't) or for whom it is at least not second nature.

WASHINGTON SQUARE, the first green tinge to the trees; you wouldn't have thought their grey skeletons capable of it. Yes spring, you're here . . . Yesterday, all I saw was decay, lepers, hordes of sick-skinned faces, young people's faces, the whole city a gigantic festering boil—what I think is never true for more than a few hours or, at the most, a day. Today, for example: this morning in this barren park in front of these delightful houses where Patricia lives, and this light, the lightness of the skyscrapers in the blue haze, and before that the kindness during a drugstore breakfast, but today I've bunked off, glad that we're here. Sitting here reading on a public bench; an old man walks past, stops and speaks to me to compare his pipe and mine, then we swap tobacco. A few young Blacks are loitering in the sun. Are they loitering? It's not clear whether something's going on. One of them sits down next to me, as close as on a bus, even though the bench is empty and long. Unfortunately, I don't have any cigarettes. He stays anyway and takes a crumpled cigarette out of his pocket without a word. I have a light. Underneath his dappled jacket is a top-of-the-range camera fitted with a telephoto lens. What does he want? A girl is walking her dog, a fine creature, and the girl is completely on trend, blonde with purple sunglasses. Now the Black man next to me has got up and saunters to the right of the fountain so that the girl will come walking towards him. What does he want? He's miscalculated, though; the dog has chosen a different path, and the pincer movement has visibly failed. No police. The girl doesn't quicken her pace, incidentally, and even stops when the dog sniffs at something, and now the other men are in the wrong positions in the park; they would have to run to block the ladylike girl's way before she disappears through the gate. I go as well; maybe my bookshop is open now. Here, on 8th Street, is another teenage girl with bad skin, begging—not from hunger. Marijuana would be fine too. Her gaze is blurry: 'YOU KNOW, DON'T YOU'. In a shop window (among other things) battery-powered plastic vibrators.

Evening with a student couple. He writes poetry and works in the daytime in Brooklyn: the fight against illiteracy. Is there any? More and more, he says, 7% now. Mainly Puerto Ricans, US citizens who talk Spanish at home; but the teachers only understand English. They can neither read nor write afterwards. NO EXIT, WALK, STOP, BUS, NO ENTRY, CLOSED, etc. They know what these signs mean from experience, of course, but they can't read the letters—people in their twenties and thirties. What jobs can they do? They can just about copy out their own names when they're written down. To test their intelligence he'll give them a camera, for example; the results are often astounding: what they see, how they see. But each year there are, as he said, more illiterate people in Greater New York.

6 April. Dinner with Jorge Luis Borges. The writer is 72 and blind, inclined to monologues: he doesn't see when the other people at the table are talking, and so he prefers talking himself. From time to time he asks politely who someone is, his open eye staring at the empty air. His great knowledge, A . He wears his fame as if he's

been famous since birth, serenely and naturally. The woman sitting next to him shows him which glass contains water and which one wine; then he relies on his memory. When it emerges that I am Swiss, he even knows some dialect: '   '—that's sad. A passionate linguist. He has read Gottfried Keller in the original. He says (trying to look at me) that he admires my country: Gstaad, Wengen, Grindelwald, none of which I've been to. But otherwise he speaks exclusively about literature in excellent English.

School of the Arts

The Black students feel misunderstood in class and that they are unjustly criticized by the White lecturers and students. The meeting is in an overheated room. Even before the debate the Black students move demonstratively away from the Whites. The head of the School, Frank MacShane, has to request that everyone move their chairs closer together into a circle. There are only six Black students there; they apologize for the absent with the accusation that an impossible time slot was chosen. It isn't possible to find another date that would suit all the Black complainants. What happened? They snigger, the Black students do, exchanging glances of agreement that the very question is ridiculous. The Vienna-born Jewish teacher cannot judge their literary work because she isn't Black. I sat in on an earlier class: the submitted texts were not clumsy but conventional, and the literary criticism extremely restrained. The spokesman for the Black students is for the time being a Black teacher, an unsuccessful writer; his theory is that all art is propaganda, and all propaganda is art. But Whites cannot grasp that. An intelligent and (as I have heard from the female teacher) very talented Black student now provides some examples: her work was praised—she laughs; praised!—whereas the work of her fellow Blacks was often criticized. What is literary merit? A White concept. An objection to the effect that there are objective literary criteria triggers faint giggling, as every objection does, a giggle with a glare directed past the other person. Even when they speak, they do not look at the Whites. Shakespeare is a racist, a White man, and thus invalid to her. A remark from a White student that it is ultimately about language and not content provokes a storm. There is open laughter when the lecturer requests at least trust in her goodwill. The debate becomes direct, but only on the Black students' part. The Whites can say whatever they like: they remain the descendants of slaveowners. Again and again: a White person cannot criticize a Black person because we come from a part of the world where White people have never lived. So what should she do in class, the lecturer asks. The response: 'We don't have to solve your problem!' with a laugh that sounds quite contented. Invited by the head of the School to perhaps add something, I try to say how Brecht imagined literature in the class struggle. They know that Brecht is White. Even my agreement that *l'art pour l'art* is always the art of the ruling class does not move them to look at the speaker. They are not left-wing; they say: Even a Black millionaire is one of us. A few of them say nothing at all, in fact; extras in arrogance. How to continue? As they admit after a lot of back and forth, the teacher never said that there was no Black literature; and yet the fact remains that she feels humiliated. Criticism of their texts is only literary on the surface, they say;

fundamentally it is racist. Demands for Black teachers. There aren't any at the moment though. Then more scorn directed at the White colleagues whose only problem is literature: 'Your short stories about nothing.' The young White man's argument (if his Black fellows will let him finish) that he too was trying to depict a conflict, just not racial conflict, causes a collective exhalation of silent contempt: 'That's exactly the problem!' Now everything just goes around in circles. The under-pressure teacher defends herself feebly; first: she is not aware of having made any derogatory comments; second: she pointed out the same artistic mistake in the same words to a White student; third: she did praise the girl, the smart one, a lot. The girl: 'Are Whites entitled to decide what offends us and what doesn't?' The praise she received is racist too: it didn't engage with Black experience, focusing on literary merit. And then she imitates the teacher's hand gesture: a White hand gesture. Her fellow Black laugh like kids. I don't discover why they come to this school regardless. Incidentally, they themselves bring up paranoia; someone, a Black student, is working on his first novel and then something happens in the street (YOU KNOW) and he cannot continue working on his novel for days, virtually paralysed . . . Eventually the meeting breaks up; the Whites stand there helplessly; the Black students appear satisfied for now.

PS

Weeks later, a party at Frank MacShane's; the Black teacher is there as well, with a hand-sized emblem of Africa on his chest. What did he make of the meeting? His schadenfreude that I proved of little use to the Whites—

23 April

Young men, both bearded and not, Vietnam vets, throw their medals onto the steps of the Capitol in Washington; every single one states his period of service and his name, then tears the medal from his neck and curses or says nothing.

24 April

An antiwar march in Washington; an estimated 300,000. Mainly people between the ages of 20 and 30. Between speeches a Pete Seeger song: THE LAST TRAIN TO NUREMBERG. Mass meeting without any fighting or destruction. The speeches are unanimous in their protest against the dirty war, against the impoverishment of the poor through the war, against injustice. Attacks on Nixon and Agnew and FBI chief Hoover, but belief in American democracy, 'ALL POWER TO THE PEOPLE', hope without a political doctrine; the tone remains moralistic, and the crowd perseveres and doesn't shout, occasionally raising their fingers in the peace sign, the odd fist here and there—'PEACE NOW'—and demands receive friendly applause. There are speeches by Martin Luther King's widow, his successor, Angela Davis's mother, a White senator, students. The faces in the crowd shown on TV are nice and square, naive. Not a revolutionary crowd, no, that it is not; it sounds more like a sect: BROTHERS AND SISTERS, serious in its confrontation of war crimes and air pollution, moving all in all. No radical critique of the system. President Nixon is staying at his far-away country residence; no representative of the administration facing up to a group of war cripples from all over this huge country.

Statics

One morning, shortly after eight, he presents himself at some counter or other. A policeman at the entrance downstairs couldn't give him directions. When his turn finally comes and he leans over the counter, hat long since in his hand, to repeat that he is supposed to report himself, the official doesn't even look at him and continues to staple sheets of paper together for reports. He should wait outside like everyone else who has parked illegally and then come in with the usual excuses. But he doesn't sit down on the yellow bench because he hasn't received a summons and so has no hope of ever being called. He looks out of the window, hat in hand, so no one sees his face. He doesn't shout.

It comes in bursts. Often it only lasts for an hour and afterwards he cannot understand his horror—the official might have laughed or maybe not; no one would have understood why it is significant that he has a married sister in Scotland and a son to whom he regularly sends money.

. . .

He's doesn't drink alcohol.

. . .

His students don't notice anything at the time. They are amused by his diligence with the chalk as he covers the blackboard with writing, always with the sponge in the other hand, so he can immediately erase any mistakes. He doesn't have very much hair, a bald patch with little sweaty curls from behind. Every time he turns around to face the class, he wipes his hands sheepishly with his eyes lowered.

. . .

Later, he sits down on the yellow bench like all the others before him. This department is probably only partially in charge of his case. Downstairs in the barred display case by the entrance are the usual wanted posters with photos of the respective murder weapon (knife), a reward of 5,000 francs, later 10,000 francs; the longer it takes to catch you, the more expensive you become. He glances at his watch: it's Saturday. He wonders if he really ought to report himself today given that the police station is obviously stretched—

. . .

His wife still thinks it's forgetfulness, absentmindedness. It's been raining all day so he must have noticed when and where he went out into the rain without his hat on—but he has no idea, a wet head but no idea.

. . .

His field: statics for architects. In practice, the calculations are left to an engineering office and the architect only needs to have a feel for statics. He always shows slides: cracks in concrete.

. . .

His nickname is 'The Crack'.

. . .

There is no second visit to the police station; he does, however, tell his wife a few weeks later that he has to step down from his job. He is 53.

. . .

He has never killed anyone, not even in a road accident. There was an accident on a building site in which a construction worker died, but he was an eyewitness, not the engineer in charge, who was in fact acquitted. He himself was only there by chance because he had to deliver some measuring instruments—and yet he's still scared he might suddenly recall that he *has* killed someone.

. . .

Not that he has confidence in the courts—

. . .

No disrespect to architecture, but stress is stress. It must never be forgotten that every stress we omit from our calculations comes back to bite us—look at the slides: cracks above the load-bearing wall, stress, torsion in the pillar, collapse. Then, every time, he says, 'Look!' During the break he stays in the auditorium, writing and drawing plans in advance. Whenever he sits down on one of the pews to help a student, he smells of stale sweat.

. . .

The first thing his loved ones notice is a nervous tic: at every opportunity he says, 'I don't know!' even if no one has asked him if he knows or what he thinks. No one pays any attention to it or they regard it as just another empty phrase, like when someone always feels he or she has to say, 'Oh right, oh right' or 'Exactly'. It isn't a filler; he is completely aware of when he says, 'I don't know!' Usually his ignorance doesn't even matter. Why should he know where the deepest part of the ocean is? It is of course virtually impossible for him to announce his ignorance immediately in all circumstances; the others have already moved on in the assumption that everyone knows, and only a while later, when the subject has been exhausted, is he able to sum up, 'I didn't know that!' How assiduously he listens and how clearly it is not an empty phrase could be deduced from the fact that he never says 'I don't know!' twice on the same point. Once is enough; his ignorance on this matter has been registered, and he never forgets anything he doesn't know.

. . .

He declines to become dean of the faculty.

. . .

His memory isn't declining; on the contrary, it turns against him—he suddenly recalls that he still owes his sister in Scotland her share of the inheritance. It's a complex matter, but what pops into his mind is: 8,000 francs. Plus interest. Or he will remember a foreign word he doesn't need just then; he simply remembers, every time, that he doesn't know what it means.

. . .

His lost hat is usually hanging in his outer office. A student who holds up the professor's coat for him once and then points to the hat is surprised when the professor claims it isn't his hat. He leaves without it.

. . .

The students like him.

. . .

It is not only that the yellow pencils, all sharpened, are lined up alongside one another on his desk; everything is that way. He is terrified of disorder. He's one of those people whose fingernails are always dirty but who can do nothing about it.

. . .

At the police station, a young policeman asks him after an hour what he is after, he just sits there on the yellow bench: like someone who doesn't know why he is waking up in a particular place—

. . .

Only his face has caved in.

. . .

His wife, who has admired him for 19 years, finds his ignorance easier to bear than his tic of thinking he has to announce his ignorance every time. Sometimes she will put her hand on his arm to stop him, at least in front of other people, from saying 'I don't know!' It's futile; he is instead startled by her friendly hand, as if she means to warn him, You don't know this! and he confirms, I don't know!

. . .

Trivial thoughts pop into his mind, especially towards morning when it's still dark outside. Then he goes barefoot into the kitchen for a snack, some cheese, stewed fruit, if necessary cold spaghetti. It isn't much consolation when the incidents that suddenly bubble up from his memory are funny. They still startle him. Often the very fact of being startled sets a whole series of similar thoughts in train . . . Failing to respond to the message from the cemeteries department that his mother's grave is due to be cancelled is an omission that has occurred to him before; but instead of sitting down at once and writing that he will gladly pay for an urn, he remembers that back in 1940 he actually did the right thing and even stood up bravely to a major. Suddenly (as he's standing there barefoot in the kitchen) his memory recreates their entire exchange, and what he said to the major was a load of nonsense. Sometimes it's merely a feeling people of his age no longer experience that comes to his mind, or a smell.

. . .

One day he tenders his resignation—

. . .

He remembers: a stolen football. He remembers: playing doctors in the cellar, homosexuality, his fear afterwards, and how the detective went into the cellar because he'd told his mother; how he betrayed the young gardener. He remembers: the young gardener giving him pocket money. He remembers: flunking a year at high school.

. . .

Later, his nervous tic stops again—now he immediately bows his head if he doesn't know something and listens. Birds sometimes tilt their heads like this and you don't know what they're looking at. He almost never says, 'I don't know!', just tilts his head and says nothing—

. . .

Yet he cannot talk about any of this or if he does try and talk about it, he immediately sounds confused; it isn't hard to prove to him that he is a full professor, not an impostor, a father who is at least well meaning, not an anti-Semite and appreciated by his colleagues for his modesty. Nor (for heaven's sake) is he a murderer, etc. He doesn't argue, nor does he nod but just stares straight ahead. They mean it in moral terms, but he is nevertheless dismayed—

. . .

His resignation is not accepted because he isn't able to justify it; he is healthy; the board of the university approves a secretary to help him.

. . .

All he knows is that it is inexorable.

. . .

He doesn't recognize his married sister from Scotland at the airport and goes home without her; she's sitting in his flat as if she's always sat there, only older. But then things go smoothly, even warmly, without any cracks.

. . .

Statics for Architects, a handbook summarizing his many years of teaching, is translated soon after its publication into three languages including Japanese.

. . .

In fact, everything is going smoothly—

. . .

His wife thinks it's mad when he reveals to her that he deserved to lose that trial . . . It's a long time ago, a case that left everyone shaking their heads. A scandal. He sued a company that had commissioned him to make a statics assessment before he was appointed a professor; the company paid him part of his fee but then they failed to comply with his recommendations during construction (a factory with large halls) to save money. He sued out of a sense of accountability. However, it turned out that the company had its headquarters in Liechtenstein and the place of trial was Vaduz. He had to employ a second lawyer, one from Liechtenstein who, as only later became clear, was the company's tax adviser. None of this he knew. By the time the halls had been completed and he was offered a so-called settlement—he would receive the rest of his fee provided he withdrew his suit—he had not only spent his whole fee on legal costs but was also reconsidering his career. The company had in fact commissioned other expert opinions in the meantime, while he was handing in his postdoctoral thesis, to strong arm him into accepting a settlement. THE SWISS SOCIETY OF ENGINEERS AND ARCHITECTS, which has a court of arbitration for such cases, warned him not to sue his colleagues for their assessments, especially as these colleagues, though unable to vote directly in the selection of a professor, obviously had influence. If it was (by his then standards) cowardly of him to spare certain colleagues so as not to jeopardize his professorship, he also rejected any settlement from the company all the more decidedly, whatever the cost—namely the share of the inheritance he still owed his sister . . . And now he suddenly admits at breakfast that he deserved to lose that trial. The disputed halls are still standing: that isn't the reason, though. He doesn't have one.

. . .

Then several stress-free weeks—

. . .

He personally arranges the slides for his lectures in the cartridge each time, holding each one up to the window, as if one might sneak its way in and make him a laughing stock. There was laughter once; it was dark in the auditorium and so he couldn't see who was laughing. He has removed one slide (collapsed warehouse with a three-hinged arch as an example of what can happen if you don't calculate for wind) from the cartridge for good.

. . .

His sister has married into wealth; when he brings up the business about the inheritance, her only concern is that her banker husband must never find out about it. He otherwise avoids mentioning any family memories. Luckily, their mother's grave has not yet been cancelled. Anyway, his sister from Scotland stays for only two days (at a hotel) and cannot figure out during this short period why she feels so sorry for her brother—he has a professorship, a lovely wife, a son who has just been promoted to lieutenant, a state pension, etc.

. . .

Then there is this congress in Brussels, a city he knows from past visits. When he has booked the hotel, which he also knows, the ticket, etc. he suddenly confesses that he has never been to Brussels before. His wife has letters from him from Brussels and even photos to prove it, but he still doesn't believe it.

. . .

The only question now is when she will realize that he knows nothing about statics; it's just a question of time. He will retire in nine years. His son already seems to know.

. . .

As he sits on the yellow bench at the police station with his hat in his hand, he doesn't know what his memory has disclosed during the night—he assumes they know and almost hopes they do.

. . .

Then again, he sometimes puts the same hat on his head. Without any hesitation. He comes home and has his hat back, easy as that. The cliche of the forgetful professor annoys him; and indeed, he forgets less and less.

. . .

One time, he takes his hat off his head in the middle of the road, stops and looks around to check no one's watching, then hangs the hat on a spike of an iron garden fence and walks away.

. . .

He sometimes marvels now at how far his head is above his feet walking along on the asphalt.

. . .

He's glad when he falls ill.

. . .

After he recovers, he can be seen being supported by his wife. He nods shyly when someone says hello but remembers his former students who have come a long way, even their names. He has recovered, he says politely, tilting his head. He still wears the same kind of felt hat with a sweat-stained band. He hasn't taken up his position again. His wife guides him across the street, also acting as if nothing has happened. The visible fact that none of his students' buildings (estates, congress halls, hospitals, steel-and-glass office blocks) has collapsed does not alter his verdict on himself: he knows nothing about statics and never understood what he was teaching—

> A trip out into the countryside, UPSTATE NEW YORK, and as always on such trips: where are we right now? Indian landscapes, but they say there are only snakes here now. A paradise without people. A sign on trees: Any crimes committed on this property will be prosecuted by the police. A wooden house, white with a green lawn in the middle of grounds that shades into wilderness on all sides, a large pond presumably full of fish, and the same sign: Any crimes committed on this property, etc. After a spell of quiet we do in fact see a fish, two even. The owner is off travelling

in Europe. Or Egypt? The sign isn't aimed at us; we have the key to the house and permission to make use of all this wilderness. A few plants are in flower. Our companion, a young sociology professor, has been a visitor here quite a few times before and finds a can opener. Sitting outside the front of the house we see a hare, some very beautiful birds, a white horse grazing on its own nearby. Private property as far as the eye can see. Two hours from Manhattan. Trains whistling in the night, but no footsteps: no robbers. The next morning, all the hills are still there, the pond too, the birds, etc.

QUESTIONNAIRE

1.

Can you remember at what age it began to seem natural that something either belongs to you or doesn't?

2.

Who do you think owns the air, for example?

3.

What do you consider to be your property:

a. things you have bought?

b. things you have inherited?

c. things you have made?

4.

Even if you can replace the stolen object (biro, umbrella, watch, etc.) does theft *per se* anger you?

5.
Why?

6.
Do you regard money itself as property, or do you need to buy something with it to see yourself as an owner? And how do you explain that you see yourself as more of an owner if you think people envy you for something?

7.
Do you know what you need?

8.
Suppose you have bought a piece of land: how long would it take for you to view the trees on this piece of land as your own, i.e. to be happy to have those trees cut down, or at least to see it as natural to do so?

9.
Do you regard a dog as property?

10.
Do you like fenced-off areas?

11.
If you stop in the street to hand something to a beggar, why do you always do it as quickly and as furtively as possible?

12.
What do you imagine it is like to be poor?

13.
Who taught you the difference between property that is used up and property that multiplies, or did no one teach you?

14.
Do you also collect art?

15.
Do you know a free country where the rich are not in the minority, and how do you explain that the majority in such countries thinks it is in power?

16.
Why do you like giving presents?

17.
How much land do you need to own in order not to fear the future? (Figures in square metres.) Or do you think that fear grows proportionally to the amount of land a person owns?

18.
What forms of insurance do you have?

19.
If we were only allowed to own things that we use up and nothing that gives us power over others: would you like to continue living in such circumstances?

20.
How many employees do you have?

21.
Why?

22.
Do you sometimes have a hard time coping with the responsibility of ownership that you can't hand over to others without putting your property at risk, or is it the responsibility that makes you happy?

23.
What do you like about the New Testament?

24.
Given that the right to own property exists but is only enforced when property is available, would you have some understanding if one day the majority of your compatriots expropriated you to enforce that right?

25.
And why not?

YALE UNIVERSITY, 5 May

Were it not for the TV set in the hotel, I would be in idyllic Gothic surroundings. Look around bookshops: everything's here: Georg Lukács, for example, Germaine Greer ( ), Beckett, Solzhenitsyn, Borges, James Baldwin, Freud, Hermann Hesse, Fanon, etc. It is a land where there is freedom of thought . . . On TV: another antiwar demonstration in Washington. No violence; the dissidents simply block access to Congress and the Supreme Court, but then law enforcement (police, National Guard, parachutists) arrest more people: 'without making specific individual charges of wrongdoing'. The members of a wedding party, for example, are also taken away to a police dormitory—they continue their celebrations there. A total of 12,700 arrests in four days.

This morning, immediately after the Swiss National Bank gave up its attempt to maintain the standard exchange of 4.2950 francs to the dollar, Swissair announced that it would no longer sell tickets for dollars . . . The central banks of Switzerland, the Netherlands, Belgium and Austria followed suit. They had been deluged with so many dollars that they could no longer absorb them under present conditions. In accepting the surplus dollars up to today, the Europeans, in effect, had been helping the United States finance the war in Vietnam and helping American companies buy European industries.

The New York Times, 5 May 1971

BROWNSVILLE

People live behind cardboard sheets that have replaced the collapsed walls of a house, surrounded by ruins, rubble, puddles, etc. A swarm of Black kids in the rubble or in a window behind a fly screen. It's familiar from photo books. What is a slum? There are middle-class house fronts (brownstone) like in any normal human town, and once I even see an avenue; here and there a public school, playgrounds with equipment including for basketball; Manhattan is visible on the horizon. Used to be a middle-class Jewish area; eastern orthodox Jews who moved out but still own the buildings, the shops, the land, which has been devalued by Black poverty. Devaluation is followed by collapse. There are ruins no one owns now because they are worthless. The synagogues have been rented out for other purposes. The only Black people who can earn a living are able to maintain the houses; there aren't many of them. What remains is the JEWISH BROOKLYN HOSPITAL for 90,000 impoverished inhabitants; COMPREHENSIVE APPROACH TO CHILD CARE, a good thing, a brave enterprise—all you can do is nod; I can't remember where I've seen all of this before, guided either by a White woman doctor or a male doctor, whom I follow with great respect—they care for 4,000 children here; one of them is in the playroom right now, a boy with frizzy hair and big eyes who, I can see, trusts the blonde woman doctor. In the corridor I learn a bit about social pathology: a populace with no identity, alcoholism, misery caused less by hunger than by neglect, unemployment due to there being no educational opportunities, disintegrating families, illiteracy, etc. and what people are striving to treat here: the mental harm caused by poverty. I note: FEDERAL PROGRAM, established with federal funds but to be continued by the individual states; but New York doesn't have any money to do this; uncertainty whether the scheme can be extended next year . . . There is no shortage of churches in the area: ALL ARE WELCOME, the architecture un-churchlike; they are usually only recognizable by a cross. There are also approaches to housing construction that seem to be improving the lot of the hopeless class. The streets are wide but riddled with potholes, and when it rains they turn into puddles; the asphalt shrinks, but we are not out in the country—there are traffic lights. A city with weeds. If, as recently, rage takes hold of them, they don't set fire to houses in the distant neighbourhoods of the elite but to the buildings here; here and there, another burnt-out ruin. It could be tactical; but sometimes children set light to an inhabited house. Who cares about homelessness? Families in a single room. We know from photo books what it looks like inside. Our guide cites figures; officials are aware of them. A hot, summery day; but we only get out of the Volkswagen if our guide knows someone from her many years working here.

WINSTON'S CHICKEN BAR; what we get isn't bad at all. A beer costs more in the ghetto than elsewhere. These customers have no choice. It isn't clear what people do all day; no factories, no offices, no manufacturing. Things of no further use are left on the edge of the road or in yards, cars with open bonnets, gutted and rusted, wrecks stripped of tyres, glass, cushions, etc. We're not far from industrial society, not in Africa; it's no surprise to see glittering jumbo jets flying over the area. Here too, an avenue with shop windows; we're not in a different country: the brands are the usual ones. There are even banks, smaller than over there but marble clad too—SAVINGS BANK. Some kids have managed to open a hydrant and delight in the resulting flood—the Manhattan skyline on the horizon again . . . Once they came to find a job, Blacks from the South; now they come to run wild, moving from one bolthole to the next, free, uneducated and unemployed. Brownsville isn't Harlem; neighbours here don't know one another. They're all refugees, but for life. There's no way out. Not even a dream of one. Apartheid through misery. Those who don't die in infancy live on and multiply, without knowing why things are as they are, and millions survive on welfare, which covers food. The state pays the rent in run-down welfare hotels, privately owned; there's no changing this: profits must be made or else nothing will happen in the world—

All of this is known.

I spot two White police officers who are not required to intervene; they go their own way, the only Whites in sight, incidentally, apart from the two White doctors I admire at the hospital; I ask them for figures: how much tuberculosis, how many suicides (not many), how many alcoholics, how many mentally disturbed children. Something is being done—no, it is not as if nothing's being done; there's just a lack of money, a lack of qualified teachers, a lack of awareness raising; incidentally, there are fewer serious riots now that drugs are common, but more crime. Also, there are crucial differences: between Puerto Rican kids and Black kids, the latter only able to vent their aggression physically, not in language.

Any other questions?

A visit to a Puerto Rican family in a tower block. Not in Brownsville this time, but Manhattan. Three rooms, kitchen and bathroom, looking onto a courtyard. A mother and six children; four daughters in two beds. One son has brain damage; he'd like to read but will never be able to learn. The other son goes to school and has a job. What kind? He doesn't really say. He does want to know what I write novels about, though. We're served beer, A Portuguese Saint Martin on top of the fridge, a blond Jesus over the sofa with ripped cushions. The father has run off to Puerto Rico, and the family is on welfare. One daughter, 15 years old, has her hair done up as if for a ball and is pretty; she's not going out, though; her childish make-up is for a dream. The son says he wants to learn something, some kind of trade. They speak Spanish together. They're Americans; but there's no hope for them back home in Puerto Rico.

We shall win because the United States has never lost a war. Woe to those who call for peace and no longer have faith in God and in the mission that God gave the American nation! says a minister with a double chin and a Bible in his hand: Jesus said . . . As soon as the young man, a Vietnam vet, tries to discuss rationally, he reads from the Bible—for example, the parable of the good Samaritan: equated to the US army in Vietnam, in Cambodia, in Laos and anywhere else; they are helping the defenceless there who have been attacked by robbers. What kind of youths are hanging around with their long hair outside the Capitol? And now he pulls Mao's little book from his pocket; it says here what Communism is: they want to win in order to destroy the world through materialism. Mao ('this guy') says it openly: they want to weaken the United States. The young man now makes a futile attempt to present some well-known historical facts about Indochina. But what does Jesus say? For example: all they who take the sword shall perish by the sword. That is equally well known, but it needs expanding upon: Communism took the sword, and it is God's manifest will that the US, as the world's most powerful country, should execute his will. This is not a zealous priest saying this but a composed minister on TV who is used to his parishioners agreeing with him. On Lieutenant Calley's case: women and children and old people are also our enemies (something the young Vietnam vet agrees with but explains this by the Vietnamese people's experiences with White people) and enemies must be killed, says the minister, thus Calley's actions were justified, good and righteous, and the cowards in this country who are appealing for peace are only helping the antichrist because peace is only possible by force of arms, peace through the victory of the US army, because God gave us freedom and one day Cuba will be free again too if we believe in God as our fathers did, which is why they never lost a war. The minister won't be put off by a bearded intellectual mentioning the extermination of the Native American population; they were victories, God's will. A third man at the table, a former ambassador in Asia, tries humour: does God only pour out his grace on one nation? followed by a question: Should we invade Cuba and Chile then? The minister is humble; he doesn't want to interfere in the president's business: as a Christian he can only hope that God chooses an unwavering president and as far as the distribution of grace between nations goes, all joking aside: God has no time for the Soviet Union in any case because God is on the side of freedom and decency and morals. What does the Bible say? There is only one thing capable of interrupting the minister—the next TV commercial: THE BEER THAT MADE MILWAUKEE FAMOUS. Well, the Bible has spoken, and the duty of every American is clear: Communists must be killed, the American prisoners freed, the bombing of North Vietnam continued and intensified. The minister has no trouble rebutting a remark that prisoners of war are only freed after a peace deal or a swap: there can be no deal with Communists until they release the American prisoners ('American lives'). The debate never descends into a bare-knuckle brawl: even if the diplomat and the minister don't agree, again and again they share a jovial laugh. Only the young bearded man remains serious, quoting figures and the Geneva Convention. Even the host is up for a neutral joke; after all, the millions of

> viewers are entitled to a bit of entertainment if they're expected to watch another batch of commercials every seven minutes. The minister thinks the fact that there are known to be areas of Vietnam where the US army doesn't take any prisoners is militarily justified because the American people have gone into war to win or else there would be neither peace nor freedom nor decency nor morals in this world 'that God has given us' . . . After an hour I turn it off.

The New York Times

Mrs. George C. Barclay is a silver-haired, 67-year-old Manhattan housewife who wants to die with dignity. So she recently signed the Euthanasia Educational Fund's 'living will', in which she requested that, if she becomes ill and there is no reasonable expectation for her recovery, she be allowed to die and not be kept alive by 'artificial means' or 'heroic' measures.

Her husband, a retired banker, and their three children know of the will, and have told Mrs. Barclay they agree with her decision and will try to see that it is carried out.

Mrs. Sydney Appel, 54, is a Brooklyn housewife who also signed the document. But her four children are vehemently opposed to the will, because they don't believe such a death could be handled in 'a responsible manner.'

'What about the woman whose children felt she was an inconvenience?' asked Mrs. Appel's son, Douglas, 17. 'If she had already signed the will, it would be no great difficulty for the children to do away with her.'

To the people who are active in this country's two major euthanasia groups (the Euthanasia Educational Fund and the Euthanasia Society of America), euthanasia generally means one thing: The right to die with dignity. Indignity, to them, means deterioration, dependence and hopeless pain. But to many other people, euthanasia (derived from the Greek for 'good death') means 'mercy killing'.

Proponents of euthanasia predict that family discussions such as those that occurred in the Barclay and Appel families are going to become quite common in the next few years as the subject of death, and whether the patient has the right to decide how and when he wants to die, is brought out into the open.

There are indications that this is on the verge of happening now. A 'right to die with dignity' bill was recently introduced in the Florida Legislature, stating that a patient suffering from an incurable, fatal and severely painful illness should have the right to ask that his life be painlessly terminated. The bill is now in committee.

Courses on death have been filled to capacity this year at both New York University and Union Theological Seminary. The technical advances in the medical arts (new life-sustaining drugs, organ transplants, artificial kidneys, auxiliary hearts, defibrillators, pacemakers and respirators) have resulted in dialogues among young medical students, who do not always agree with these artificial means of keeping dying patients alive.

Making own decisions

And the recent liberalization of abortion laws in several states has added fuel to the arguments of those who believe that people should have the right to make their own decisions regarding life and death.

'All of my friends like to talk about death nowadays,' said Mrs. Henry J. Mali, 67, of Manhattan, president of the Euthanasia Educational Fund. 'It's even a subject of conversation at cocktail parties. People seem charmed to find somebody else who wants to talk about it.'

Almost 20,000 persons have requested the 'living wills' in the 18 months that they have been available, according to Mrs. Elizabeth T. Halsey, executive secretary of the Euthanasia Educational Fund, at 250 West, 57th Street. She said that she received 50 requests a day for the wills, which are not legally binding, and recently ordered 10 000 more.

How does one die with dignity? One of the lines in the 'living will' says: 'I ask that drugs be mercifully administered to me for terminal suffering even if they hasten the moment of death.'

At present, doctors who carried out this wish could legally be charged with murder. This is perhaps the major reason why people consider euthanasia abhorrent—or because it is often used interchangeably with the term, 'mercy killing', which in turn is usually associated with the killing of babies who are born with mental or physical defects. (To many others, euthanasia is equated with Hitler's program of killing mentally and physically handicapped persons.)

'It is a common misunderstanding that we advocate mercy killing,' said Jerome Nathanson, chairman of the board of leaders of the New York Society for Ethical Culture, and a strong proponent of euthanasia. 'But actually, mercy killing is the complete antithesis of what we seek.'

'The question is not one of killing people,' he added, 'It is the question of letting one die.'

Mr. Nathanson, whose wife died of cancer in 1968, said he believed that the new honesty and openness among American youth might help change public attitudes about euthanasia.

'Sexual relations are one's private affair,' he said, 'and one's attitudes on death should be a private affair.'

Mr. Nathanson said he knew of a doctor who, if a patient is suffering from a terminal illness, leaves three pills on the bedside table and tells the patient, 'Take one every four hours. If you take them all at once, they will kill you.'

'I don't know why all doctors can't be that way,' he said, 'and leave the decision up to the patient.'

Many doctors make a distinction between 'active euthanasia', where a drug or other treatment is administered to hasten death, and 'passive euthanasia', in which therapy is withheld and death is hastened by omission of treatment.

Most religious groups condemn active euthanasia, especially the Roman Catholic Church. Last October, Pope Paul VI said in a statement to Roman Catholic physicians that euthanasia, without the patient's consent, was murder; and with his consent, suicide. 'What is morally a crime cannot, under any pretext, become legal,' he added.

But the Pope also seemed to espouse the religious community's more lenient attitude towards passive euthanasia when he said that while doctors have the duty to fight against death with all the resources of science, they are not obliged to use all the survival techniques developed by science. Prolonging life in the terminal stage of incurable disease could be 'useless torture', he said.

A statement by Pope Pius XII is included in the literature distributed by the Euthanasia Educational Fund. It says: 'The removal of pain and consciousness by means of drugs when medical reasons suggest it, is permitted by religion and morality to both doctor and patient; even if the use of drugs will shorten life.'

The Euthanasia Educational Fund is a non-profit, educational organization that finances studies and seminars on euthanasia for physicians, clergymen, social workers, nurses and lawyers. Contributions to the fund are tax deductible, while contributions to the Euthanasia Society of America, an action organization seeking political change, are not. Both groups have offices in the same room at the West 57th Street address, and claim 1200 joint members. Last year, the membership was 600.

The Rev. Donald W. McKinney, pastor of the First Unitarian Church of Brooklyn and vice-president of the Euthanasia Educational Fund, said he believed that the fact that the 'living will' was not legally binding was 'rather irrelevant'.

'Its great value,' he said, 'is that a tremendous burden of guilt is lifted from the family and children when a person signs the will. And it is also a great deal of help to doctors.'

He said that more and more clergymen had to wrestle with the moral question posed by euthanasia: Whether it can be reconciled with the commandment, 'Thou shalt not kill.'

'The primary commandment is reverence for life,' he said. 'It is not a question of killing, but a question of honoring life, a question of dignity.'

'The process of dying is changing today,' he went on. 'With all the new medical advances we have, we have to determine if life is really being served by prolonging the act to dying.'

The fact that there is no clear definition of death that is acceptable to everyone is one reason why many doctors are opposed to euthanasia. Some doctors consider death to occur when the brain dies; others, when the heart stops functioning. Sidney D. Rosoff, legal advisor for both euthanasia groups, said: 'A patient is dead when a doctor says he is.' But even this definition has not always helped up in court cases.

'I tend to be basically moved toward it (euthanasia),' said Dr. Barry Wood, a Manhattan internist who is also an ordained Episcopal priest, 'but I become more conservative as I see the possibilities. One possibility is to declare certain people unfit—and this has happened in the past.'

Dr. Fred Rosner, director of hematology at the Queen's Hospital Center and a leading critic of euthanasia, said: 'If euthanasia were legalized, the next logical step would be the legalization of genocide and the killing of social misfits.' 'And who can make the fine distinction between prolonging life and prolonging the act of dying?' he added.

Another argument

Other opponents of euthanasia frequently argue that a dying patient should be kept alive as long as possible because a cure for his illness could be just around the corner.

'There is a paucity of overnight miracles,' Mr. Nathanson rebutted. 'Physicians generally know what's going on in the field.'

'And what if a person can't stand the pain for five years? If I say, "I can't stand it," and the doctor says, "Look, your suffering may help other people," that's the worst ethical indignity that can be done to a person.'

The Hippocratic oath that all physicians take when they graduate from medical school is used as an argument by both proponents and opponents of euthanasia. The oath states that it is a physician's duty to relieve suffering, but it also says he must preserve and protect life.

In Great Britain, which has an active Euthanasia Society, there have been two recent controversial proposals by doctors that an age limit should be set at which doctors should stop 'resuscitating the dying'. Dr. Kenneth A. O. Vickery suggested the age of 80; another said that anyone over 65 should not be resuscitated if his heart stopped.

Dr. Vickery, who said he thought geriatric patients were overloading hospital and welfare services in Britain, recalled the frequently quoted lines of Arthur Hugh Clough, the 19th-century English poet, who wrote:

> Thou shalt not kill;
> but need'st not strive
> officiously to keep alive.

This country's two euthanasia groups are opposed to age limits.

'The people in Britain are thinking of society,' the Rev. McKinney said, 'we're thinking of the individual. We believe that even people in their twenties and thirties should have euthanasia, if they need it.'

Mrs. Appel, whose children are opposed to her desire for euthanasia, said she came to her decision after watching her senile, 87-year-old mother die a painful death after suffering a broken hip.

'I made up my mind I didn't want my children to see me that way,' the darkhaired woman said. 'I don't want to leave them with the mental image of deterioration.'

Mrs. Appel's son's argument that families might let a patient die for ulterior motives is another frequently used argument against euthanasia. Some family members, the opponents reason, may wish to believe their own suffering rather than the patient's; or else the heirs may have their eyes on the patient's estate.

Most people who have signed the 'living will' have chosen doctors who are sympathetic to their wishes. Mrs. Barclay said she picked her doctor because she knew he was a contributor to the Euthanasia Society of America. Mrs. Mali, who is the wife of a retired textile executive, said her physician was a man who had promised he would let her die 'peaceably, rather than having my arms stuck full of tubes.'.

'Now that I'm old, the next celebration is death,' Mrs. Mali said in her East Side town house. 'And what I'm most interested in is how my death can be made an honorable estate, like matrimony.'

By Judy Klemesrud

Copyright: *The New York Times*, 1971

[1971]

Note for the Handbook

One advantage of being old is that since being considerate no longer pays, an elderly person no longer requires rage—the impetuosity of rage—to tell the truth. Sometimes it really is as he sees it, and of course the others know this too; they are just showing consideration for themselves, that's all. Not that this makes the old man a prophet, just fearlessly calm. What the prophets of the ancient world, most of whom were blind, had to say was seldom more than the obvious things other people could not afford to see—out of consideration for themselves and to their detriment.

So this is what petty criminals look like, today's thieves, the burglars and the drug dealers and the bandits and the robbers in the lift, etc. the people the police catch day in, day out—they are waiting on the long bench on the right-hand side of the room. The expedited NIGHT COURT is open to the public. The Stars and Stripes behind the judge and engraved above it in marble: IN GOD WE TRUST . . . Almost without exception they are Blacks or Puerto Ricans, some of them in brightly coloured tops, some in tattered grey clothes, female criminals too. Many seem familiar with the procedure. Routine for both sides. Four prosecutors and attorneys, all young and Jewish, do their job without any fuss. Unfortunately, it remains largely a pantomime, almost impossible to hear who is speaking; the murmur of routine. Only the verdict after 5 or 7 minutes is audible to the public: 1,000 dollars, 50 dollars, presumably bail, then another sentence: 5 days in prison, 3 days in prison. A thug, in shirt sleeves and fat, holds the reports in his hand: from time to time he says, 'Quiet!' Everything proceeds smoothly, normally, without ceremony. The clerk is an African American with sideburns wearing a white shirt and a tie and pop-art glasses; he looks dated somehow and sits there as motionless as a monument, his forehead gleaming like bronze, but now and then he yawns. Only the judge is wearing a gown. It looks like a theatre rehearsal, not quite in sync yet, especially the sinners' entrances, people interrupt, a back and forth; but the sentences are real. Then the look back at the public: are their families there to pay? Sometimes they are. Someone waves a handful of dollar bills; but sometimes there's just a shrug if they don't have enough, or there's no one in the courtroom: then it's out through the doors beyond which there are lots of blue-shirted police officers and for a second you see bars opening and closing. Like chicken coops. Only once does a White man become unruly when the man in his shirt sleeves with the cockade grabs his arm to show him the way even though he knows it already. When the long bench is empty, they let the next ones in. Lots of young people. The procedure looks a bit like a job placement service. No fuss. The night judge skims through the reports pushed towards him, without glancing at the delinquents. Meanwhile the attorney asks the delinquent something, quite amiably, and says something to the judge who rarely asks any questions: he already knows the answers. Only one Black pupil states clearly and doggedly that he is innocent. It doesn't seem to be true, though. Unfortunately, because the prisons are packed and everyone knows this: four people in a single cell at the moment. It's midnight. In most cases it's drugs, currently the best way for people with no qualifications to earn some money. An old man as Black as the first slaves doesn't seem to understand his attorney; hat in hand, as if he is honoured by this official ceremony, he looks one moment at the attorney, the next at the plaintiff and the next at the judge, as devoutly as if he were in hospital; the outcome is three days in prison, and he nods like a patient. It isn't a sham: proper procedure is observed. Next to me a baby is sleeping with its Black mama who's still waiting for her son. There is also the occasional acquittal; a girl who is slightly crippled and slovenly is allowed to go. It looks as if she doesn't have any cash for the subway though, and no begging is permitted in the courtroom. How is she going to get to, for example, Brownsville? When we leave at around one o'clock in the morning, the court is still in session; there is still a mountain of blue reports——

PS

Something I didn't know, but which the trustworthy Uwe Johnson tells me in Berzona: outside that building (courtroom and jail under one roof) there are places offering short-term, high-interest bail money loans. 500 dollars on the table today and you don't have to go to jail but you do have to get hold of 600 dollars by Saturday. How? The Stars and Stripes (IN GOD WE TRUST) doesn't interfere in such things; that is FREE ENTERPRISE for you, the natural order of things: the bedrock of Western freedom.

A wholesaler from Hamburg who has been in business here for many years explains his respect for this country: there are no class distinctions here, only differences in ability.

'You have the right to defend yourself. No charge has been brought against you, but you may wish to defend yourself anyway. For instance, you have lived in a society that you regard as disreputable, you have demanded reforms, etc. That is clear from your many statements, if not from your actions. Or do you consider by your own explicit confession that you did act? There is nothing in your case file. Your beliefs as such are not at issue, nor is your career as such. By the standards of the society you are suing, you have committed no major crime; according to your case file, however, your life is no different to that of any other profiteer who finds this society to their liking.'

. . .

'Are you pleading resignation?'

. . .

'You were able to pick the jury members you see here. There could have been different people, but you picked them: an old school friend to whom you think you owe a great deal; Tolstoy and Kafka and Brecht and other authors, your biological children, also neighbours who know a great deal about your daily life, a few mates, colleagues too, women, a Jew, a worker, a Negro; in short, people from all walks of life, a few philosophers insofar as you think you understood them, a dead teacher, and also a hippie who didn't show up.'

. . .

'Although you deem society despicable, you have never exercised power or even tried to exercise power. You might have been able to achieve some modest changes. Why did you never seek to exercise power?'

. . .

'There is no charge against you, unless you lay charges against yourself. So you were content to be comparatively blameless?'

. . .

'You are silent.'

NEW YORK, May

Donald Barthelme says, 'You (Europeans) are happier than us.' Why? Marianne is making her popular bacon-onion-veal-rosemary skewers, and I get the fire going, albeit with unfamiliar wood. What is different here from Ticino? The nearby stream doesn't roar any differently; it's wise to be wary of snakes in Ticino too . . . Jürg Federspiel turned up recently, Jörg Steiner came to visit a bit later, and the reports on events back home were soon over; we have more to discuss abroad . . . I am occasionally surprised by how easy it is to call everyone only by their first names after less than an hour: Donald, Mark, Elisa, Joe, Frank, Lynn, Harrison, Ted, Patricia, Stanley, Steven, etc. I couldn't say whom I would call 'Du' in German and whom I wouldn't. A compatriot who has lived here for years immediately switches to 'Du' when he uses my first name (anything else would seem stiff and unnatural to him, he says); it sounds like a bad translation. They don't mean it when they say: Max, do you know . . . It's a turn of phrase that we have too:

. . . American friendliness is not more superficial, as is so often claimed; their way of expressing it is more ambivalent than 'Du' in our language, which is devalued by premature familiarity . . . Sometimes you meet someone you know in the street, among the millions, as in a village; it isn't a village, though: everyone knows that the others will get by without him or her, and no one is hurt by this knowledge. It makes both parties act warmly towards one another. They are more helpful than in small cities, and so you become more helpful too—out of reciprocal gratitude. If you happen to meet someone by chance after several weeks in a crowded party, you greet each other like two people boring a tunnel and meeting at the breakthrough point: 'HOW WONDERFUL TO SEE YOU!' you say, and it's true.

End of the seminar.

Afternoon in a bar by the Hudson. Port workers playing pool and drinking beer out of cans. As early as your second or third visit, without us ever having spoken, they say hello—

Questionnaire

1.

Are you afraid of death and if so, at what age did this start?

2.

How do you deal with this fear?

3.

Are you not afraid of death (because you're a materialist; because you're not a materialist) but of dying?

4.
Would you like to be immortal?

5.
Have you ever thought you were going to die? And if so, what did you think about at the time:

a. what you were leaving behind?
b. the state of the world?
c. a landscape?
d. that it was all in vain?
e. the things will never be accomplished without you?
f. how messy your drawers are?

6.
What do you fear more: that on your deathbed you might insult someone who doesn't deserve it, or that you might forgive all those who don't deserve it?

7.
When another acquaintance dies: does it surprise you how you take others' deaths in your stride? And if not: do you have the feeling that the deceased has an advantage over you or do you feel superior?

8.
Would you like to know how it feels to die?

9.
If you have previously, under certain conditions, wished to desire but didn't get round to it: do you think that you were wrong, i.e. do you judge the circumstances differently as a result?

10.
Who do you sometimes think would be pleased if you died?

11.
If you are not currently afraid of dying: is it because life is onerous at the moment or because you are enjoying the moment?

12.
What bothers you about funerals?

13.
If you have pitied or hated someone and hear that he is dead: what do you do about your previous hatred of him or with your pity?

14.
Do you have any dead friends?

15.
If you see a dead person, do you get the impression that you knew the person?

16.
Have you ever kissed a dead person?

17.
If you think about death not in general but about your own death: are you shocked, i.e. do you feel sorry for yourself or for those who will outlive you?

18.
Would you rather die fully conscious or be surprised by a falling brick, a heart attack, an explosion, etc.?

19.
Do you know where you would like to be buried?

20.
When someone's breathing stops and the doctor confirms this: are you sure we stop dreaming at this point?

21.
What kinds of agony would you prefer to death?

22.
If you believe in a realm of the dead (Hades), are you reassured by the idea that we will all see one another for ever, or is that why you're afraid of death?

23.
Can you imagine an easy death?

24.
If you love someone, why do you not wish to be the one who survives rather than leaving the grief to the other person?

25.
Why do the dying never weep?

NEW YORK, May

The trees in the courtyards are turning green; trees like proper trees; you look down on their green leaves with some emotion: this brave chlorophyll!

A phone call from a compatriot who lives here, and I invite him to speak Swiss German because his English is confused. Even more confused now, he asks, 'But who are you?' He has called on behalf of a friend from Gockhausen (Switzerland), doesn't believe it is me on the phone and would rather speak with my wife, but she is out. He repeats, 'Who are you?' Even in Swiss German he still doesn't believe me and would rather check with my wife that the death announcement on the United Press wires definitely isn't true. He has never heard of Mark Twain's words in the same situation ('The reports of my death have been greatly exaggerated.'). We have then been talking for quite some time when he asks again, 'But who are you?' Incidentally, Mark Twain lived on the other side of this street.

A Black household help working for friends of ours is learning to read and write, taking four lessons a week, and asks me for one of the books I've written—her first book. She's 65. Our maid, who is also Black, doesn't come any more; I heard her laughing loudly, then talking, and she was standing in the room, smoking a cigarette with her almost toothless mouth and staring out through the wall; she hears voices. The new help, a Black woman from the West Indies, cleans very thoroughly but doesn't enjoy it, as she politely puts it; she writes songs and sings them, is looking for an agent to get into the record business; she would like to play us her music on a tape one day. Music is all that counts in the world. She's probably 50 and lives in Brooklyn.

A death in the street (Bowery) in the afternoon; the police are already there, two officers, which is quite enough and we continue our journey like everyone else.

Rip Van Winkle

He always feels like this when he returns home after a spell away. He is surprised to find everything in its usual place.

. . .

The ravine in which the all-male revelling and bowling party made the lost Rip Van Winkle their skittle-arranger and butler could be in modern-day Morningside Park or somewhere farther out of town where the Rockefeller monastery lies. The legend says simply: Manhattan.

. . .

Waking on the black rocks of Manhattan, his musket by his side, he runs his hands over his face in fright but is alert despite the smell of brandy on his breath. It was probably a distant thunderstorm he heard in his sleep. It wasn't the sounds of bowling balls. The brandy, on the other hand, is not a dream. The storm has moved on. Evening light on the Hudson. It cannot have been a matter of years; his dog, for example, is still young.

. . .

He has a wife and even in his dreams he hasn't forgotten this, telling the gentlemen in Dutch traditional costume about her for years; but he couldn't escape in his dreams.

. . .

The path (now Broadway) is a long path; as he travels night falls and he is gripped by fear that there will be no one left who knows him. How would he react?

. . .

Those gentlemen playing bowls!

. . .

When he reaches the village (New Amsterdam) and looks around in the dawn light, it is unchanged. The chickens are still there, every one of them. His contemporaries are merely asleep. Ships in the harbour: one has set sail in the meantime; another now lies at anchor. What else? Time has stood still. His wife doesn't believe a word of it and says it is Wednesday. Of course she was worried about him; something nasty could have happened to him out there.

. . .

No one believes his fairy tale—

. . .

His house with its small windows and steep stairs, the familiar crockery, etc. He doesn't take stock, already sure that everything is in its rightful place. Edam or herrings from the barrel or sausage, he wolfs down anything and everything, staring out of the window. Everything is as it is; this, then, is his home.

. . .

Not a single death in the village.

. . .

It's not as if they don't recognize old Rip. His assistant says that a customer has raised hell twice already. Nothing new. He's known as a drinker; they've frequently had to show him where Rip Van Winkle lives. He's sober now, though.

. . .

Why is he telling these fairy tales?

. . .

He continues as before: making barrels, as he has trained to do. After work he plays cards, talks Dutch and drinks, on Sundays he goes to Coney Island to shoot rabbits or to the black rocks of Manhattan. His life. He's amazed when people greet him as if nothing has happened. Everyone else, his good wife and his neighbours, his customers, his mates who laugh at his famous fairy tale, all believe that this is his life—

SS FRANCE, 8 June

Europe in sight. The ship is following a pilot now, people stand on deck, suitcases packed, but we're still moving and no one is in any rush, happy to see that it's still moving—

THE COLUMN

The Grosse Brockhaus encyclopedia refuses to include it. From time to time a guest touches it with his or her hand to discover. Granite? Yes, it's granite. A rough and touching column. Some ask when they first see it: Was this always here? There's no chronicle of our village, only engravings on the abandoned chapel and a few houses: 1682, 1664, etc. The column was probably sculpted for his own pleasure by a stone mason who was working away from his native valley, which has no details about him. He has done nothing novel; he's no Carlo Madermo, who is also from around here. In fact, there's nothing to say when you've touched it with your fingers and realize: Tuscan! A bit has splintered off the base, incidentally, but nothing terrible. It will outlast us. Grey, brittle stone, local. The encyclopedia contains a reliable list: the Doric column, the Ionian column, the Corinthian column, just as we were taught at school and later saw at Sounion, Corinth, Olympia, Athens, Delphi, Paestum, Selinunte, Baalbek, etc.; but the column that supports our little loggia never puts me in mind of my travels. When we drink coffee, it divides the valley for us. Its lower half is a little rounded, its proportions not at all graceful. We sit in our wicker armchairs, looking out at the sheet lightning in the night, in the foreground the column of which we know only that someone carved it, because there it stands as a support. I assume that in the summer he used to carve for foreign lords or at churches in southern lands where he had a master; in winter he had to go home and had time—lots of time for granite. Why he had to go home I don't know; he probably had family here. Granite isn't marble; the form he has in mind is still weaker than the granular stone. And the main thing is: it is alone. Everything else about the house is usual and proper: the rustic beams, the window seats made of the same granite, the big fireplace, etc. bear no relation to it. The column is like a guest. It is not quite head high, but it stands on a balustrade; when talking to someone, you can stand and rest your hand on the capital, and I sometimes do because there's nothing ceremonial about it. I occasionally tap out my pipe on it. We know its wider family, of course, including the smooth bastardized offspring on the fronts of banks around the world. This one doesn't know its heritage, though. Some people don't even notice it, it seems, and if so I don't bother introducing the column. Then later, if our conversation falters for a moment, there comes the question for the umpteenth time: Was that funny column always there? Not always; someone carved it once. I can imagine he was proud of it. Only the wreath below the capital is classical, but it too bulges remarkably like a sausage. If you put the day's newspapers aside after reading, idling for a while in the knowledge of our helplessness, still the column stands there, unshaken, not proud but upright. If you touch it: grainy, the stone warmth of the past day. Against the pale evening sky it presents its apology: centuries of weathering, its blurred outline black against the precise twilight that is just letting through the first star.

Vereinigung Freitod
(End)

Every association has its time. If we need to remind candidates at the annual meeting of the purpose of our association (conscious suicide as an ethical commandment), then it is the same as with all necessary and solemn reminders of the statutes: there are no possible objections, even if the rules have never been tested.

The more ancient the members become, the less the ageing of Western society shocks them; they think there are enough young people, more than enough—

The youth revolts are having a rather negative effect because it is precisely those members who have no intention of taking their leave that are particularly put out by their sons. They feel misunderstood. They feel that they have to hang around until they are proved right, and this means: until their sons have passed 50 too.

Even members with slim faces have bloated bellies. It is usually when they are sitting, always with their jackets hanging open from their scrawny shoulders like a scarecrow's clothes, and it looks as if they're carrying a balloon under their hoicked-up trousers. The waiters who serve at our gatherings have the patience of zookeepers, and as for the waitresses they talk like nursery-school teachers. We get on one another's nerves; everyone thinks the others are always interrupting him and yet talks incessantly; we simply don't listen to one another. The more someone knows, the worse it is; they can't keep their knowledge to themselves. I'm sick of hearing about BAUHAUS, ZURICH SCHAUSPIELHAUS, etc.

The planned HANDBOOK will not be completed. I cannot think what else to write, and when I look back over my notes, the observations and conjectures that occupied my thoughts years ago strike me as inaccurate. Also, my fear of ageing is diminishing. That's part of the problem.

According to statistics, average life expectancy has risen further; by the time I am 73, the average life expectancy is 74—I announce that I am leaving the association . . .

HANDBOOK FOR MEMBERS

Grow old and you only have yourself to blame.

Notes

All notes are supplied by the translator.

PAGE **18** | '`Mecklenburg can count on it`': Uwe Johnson, author among other things of *Anniversaries: From a Year in the Life of Gesine Cresspahl* (Damion Searls trans.) (New York: New York Review of Books, 2018), was writing a trilogy about the eastern German province where he grew up.

PAGE **18** | 'An account of the "hearings" ': Brecht testified before the House Un-American Activities Committee in 1947, accused of writing 'a number of very revolutionary poems, plays, and other writings'.

PAGE **19** | Peter Suhrkamp (1891–1959) was a German publisher and founder of the eponymous publishing house.

PAGE **20** | Paul Dessau (1894–1979) was a German composer and conductor. He collaborated with Brecht and composed several operas based on his plays, like *Herr Puntila und sein Knecht Matti* (1948) and *Die Verurteilung des Lukullus* (1951).

PAGE **20** | Caspar Neher (1897–1962) was an Austrian-German set designer and librettist, and a frequent collaborator of Brecht.

PAGE **29** | Heinz Hilpert (1890–1967) was a German actor, screenwriter and film director. He was head of the Deutsches Theater during the Third Reich.

PAGE **31** | Władysław Gomułka (1905–1982) was a Communist politician and de facto leader of Poland from 1947 to 1948.

PAGE **35** | Boleslaw Barlog (1906–1999) was a German stage, film and opera director, and the manager of West Berlin's Schiller Theater.

PAGE **37** | Konrad Farner (1903–1974) was a Swiss art historian and Communist intellectual from Zurich. He was declared *persona non grata* for his support for Communism after the 1956 Hungarian uprising.

PAGE **69** | 'The most dangerous people [. . .] life draws nearer and nearer.': Leo Tolstoy, *The Law of Violence and the Law of Love* (Vladimir Tchertkoff trans.) (London: Concord Grove Press, 1983[1908]), p. 74.

PAGE **72** | 'I cannot and will not [. . .] crimes committed around me.': Leo Tolstoy, 'I Cannot Be Silent' [1908] in *Recollections and Essays* (Aylmer Maude trans.) (London: Oxford University Press, 1946), p. 409.

PAGE **72** | 'Strange as it seems [. . .] what I have.': Tolstoy, 'I Cannot Be Silent', p. 410.

PAGE **73** | 'That is why I write this [. . .] noose round my old throat.': Tolstoy, 'I Cannot Be Silent', pp. 410–11.

PAGE **73** | 'Violent revolution [. . .] already given them.': Leo Tolstoy, *The End of the Age* (Vladimir Tchertkoff trans.) (London: Heinemann, 1906[1905]), p. 29.

PAGE **74** | 'Every revolution begins [. . .] under former conditions.': Tolstoy, *End of the Age*, p. 28.

PAGE **74** | 'The signification of the revolution [. . .] *actual freedom.*': Tolstoy, *End of the Age*, p. 30.

PAGE **75** | 'Freedom not imaginary [. . .] any human authority whatever.': Tolstoy, *End of the Age*, p. 30.

PAGE **75** | 'To deliver men [. . .] humanity's greatest evils flow.': Leo Tolstoy, 'Patriotism and Government' [1900] in *Essays and Letters* (Aylmer Maude trans.) (London: Oxford University Press, 1911), p. 252.

PAGE **76** | 'The error at the root [. . .] conduct flowing therefrom.': Tolstoy, *Law of Violence and Law of Love*, pp.15–16.

PAGE **78** | 'However much they may assure themselves [. . .] attainment of their aims.': Tolstoy, *Law of Violence and Law of Love*, p.77.

PAGE **110** | Heinrich Lübke (1894–1972) was the second president of the Federal Republic of Germany from 1959 to 1969. After stepping down, he suffered from cerebral sclerosis, engendering memory loss.

PAGE **116** | Alexander Dubček (1929–1992) was First Secretary of the Communist Party of Czechoslovakia from January 1968 to April 1969. His attempts to reform the Communist government paved the way for the Prague Spring and provoked a Soviet-led invasion and crackdown.

PAGE **117** | Peter Weiss (1916–1982) was a German-born Swedish author and dramatist principally known for his play *Marat/Sade* and his novel *The Aesthetics of Resistance*.

PAGE **118** | Sozialistische Deutsche Studentenbund (SDS) or the German Socialist Students' Association was the collegiate branch of the Social Democratic Party of Germany.

PAGE **137** | 'One day of war in Vietnam costs $79,795': It is unclear how Frisch came to this figure, although his correspondence with his editor, Uwe Johnson, reveals that he did not include it in earlier versions of the text; he merely asked the question of how much the war cost. The US Department of Defense estimated that the United States spent approximately US$168 billion over the course of the Vietnam War (1953–1974), of which US$111 billion was allocated to military operations. Dividing this latter figure by 3,000 days for the main period of US military engagement (1965–1972) equates to US$ 37 million per day.

PAGE **162** | *Sinn und Form* was a bimonthly literary and cultural magazine founded in East Berlin in 1949

PAGE **163** | The city of Nizhny Novgorod was renamed Gorky in 1932 to honour the writer, born there in 1868. Its original name was restored in 1990.

PAGE **190** | 'Suppose you harbour the Ultimate Hope': Brecht's vision of man as man's helper: '*Wenn es so weit sein wird, dass der Mensch dem Menschen ein Helfer ist*'

PAGE **193** | The Federal Council is the executive branch of the Swiss government.

PAGE **198** | '*I cannot allow* [. . .] *eight-and-forty years.*': Michel de Montaigne, *Essays* (Charles Cotton trans., Charles Cotton ed.) (Auckland: The Floating Press, 2009 [based on the 1877 edition]).

PAGE **198** | 'BOURGEOIS VOUS N'AVEZ RIEN COMPRIS': 'Bourgeois, you don't get it'

PAGE **198** | 'FEU LA CULTURE': 'Dearly deceased culture'

PAGE **198** | 'L'ART C'EST DE LA MERDE': 'Art is shit'

PAGE **203** | 'Freigeld Theory': A theory advanced by the economist Silvio Gesell (1862–1930) for a currency that people would have no incentive to store as it lost its value over time.

PAGE **255** | Gustáv Husák (1913–1991) was elected First Secretary of the Communist Party of Czechoslovakia in 1969 and was responsible for reversing the reforms of the Prague Spring during the period known as 'Normalization'.

PAGE **261** | 'Reich Literature Chamber': The Reichschriftums-kammer was founded by Joseph Goebbels as part of the Reich Chamber of Culture to ensure Nazi control of the book industry.

PAGE **271** | '`Like landowners [...] "a government with no plan", etc.`': 'Bundestag elections and appointment of Chancellor in West Germany. The so-called Christian parties, which since the setting-up of the Federal Republic have governed alone, (in the end with a former Nazi as Chancellor) have lost votes so that Willy Brandt, a Social Democrat, becomes Chancellor.' (From Geoffrey Skelton's 1974 translation of Frisch's *Sketchbook, 1966–1971* [New York: Harcourt Brace Jovanovich, 1974])

PAGE **309** | Heinar Kipphardt (1922–1982) was a German writer and initiator of the 'documentary theatre' movement.

PAGE **314** | 'United Fruit Company': This archetypal monopolistic transnational company heavily dictated the political and economic situation in many Central American 'banana republics'.

PAGE **319** | Stylianos Pattakos (1912–2016) was a Greek army officer and member of the military junta that ruled Greece from 1967 to 1974.